# DIGITAL VIDEO AND TELEVISION

# DIGITAL VIDEO AND TELEVISION

Ioannis Pitas

Published by  :  Ioannis Pitas, Hortiatis 57010, Greece
    Contact  :  Ioannis Pitas, Department of Informatics, Aristo-
                tle University of Thessaloniki, Thessaloniki 54124,
                Greece
Tel. +302310996304
Fax +302310996304
e-mail: pitas@aiia.csd.auth.gr
http://www.aiia.csd.auth.gr

The front cover image of UCCA café is courtesy of the Ullens Center for Contemporary Art, Beijing, China. The back cover images are courtesy of the i3DPost FP7 project.

ISBN 978-960-91564-4-8

# PREFACE

We have fairly recently witnessed a major breakthrough in the field of electronic mass media: the transition from analog television to the era of digital television. The impact of this tremendous technological development is comparable to that of the introduction of analog black-and-white television more than half a century ago. More specifically, this is the beginning of a series of developments and innovations that will have a tremendous impact in broadcasting, cinema and media industry worldwide. Currently, media streaming and social media have become very popular, because of the ease of data recording by mobile devices and digital video cameras and their dissemination through the web with services like, for instance, well-known web sites like Google YouTube. Social media have already contributed in this direction as well. Many households are now equipped with home theater systems, where anyone can view digital movies in high resolution and at a high audio quality. High Definition TV (HDTV) is now widely distributed, e.g., by satellite broadcasting. 3D television follows HDTV as the next technological advance.

The technological revolution that we have witnessed in the course of the past decades has lead to dramatic changes in the way we collect, store, disseminate and consume audiovisual information. Enormous volumes of such data are stored and communicated each day. Today, our weak point is rather our inability to efficiently analyze and search such information, so that we can effectively uncover and retain only the relevant information that we actually want to consume. Therefore, there is a pressing need that not only experts in the field, but also the wider audience as well, are acquainted with the power of the digital audiovisual technology, so that it is massively adopted and harnessed. In this direction, several undergraduate and graduate-level courses are available in universities, colleges and schools of art, ranging from purely technical ones to courses covering the creative side of digital video. This book provides a general introduction to digital television and digital video. It can readily be comprehended by both university/college students and the general audience, who usually do not have a strong mathematical or technical background. It explains digital video acquisition, video compression, digital TV broadcasting and media streaming / webcasting. It describes digital video interfaces and storage / display peripherals. Finally, it provides an introduction to digital cinema and 3DTV.

This text on Digital Video and Television is the result of teaching a graduate-level course on *Digital Television* for more than a decade in the MSc specialization of Digital Media in the Department of Informatics at the Aristotle University of Thessaloniki, Greece. My experience in intelligent digital media research over the last thirty years has also left its mark in the formation of this textbook. I am very grateful to the following people, who have contributed to the collection of scientific material related to this book, under my supervision, in the undergraduate and graduate courses I have taught on *Digital Video Processing, Digital Image Processing* and *Digital Television* or helped in its preparation: J. Agaliadis, N. Arvanitopoulos-Darginis, D. Bouzas, G. Chantas, C. Charalampous, K. Chatzistavrou, I. Costavelis, A. Damtsa, S. Delis, A. Iosifidis, E. Kakaletsis, S. Karavarsamis, S. Manolopoulos, E. Marami, S. Nikitidis, G. Orfanides, C. Papachristou, C. Sagonas, N. Tsapanos, I. Tsingalis, B. Tsitlakides, M. Tsourides and O. Zoidi. I would also like to thank my colleague, Prof. G. Papadimitriou, for reviewing Chapters 8, and 9 and Ms E. Mouratidou, for the cover image artwork.

**Trademark disclaimer.** Company and product names mentioned in the text are trademarks of their respective owners.

**Acknowledgements.** Several of the images included in this book are courtesy of the EU funded FP7 R & D projects 3DTVS, 3D4YOU, i3DPost, IMP·ART, MOBISERV, MUSCADE and their partners. Other images are courtesy of the Science Center and Technology Museum NOESIS (Greece), University of Surrey (UK), Hertz Heinrich Institute (HHI, Germany), ARRI (Germany), Zaxcom (USA), Mediascreen Gmbh (Germany) and Optics for Hire (USA). Chapters 13 (3DTV) and 14 (video storage) are related to the research done within the EU funded FP7 R & D project 3DTVS. The rest of the chapters are related to the research done within the EU funded FP7 R & D project IMP·ART.

Ioannis Pitas

# Short author biography

Ioannis Pitas, IEEE fellow, received the Diploma and PhD degree in Electrical Engineering, both from the Aristotle University of Thessaloniki, Greece. Since 1994, he has been a Professor at the Department of Informatics of the same University. He served as a Visiting Professor at several Universities. His current interests are in the areas of intelligent digital media, image/video processing (2D/3D) and human-centered interfaces. He has published over 700 papers, contributed in 39 books in his areas of interest and edited or (co-)authored another 9 books. He has been invited speaker and/or member of the program committee of many scientific conferences and workshops. In the past, he served as Associate Editor or co-Editor of eight international journals and he was General or Technical Chair of four international conferences (including ICIP2001). He participated in 67 R&D projects on digital media, primarily funded by the European Union and is/was principal investigator/researcher in 40 such projects. He has 16500+ citations to his work and h-index 63+ (2013).

Communication:
Prof. Ioannis Pitas, Department of Informatics
Aristotle University of Thessaloniki,
Thessaloniki 54124, Greece

http://www.aiia.csd.auth.gr/
Email: pitas@aiia.csd.auth.gr

# CONTENTS

# 1

# INTRODUCTION TO

# DIGITAL VIDEO

## 1.1 Introduction

Digital television is a reality that changes the way we record, process, transmit and enjoy audiovisual information. It is the successor of analog television that dominated the electronic mass media in the last sixty years (approximately between 1950 and 2000). This book presents digital television technology, especially that of digital video, without entering into technical or mathematical details, so that a large audience, ranging from university/college students to video amateurs, can grasp its essentials.

Figure 1.1.1: Video sequence (*courtesy of the i3DPost FP7 project*).

A *picture* (still image) is a two dimensional spatial distribution of light intensity, which is constant over time. Video is a time varying image, in which the spatial light intensity changes over time, as shown in Figure 1.1.1. Basically, the video is a spatiotemporal signal $f(x, y, t)$, where $x, y$ are the spatial coordinates and $t$ is time. It is sometimes called *motion picture*. Another term that is used for video is image sequence or video sequence, since it can be represented by a temporal sequence of static images, called *video frames*. In the past, video traditionally was recorded, stored and broadcasted in analog form. Nowadays, this is performed digitally. In Section 1.2, we provide a brief description of analog video signal standards that enable video storage and transmission. In Section 1.3, we discuss digital video formats and standards that enable video storage and transmission.

## 1.2   Analog video

Until recently, video recording, storage and broadcasting were performed in an analog way. For instance, the TV pictures were recorded or stored as analog signals in magnetic tapes, using analog videotape recorders. Furthermore, cinema movies were traditionally recorded on film, which was the 'analog' way of recording high quality audiovisual material for cinema. In the following subsections, we shall briefly describe the nature of analog video signals and standards.

## 1.2.1    Analog video signal

The analog video is an one-dimensional electrical signal over time. The video signal captures the time-varying image intensity along the scan lines, as shown in Figure 1.2.1. It also includes synchronization signals that are necessary for the correct image alignment and display at the TV receiver and monitor. *Scanning* essentially discretizes a fully analog spatiotemporal video signal along time $t$ every $\Delta t$ sec (as shown in Figure 1.1.1) and along its vertical spatial dimension $y$. The most common video scanning methods are the progressive and the interlaced ones. In *progressive video*, all image lines are scanned in one step, forming one video *frame*. The computer industry uses progressive video scan for high-definition computer monitors with $\Delta t = 1/72$ sec. The television industry uses 2:1 *interlaced video*, which consists of *field* sequences. The odd/even image lines are scanned separately and form the odd/even video fields, respectively, that alternate over time. Two consecutive video fields can be used to form a video frame. A 2:1 interlaced video scan is shown in Figure 1.2.1, where the continuous and the dashed lines form the odd/even fields, respectively. In every video field, the scan begins at point $A$, returns from point $B$ to point $C$ (*horizontal return*), and from point $D$ to $E$ (*vertical return*). It continues from $E$ to $F$ by forming the next video field, and returns vertically to $A$.

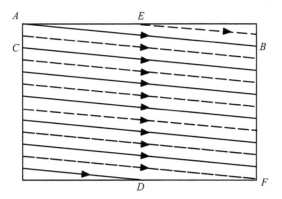

Figure 1.2.1: Interlaced video scan.

Significant video signal parameters are its vertical resolution, aspect ratio and frame/field rate. The *vertical resolution* refers to the number of scanned lines per frame, e.g., 525 lines/frame. The *aspect ratio* is the ratio of the frame width to its height, e.g., 4:3 or 16:9. The *frame/field rate* defines the number of frames (or fields) per second, e.g., 60 fields/second or 30 frames/second (fps). Psycho-optical studies show that the human visual system does not perceive flickering, if the monitor refresh rate is over 50 Hz. However, for television systems, such a high frame rate, combined with a high vertical resolution, requires a very high transmission bandwidth. Thus, the traditional analog television systems employ the interlaced scan, which trades vertical resolution to reduced flickering, within a predefined frequency bandwidth. Hence, when the image is almost still, it is displayed with high spatial resolution. When the picture has vivid motion, this motion is properly displayed at a double sampling ratio, in the form of fields.

## 1.2.2    Analog video formats

In the previous section, we dealt with black and white video signals. However, nowadays, most video signals are color ones and can be represented by a superposition of the three basic $RGB$ color components. Colorimetry supports that almost all colors can be represented by an appropriate mixture of three basic colors, namely red $R$, green $G$ and blue $B$. Since imaging devices can reproduce only specific non-negative basic colors and require a significant amount of luminance, there is a limit in the color gamut that can be reproduced. There are various analog video formats, which have different image parameters, e.g., spatial and temporal analysis and also differ in the way they handle color information. These formats can be distinguished in the following categories: component video, composite video and S-video.

In *component video*, every basic color component is handled as a separate single-color video signal. The basic colors can be either the basic $R, G, B$ signals, or their luminance-chrominance transformation. *Composite video* signal formats encode the three color components, by superimposing the chrominance information on the luminance signal. The result is one video signal, which has similar bandwidth with that of the luminance signal. Composite video signal formats may suffer from wrong color rendering, also commonly known as color errors, because of their inaccuracy in color signal separation. There are various composite analog video formats, like the American *National Television Systems Committee* (NTSC) and the European *Phase Alternation Line* (PAL) and *System Electronique Color Avec Memoir* (SECAM) systems, which were used in various countries worldwide. The *S-video* format is a compromise between composite video and component-analog video, where the video signal is represented by two components: one luminance signal and one composite chrominance signal. S-video was used in analog videotape recorders (S-VHS) and in analog consumer quality cameras for achieving better image quality, compared to that of the composite video.

The NTSC composite video format was defined in 1952. It was primarily used in North America and Japan. An NTSC signal is a 2:1 interlaced video signal with 262.5 lines per field, 60 fields per second and 4:3 aspect ratio. As a result, the horizontal frequency scan is $F_h = 525 \times 30 = 15.75$ kHz. This means that $\frac{1}{15750} = 63.5$ msec are required to scan one horizontal line. Only 485 out of the 525 lines are active, because 20 lines per field are empty, to be used for the vertical return. While there are 485 active lines per frame, the *vertical analysis* (number of horizontal lines perceived by the viewer) is $485 \times 0.7 = 339.5(340)$ lines per frame. The coefficient 0.7 (also called *Kell ratio*) is the ratio of the perceived horizontal line number to the total number of horizontal active scan lines. *Horizontal analysis*, which is defined as the number of perceived vertical lines, should be $339 \times (4/3) = 452$ elements/line. The spectral characteristics of the NTSC video signal are shown in Figure 1.2.2.

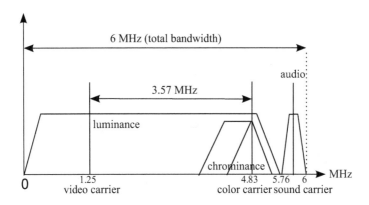

Figure 1.2.2: NTSC video signal spectrum.

The previous analysis refers to black and white (BW) video. The spectrum of the chrominance signal and the stereo sound signal are appended to that of the BW video, as shown in Figure 1.2.2. A total bandwidth of 6 MHz results. PAL and SECAM formats were developed in the '60s and were primarily used in Europe. They also describe 2:1 interlaced video, but have different spatiotemporal resolution than the NTSC signal. Both PAL and SECAM have 625 lines per frame and 50 fields (25 frames) per second. Thus, they have higher vertical analysis and smaller frame rate, in comparison to NTSC. One difference between PAL and SECAM systems is the way they represent chrominance information. Both these systems provide better color representation than NTSC.

# 1.3   Digital video

In the past two decades, we experienced a digital revolution in audio-visual media. This revolution has offered quality digital sound on CDs or MP3 devices and digital video in DVDs, Blu-rays, or by Internet streaming. The durability of digital media over time and the easiness in copying them are their main advantages. Furthermore, their streaming and/or broadcasting capabilities allow the provision of various services over the same platform, notably interactivity. Furthermore, digital video brings together computers, telecommunications and mass media in a really revolutionary way. The same device can function as a personal computer, high definition television, video conference platform or streaming device. Many such devices, for example mobile phones, have a digital video camera. Thus, users can record, edit and share live video with friends, or print static frames on a local printer.

## 1.3.1   Advantages of digital video

In the analog video world, we deal with analog video devices, e.g., videocassette recorders (VCR) and video cameras. Video distribution depends primarily on TV broadcasting (satellite, cable, terrestrial), which broadcasts preset TV programmes at a constant transmission rate. Only limited interactivity is allowed, e.g., TV zapping and forward/backward or slow motion playback on VCR. Moreover, analog composite video signal formats (NTSC, PAL or SECAM) do not offer good picture quality. Video material recorded on VCR should be in NTSC/PAL/SECAM format and, hence, is of low still and moving picture quality. Analog video database search for specific recordings is a tedious and time consuming visual search in a multitude of videocassettes. Furthermore, analog video editing is not an easy task. Usually, analog video is first digitized, edited digitally and then recorded again in analog form, by means of a D/A converter.

Recent developments in digital image technology, television, computers and telecommunications tend to merge the respective market sectors. The appearance of better compression algorithms, high-speed broadband networks, mobile devices, digital recording and faster computers created a variety of digital video and optical communication products and services. Some commercial and consumer applications that lead the research and development in this sector are: digital TV (DTV), High Definition TV (HDTV), interactive TV, Video-On-Demand (VOD), multimedia, video-conferencing, mobile video, social media and video streaming. Other digital video applications include smart systems for traffic monitoring or for surveillance. Furthermore, video has also been applied in scientific imaging, medical imaging and human-computer interaction.

Digital video representation offers many advantages, such as:

- availability of videos in multiple spatial and temporal analysis;

- variable video transmission rate based on user demands or on channel characteristics;

- easy video format conversion;

- combination of various video applications, such as television, video-conferencing, etc., on a common multimedia platform;

- easy video editing capabilities, such as cut, collage, zooming, denoising and deblurring;

- tolerance in channel noise, easy encryption, authentication control;

- easy querying in video databases;

- interactivity, which allows the expression of consumer/viewer preferences.

A basic advantage of digital video is its ease in processing and analysis. Basic video processing functionalities include noise reduction, quality improvement, color manipulation, video effect creation, video editing and conversion to various formats. Video analysis includes motion detection and estimation, object tracking and three-dimensional scene/motion acquisition and representation.

A basic disadvantage of digital video is illegal copying (piracy). Several techniques, such as video watermarking or fingerprinting, have been developed to protect digital content. Furthermore, access control systems have been developed for digital television for distribution control, through encryption and/or scrambling. Another big problem encountered in digital video is the enormous storage and transfer rate requirements. For example, digital video requires much higher transfer rates than digital sound. Therefore, the wide use and commercial viability of digital video depends strongly on the use of proper video compression technologies.

## 1.3.2 Digital video signal

Digital video is usually produced directly by digital video cameras that typically offer compressed digital video, which can be easily decompressed to its RGB components. Most digital video processing systems use component color representation, which avoids the artifacts that are created by composite video encoding.

The *horizontal resolution* and *vertical resolution* of a digital video signal are the number of *picture elements (pixels)* per line and the number of lines per frame, respectively, e.g., 640 pixels/line×480 lines. *Color depth* refers to the number of bits dedicated to represent each pixel. The usual color depth is 24 bits/pixel (8 bits per color channel), which allows for $2^{24}$ (approximately 16 million) colors. Nowadays, digital video recording can deliver up to 36 bits per pixel, which allows for $2^{36}$ (68 billion) different colors. Optical artifacts in digital video, due to insufficient spatial resolution, are much different than the ones encountered in analog video. In analog video, insufficient spatial analysis leads to image blurring along the corresponding spatial direction. In digital video, we can have *pixelation* artifacts, because of insufficient spatial resolution. These artifacts are manifested either as jaggy edges along region borders, or by image blocks having equal luminance/color. The visual perception of such artifacts depends on the monitor size and the distance between the viewer and the monitor device.

## 1.3.3   Digital video formats

The use of digital video in various applications and products dictates the definition of digital video formats. Video data must be transmitted in compressed form for financial reasons, a fact that leads to the definition of video compression formats. Furthermore, there are already established computer monitor resolution formats in the computer industry, digital studio formats in the television industry and video streaming formats for Internet video transmission. Since digital video brings these three industries even closer, there must be a format interoperability to facilitate cross-platform video distribution. This section presents a summary of some digital video formats and the relevant format prototyping efforts.

Digital video is quite old in television broadcasting studios. In such environments, editing and special effects are applied to digital video, because it is easier to edit digital images, rather than analog ones. Furthermore, digital video editing does not suffer from consecutive analog video read/write operations from/to magnetic tapes, during the various video production stages. Significant digital video format specifications result from the conversion of analog PAL or NTSC video to digital one, because huge amounts of archived audiovisual material is (even at present) in analog format. The 601 Recommendation of *Comite Consultatif International pour la Radio* (CCIR) defines a digital video format for television studios and systems with 525 lines and 625 lines. It is also known as the BT.601 Recommendation of the *International Telecommunications Union-Radio Sector* (ITU-R). This format aims at facilitating the exchange of

Table 1.3.1: Digital video formats.

| Parameter | BT.601 525/60 NTSC | BT.601 625/50 PAL/SECAM | CIF | SVGA/ SXVGA |
|---|---|---|---|---|
| Luminance $Y$ | | | | RGB |
| Active pixels/line | 720 | 720 | 360 | 1280/1024 |
| Active lines/image | 480 | 576 | 288 | 1024/768 |
| Chrominance $U, V$ | | | | |
| Active pixels/line | 360 | 360 | 180 | |
| Active lines/image | 480 | 576 | 144 | |
| Interlacing | 2:1 | 2:1 | 1:1 | 1:1 |
| Field/frame rate | 60 | 50 | 30 | 72 |
| Aspect ratio | 4:3 | 4:3 | 4:3 | 4:3 |

broadcasting quality of audiovisual material at an international level. The BT.601 format parameters are shown in Table 1.3.1. The uncompressed video data rate for the BT.601 formats is 165 Mbps. Because this rate is very high for many applications, the *Consultative Committee for International Telephone and Telegraph* (CCITT) suggested another digital video format, called *Common Intermediate Format* (CIF). Its parameters appear in Table 1.3.1. The CIF format is progressive (non-interlaced), demands a data rate of 37 Mbps and offers rather low spatiotemporal video resolution.

Although digital video is usually produced in the three Red-Green-Blue (RGB) color components, in most cases, it is converted to other color coordinate systems, typically for compression or transmission. The most commonly used color systems are $YIQ$ (NTSC), $YUV$ (PAL/SECAM) and $YC_bC_r$, which is a digital version of YUV. $Y$ denotes the luminance component, which can be estimated as the weighted mean value of the $R$, $G$, $B$ components: $Y = k_rR + k_gG + k_bB$, where $k$ are weight coefficients. Chrominance information can also be represented as a chrominance difference between the $R$ or $B$ component and the luminance component $Y$: $C_b = B - Y, C_r = R - Y$.

The BT.601 recommendation suggests a $YC_bC_r$ version, where the components $Y$, $C_b$, $C_r$ result from scaling the $Y$, $U$, $V$ components, so that their values are in the range $[0, \ldots, 255]$.

The main advantage of the $YC_bC_r$ system, in comparison to the $RGB$ system, is that the components $C_b$, $C_r$ can be represented under lower resolution, because the human visual system is less sensitive to chrominance than to luminance information. This reduces the required resolution for representing the chrominance information, without a perceptible visual dif-

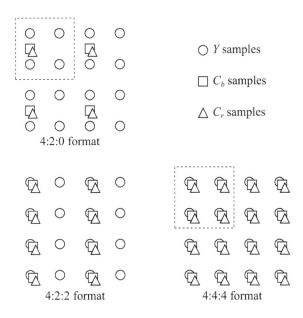

Figure 1.3.1: Chrominance subsampling formats in BT.601.

ference to the user. Usually, for compression reasons, we subsample the chrominance components $C_b$, $C_r$ with respect to the luminance component $Y$. The most known subsampling systems that exist in the BT.601 Recommendation are presented in Figure 1.3.1:

- *4:2:0 system.* For each $2 \times 2$ $Y$ pixels, there are 1 $C_b$ and 1 $C_r$ pixels (2:1 horizontal and vertical subsampling).

- *4:2:2 system.* For each $2 \times 2$ $Y$ pixels, there are 2 $C_b$ and 2 $C_r$ pixels (only 2:1 horizontal subsampling).

- *4:4:4 system.* For each $2 \times 2$ $Y$ pixels, there are 4 $C_b$ and 4 $C_r$ pixels (there is no subsampling).

In the computer industry, the video display formats were defined by the *Video Electronic Standards Association* (VESA). In the past, VGA was the graphics card format of preference for personal computers, offering an image resolution of 640 pixels/line×480 lines. Today all personal computer displays are compatible with the SVGA/SXVGA format, which supports at least two basic resolution levels: 1280 pixels/line×1024 lines, or 1024 pixels/line×768 lines. There are also formats of much higher spatial resolution, like the WQSXGA, supporting 3200×2048 pixels. In these cases, the refresh rate is 72 frames/second. Considering the fact that, till recently, television picture resolutions were far behind the present state-of-the-art

Table 1.3.2: Industrial digital video formats.

| Name | Video types |
|---|---|
| D1 | Uncompressed component |
| D2 | Uncompressed composite |
| DV | Compressed interlaced NTSC (480i)/PAL(576i) |
| Digital Betacam | Compressed component NTSC/PAL |
| XDCAM | DVCAM, MPEG IMX, MPEG HD, ProxyAV (MPEG-4) |
| XDCAM HD | High resolution video |

technology, many high-definition television formats have been proposed. These formats support at least double the spatial resolution of the BT.601 formats along both spatial axes $x, y$, as described in Chapter 8.

Various digital video applications, e.g., fully digitalized high-definition television multimedia services, videoconferencing and mobile video have various transfer rate demands. Most probably, these applications can reach possible users through a telecommunication network. The study of the available bit rates show that the commercial viability of digital video depends on its compression efficiency. As video compression is a significant technology for developing digital video services, various video compression formats have been developed for various bit rates, e.g., MPEG-1, MPEG-2, H.264 and MPEG-4. This area is still active and new formats are being developed. The more recent format is MPEG-4 part 10 AVC and HEVC. Video compression prototyping ensures the compatibility of digital video equipment produced by various manufacturers and facilitates market development. Digital video product and service interoperability demands not only compression but also video display format standardization. There is a whole range of industrial digital video formats, besides the BT.601 and CIF ones, as shown in Table 1.3.2.

# DIGITAL VIDEO

# ACQUISITION

## 2.1 Introduction

A video sequence (moving image) is the visualization of a moving object or scene that is illuminated by a light source using a still or moving video camera. Camera or light source motion can also produce a moving image. The light that is reflected on a scene and its objects enters the video camera through its optical (lens) system for recording. The image sensor transforms the incident light to electric current (or charge). It is sampled and digitized to form a digital video stream, which is subsequently stored on a digital storage device, e.g., a hard disk. The light can be of various kinds, e.g., white light (sun light), x-rays (in the case of radioscopy), infrared radiation, or even ultrasound (in the case of medical ultrasound video). The only thing that differs, in each case, is the set of physical laws governing the formation of the moving image. Changes in the three-dimensional scene over time usually occur due to object motion. Thus, moving images are the projection of moving 3D objects on the camera image plane, as a function of time. Digital video corresponds to a spatiotemporal sampling of such moving images. A schematic diagram of the creation and recording of digital videos is shown in Figure 2.1.1.

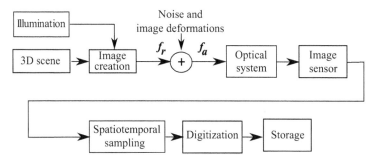

Figure 2.1.1: A model for the creation and recording of digital video.

## 2.2  Image formation

Typically cameras record objects that reflect light. The perceived color depends on the range of the reflected light wavelengths. In general, the reflection can be decomposed in two components: *diffuse reflection*, which distributes light energy equally in all directions and *specular reflection*, which is the strongest along the direction of the incident light. Surfaces performing only diffuse reflection, known as *Lambertian surfaces*, are described as dull and matte (for example, cement surfaces). In the case of diffuse reflection, we can perceive the object color. Specular reflection can be observed on glass surfaces and mirrors. In this case, we do not see the object color; instead, we see the color of the incident light. Image formation also depends on the type of light source. *Ambient illumination* sources emit the same light energy in all directions. In this case, the position of the source relative to the reflecting surface is not very important. Such a light source can model quite well the room illumination, coming from white

walls. Similarly, in the outdoor scenes, a cloudy sky produces ambient illumination. The *point illumination* sources emit light energy isotropically or
anisotropically along different directions. In this case, the position of the
light source, in relation to the reflecting surface, is important. Ordinary
light bulbs are such anisotropic light sources, emitting different light energy
along different directions. The sun can be considered as an isotropic point
light source. The mathematical modeling of light reflection is different for
the various light source types.

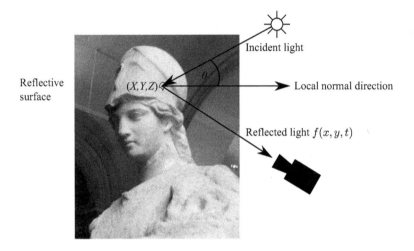

Figure 2.2.2: Diffuse reflection geometry.

The reflection geometry for image formation is shown in Figure 2.2.2. In
diffuse reflection, the luminance $f(x, y, t)$ of pixel $(x, y)$ at time $t$, depends
on the incident light intensity at the object point $(X, Y, Z)$ corresponding
to pixel $(x, y)$, the surface reflectivity $r(X, Y, Z)$ at this point and on the
incidence angle $\theta$. As the object moves over time, angle $\theta$ changes, resulting
in recorded image changes (moving picture). The same happens, when the
illumination source position and/or intensity changes or when the camera
moves.

The reflected light hits the video-camera lenses for recording, as shown
in Figure 2.2.3. Typically, a *pinhole camera* model is assumed, even in the
case the camera has a very sophisticated lens system. Video-cameras capture the two-dimensional projections (views) of a three-dimensional time-
varying scene on the so-called *camera image plane* lying at the back of the
camera. The photosensitive surface (typically a CCD chip) is located on
the image plane.

The perspective projection describes image formation in an ideal pin-

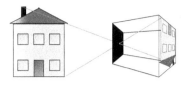

Figure 2.2.3: Pinhole camera model.

hole camera. Each camera has a *projection center*, also called *focal* or *camera* or *lens center*, in accordance with the principles of optics, as shown in Figure 2.2.3, which corresponds to the lens center. The projection center is located between the object and the image plane $(x, y)$. All light rays emanating from an object pass through the projection center. For this reason, the perspective projection is also known as *central projection*. The image plane $(x, y)$ coincides with the $(X, Y)$ plane of the *world coordinate system* $(X, Y, Z)$. The distance $f$ of the image plane from the camera center is called *focal length* of the camera. During camera zooming, the focal length changes (increases/decreases). Let an object point be located at the position $(X, Y, Z)$ in the world coordinate system. It is recorded (viewed) at the point $(x, y)$ on the image plane, as shown in Figure 2.2.4. The image plane $(x, y)$ coordinates are proportional to the focal length $f$ and the world object coordinates $X$, $Y$. They are inversely proportional to the object depth $Z$.

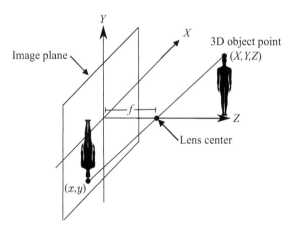

Figure 2.2.4: Perspective projection for image formation.

## 2.3   Digital video cameras

Today, the most prevalent digital camera fabrication methods are *Charge Coupled Device* (CCD) and *Complimentary Metal Oxide Sensor* (CMOS) technologies. They have replaced vacuum tube video cameras and, to a great extent, the conventional film cameras. CCD cameras are widely used in a variety of scientific, surveillance and biomedical applications of digital imaging. A high-resolution digital camera contains a photo-sensitive integrated CCD chip, a suitable lens, a cooling method and other functional electronics. A CCD chip consists of a photosensitive cell matrix, as shown in Figure 2.3.1. The incident light induces an electric charge in the semiconductor cells, each corresponding to one pixel. Therefore, CCD directly produces a *discrete* (sampled) *image* $f(i\Delta x, j\Delta y)$, where $i, j$ are the pixel coordinates and $\Delta x, \Delta y$ are the *sampling intervals*, corresponding to the pixel size. These electric charges (one for each cell) are shifted to the right and are stored on an output register. There, they can be digitized. The corresponding numbers $f(i, j)$ (one per pixel) can be stored on secondary storage, e.g., on a hard disk.

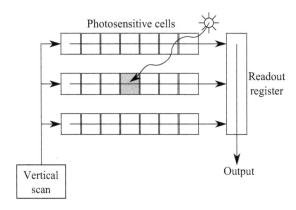

Figure 2.3.1: CCD camera structure.

A CCD pixel cell structure is shown in Figure 2.3.2. It consists of three *polycrystalline silicon (polysilicon)* gates that are placed perpendicularly, with respect to two channel stops. Between the channel stops, which insulate each photodiode, one CCD cell is formed. If the electric potential in the middle electrode is higher than that applied to each of the other two gates, a minimum of the local potential is formed under the middle gate. When photons hit a cell, electron-hole pairs are generated due to photoelectric energy conversion. The electrons generated in the channel stop area or the substrate beneath the cell cannot be dispersed and can be collected. In any case, the holes are dispersed and collected on the

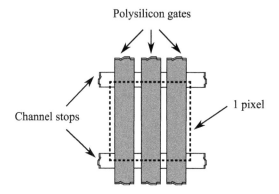

Figure 2.3.2: Three-phase CCD pixel.

type $p$ substrate. The electric charge collected in a potential well in each cell is directly related to the photon flow (incident light intensity) and the *exposure time* (*integration time*). CCDs are essentially an array of shift registers. The charges of the various cells are shifted across cells in parallel, by proper clocking and changing the well potential. There are CCD structures using from one up to four polysilicon gates to define a pixel. Typically, cells are square shaped and are arranged in a rectangular grid. However, there are CCD sensors with octagonal cells that are arranged in a rhombus configuration (square layout rotated by $45^o$), as shown in Figure 2.3.3.

CMOS cameras are generally cheaper than CCD ones, since they can be produced in classical silicon production lines. They tend to produce more image noise and have less light sensitivity, since light hits not only the CMOS image sensors, but also the adjacent transistors. However, nowadays, CMOS cameras appear in a wide spectrum of price and quality ranges.

Three CCD or (CMOS active pixel) image sensors are used for acquiring

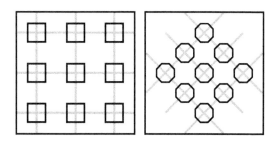

Figure 2.3.3: Rectangular and rhomboid CCD cell arrays.

color digital images. A properly placed prism refracts light and different wavelengths stimulate each of the three CCD sensors, thus creating RGB color images of very good quality. There are color cameras with a single CCD sensor and three optical RGB filters, which produce lower quality images.

Web and mobile phone cameras have very cheap lenses and electronic parts. Therefore, they produce low-quality video. Yet, they are widely spread. In particular, mobile cameras are often used to produce user-fed content, e.g., in social media sites. Professional video-cameras are equipped with quality lenses and other support devices, e.g., viewfinders and special camera rigs for camera motion control. Such cameras can be mounted on tripods, dollies or cranes, to facilitate camera control.

A video sequence (moving picture) can be produced not only due to object/scene motion, as already explained, but also due to camera motion. Video-cameras typically have three controls, that are widely used in cinematography. *Panning* refers to horizontal camera rotation. *Tilt* refers to vertical camera rotation. *Zooming* refers to a change of the camera focal length.

The recorded (compressed or uncompressed) digital video is stored in various storage devices, local (in the case of *camcorders*) or remote ones. The storage needs are huge, particularly if high definition uncompressed video is recorded in professional applications, e.g., for movie production. Various digital video formats are used to this end. In the past, D1 or D2 and Digital Betacam formats were used. XDCAM, XDCAM HD video recorders employ various uncompressed (DV) and compressed (MPEG-2 and MPEG-4) video formats. IMX (the successor of DigiBeta) offers MPEG-2 Part 2 encoding. AVC-Intra supports MPEG-4 AVC compressed video storage. DVCPro is a variation of DV video for SDTV recording. HDCAM SR supports 10 bit 4:2:2 or 4:4:4 RGB video recording. More on compressed video formats can be found in Chapter 7.

## 2.4 Video digitization

An analog video signal is a time-varying image of the form $f(x, y, t)$, where $x$ and $y$ are the horizontal and vertical coordinates, respectively and $t$ is the time variable, as shown in Figure 2.4.1.

Analog video signal is obtained by sampling the time-varying image luminance along the vertical $y$ axis and time $t$, by employing a two-dimensional sampling process, known as *video scanning*, as already described in Chapter 1. Essentially, the analog video signal is discrete along $y$ and $t$ axes and continuous along $x$ axis. The luminance information

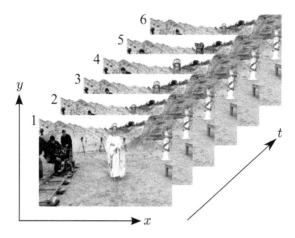

Figure 2.4.1: Spatiotemporal analog video signal (*courtesy of the i3DPost FP7 project*).

along each scanned horizontal image line is serialized (together with appropriate sync information) to form an one-dimensional analog signal as a function of time that can be broadcasted over single telecommunication channels. Digital video can be obtained either by sampling legacy analog video along the horizontal scan lines or by using a discrete two-dimensional sensor grid, e.g., in CCD chips. Sampling geometry defines the sampling intervals along each coordinate $\Delta x, \Delta y, \Delta t$, as shown in Figure 2.4.2. Spatial sampling intervals $\Delta x, \Delta y$ define *image resolution*: the smaller they are, the smaller the pixel size is and the larger the image resolution is, for the same CCD physical size. The temporal sampling interval $\Delta t$ defines the video frame rate, e.g., 24/25/30 frames per second (fps).

The simplest way to digitize an analog video signal is by using the so-called *progressive sampling grid*, which leads to uniform spatiotemporal sampling along the three spatiotemporal coordinates $x$, $y$ and $t$, as shown in Figure 2.4.2a. The progressive digital video consists of a series of *video frames*. An alternative form of analog video sampling is the 2:1 interlaced video sampling, shown in Figure 2.4.2b, producing digital interlaced 2:1 video, which consists of odd/even *fields*, rather than frames. Several other video sampling grids exist, as shown in Figure 2.4.3. In these diagrams, each circle represents the position of a pixel. The number inside the circle indicates odd/even field sampling. These fields are $\Delta t/2$ sec apart. A visual 3D representation of the first two grids is shown in Figure 2.4.2.

After discretization, image pixel values undergo a quantization procedure, so that they are represented by numbers to be stored in a file. 8 bits are typically assigned to one black and white pixel, leading to 256

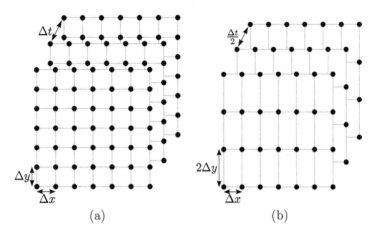

Figure 2.4.2: Sampling grids for: a) progressive and b) 2:1 interlaced video.

gray shades (0 denoting black and 255 denoting white). In color images, 8 bits are assigned to each color channel, leading to 24 pixels per pixel. Sometimes, up to 36 bits per pixel are used to produce superior quality color video.

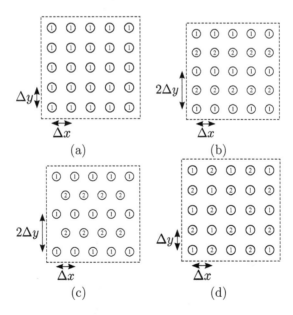

Figure 2.4.3: a) Rectangular sampling grid, b) vertically aligned interlaced 2:1 grid, c) quincunx grid, d) orthorombic grid.

## 2.5   Image distortions

A digital video-camera samples a moving scene at regular sampling intervals $\Delta x, \Delta y, \Delta t$ along the horizontal, vertical and temporal direction, respectively. If the sampling frequencies $F_x = 1/\Delta x$, $F_y = 1/\Delta y$, $F_t = 1/\Delta t$ are not high enough, then digital video suffers from aliasing artifacts, since content having high spatiotemporal frequencies (e.g., image details and/or fast motion) cannot be visualized well any more.

Figure 2.5.1: Directional (motion) image blur.

Pixel luminance corresponds to the average illumination of the corresponding sensor cell within a given exposure (integration) time period. Therefore, a camera blurs the recorded video, if the exposure time is relatively long. Even for small exposure times, the image of a fast moving object is blurred along the motion direction (*motion blur*), as shown in Figure 2.5.1. The same thing happens, when the camera moves. Motion blur is proportional to motion speed. Furthermore, due to camera imperfections and/or poor focus, the luminance of each image pixel is essentially the weighted average of the incident light luminance in a small window around this pixel (*spatial aperture*). Therefore, camera lens performs spatial (isotropic) image blur (e.g., in the case of defocused images). In most cameras, the spatial aperture has circular shape, producing *defocus blur*, as shown in Figure 2.5.2. Defocus blur is inversely proportional to the camera focal length. A camera having a small focal length produces low *focus depths*, i.e., focuses only on objects lying in a limited depth $Z$ range and can easily record defocused images. It was found that the human eye is more sensitive to spatiotemporal blur, rather than to aliasing artifacts.

(a)                                                    (b)

Figure 2.5.2: A defocused image (a) vs a sharp image (b).

Lens spherical shape creates geometrical image distortions. The so-called *spherical aberration* is due to the fact that light rays hitting lens periphery are more refracted than the ones hitting the lens center. Therefore, they do not focus at the same focal point. This fact creates image blur. Aspherical lens surfaces minimize spherical aberration.

Radial distortion distorts the geometric patterns of the incoming light. It is radially symmetric and increases with the square of the pixel distance from the image center. *Fisheye lenses* employ this distortion to provide a wide field view. Finally, *chromatic aberration* is due to the fact that different light wavelengths are refracted in a different way in the camera lens, since the refractive index decreases, as the wavelength increases. Hence, they are not focused at the same focal point.

Photoelectric conversion produces nonlinear image distortions. A simplified model for a CCD image sensor is of the form $i = b^{\gamma}$, where $b$ is the input luminance, $i$ is the recorded digital image luminance and $\gamma$ is the *gamma* sensor gain, which can be automatically adjusted. The coefficient $\gamma$ ranges between 0.55 and 1. Figure 2.5.3 shows the input-output response curve of CCD sensor. The central part of the response curve corresponds to the $b^{\gamma}$ form. Gamma is the slope of the linear part in Figure 2.5.3. For very low incident light, we have the so called *dark current effect*. For very high input luminance, we have CCD *sensor saturation*. Generally, CCD sensors have great dynamic range.

Similarly, most display devices suffer from a similar non-linear relationship between the digital pixel luminance $i$ and the displayed luminance $b = i^{\gamma'}$. In most monitors, the gamma value $\gamma'$ ranges from 2.2 to 2.5. Therefore, the camera output luminance $i$ must be corrected, in order to get correct pixel values. Furthermore, the pixel values must be further corrected, before display, to counter the display gamma effect. This process is known as *gamma correction*. It is even more complicated in the case of color images, because all three RGB channels must be corrected.

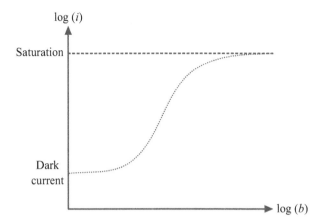

Figure 2.5.3: Input-output response of a photoelectric sensor.

It becomes even more difficult, if the digital image has undergone a color coordinate system change, e.g., from RGB to $YC_bC_r$.

Digital images suffer from *photoelectric noise*, due to the randomness of photon hits on the photoelectric cells. Furthermore, camera electronics produce additive white noise that further deteriorates the created image. Image noise can be significant in twilight conditions or in night vision.

Pixel quantization produces errors (noise) as well. *Quantization noise* can be severe, if few (e.g., less than 24) bits are assigned to each color image pixel. This noise is particularly evident, when the image is displayed in big screens. High quality video typically uses up to 36 bits per color image pixel to reduce quantization noise.

# 3

# HUMAN VISUAL

# PERCEPTION

## 3.1 Introduction

This chapter deals with the human visual perception of moving images. The first section presents human vision modeling approaches. It is followed by color theory, color perception by humans and color representation in various coordinate systems. Depth perception and stereopsis are subsequently presented, since they are very important issues in 3DTV. An analysis of the frequency response of the human eye at various spatiotemporal frequencies follows. Such an analysis helps to understand better the

35

perception of the video spatiotemporal frequency content by humans. Finally, there is a reference to various approaches for assessing video quality.

## 3.2   Human vision modeling

In many applications, digital image and video processing aim at improving image quality, so that an image is pleasant to humans or that it can provide more reliable information on the image content. To achieve this, we must understand human vision and create its functional and, possibly, mathematical model. Of course, modeling the *human visual system* (HVS) is a very difficult task, because the human eye and visual cortex has a very complex structure.

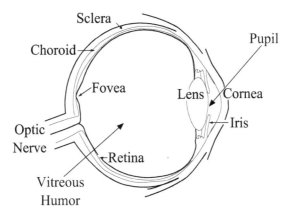

Figure 3.2.1: Human eye.

A schematic cross-section of the human eye is shown in Figure 3.2.1. It is almost spherical and has a diameter of 20mm. The light enters the eye from the *pupil* of the *iris*. Pupil diameter can range from 2 mm to 8 mm, depending on lighting conditions. The light passes through the focusing *lens* and *vitreous humor*, which consist primarily of water and are transparent. Over 90% of the lens proteins are water solvable *crystallines*. Finally, it stimulates the optical nerve endings (rods and cones) on the retina. The similarities with the pinhole projective camera model are obvious. The eye lens is adjusted by the small *cilliary muscles* using the so-called *zonules*. Thus, the focal length of our biological camera changes, according to scene viewing demands. This process is called *accommodation*. The retina is directly related to the image plane, which is sometimes called *retinal plane* to emphasize their similarity. In Figure 3.2.2, we can see the perspective

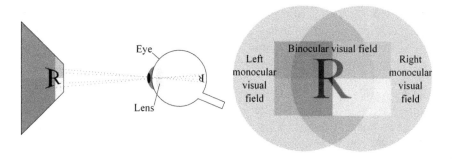

Figure 3.2.2: Perspective projection in the human eye.

projection onto the retina surface. The light rays pass through the optical elements of the eye and result in images that are inverted and left-right reversed on the retinal surface. Furthermore, we can see the perspective projection of the visual stimulus onto the left- and right-eye retinas.

*Retina* consists of two types of light detectors: *cones* and *rods*. Both of them are photo-sensitive neurons. The cones are sensitive to color. Their number is 6-7 millions and are mostly distributed in the central part of the retina. Each cone is connected to one nerve. The vision attributed to cones is called *photopic* or high-brightness vision. It is characteristic that we do not recognize colors at low brightness levels. The rods give a general idea of the content in the visual field. They are sensitive to low light, but they can not distinguish color. For this reason, rods provide *scotopic* (low-light) vision. The number of rods is between 75 and 150 millions. They are evenly distributed throughout the retina. Many rods are connected to one nerve ending. This explains the low visual resolution in scotopic vision. Both rods and cones convert visual information into electrical stimulation, which is transferred to the brain through the *optic nerve* for further processing. However, a first visual signal processing is already made in the retina and the optic nerve. A crude model of the eye, based on this description, is shown in Figure 3.2.3.

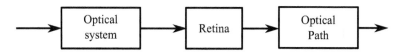

Figure 3.2.3: Model of the human eye.

Human vision is very complex. Only a few characteristics have been studied in detail. Such a phenomenon, which is important for artificial vision, is visual sensitivity to image contrast. Consider an image consisting of a constant background intensity $I$ and a pulse at its center, having intensity $I + dI$, as shown in Figure 3.2.4. $dI$ increases from 0 until the pulse is clearly perceived by the viewers. The fraction $dI/I$ is called *Weber ratio* and is constant at around 2% over a large image intensity range, as shown in Figure 3.2.4. If the experiment becomes more complex, the findings change but the basic conclusions persist. Weber ratio is, in fact, the derivative of the logarithm of intensity $d[\log(I)] = \frac{dI}{I}$. Therefore, same changes in the logarithm of image intensity create the same perceived image intensity changes. This experiment demonstrates that the human eye performs an analog nonlinear (logarithmic) image transformation.

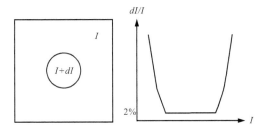

Figure 3.2.4: Weber ratio measurements for image background intensity $I$.

Another particularly useful phenomenon of human vision is *Mach phenomenon*. The image in Figure 3.2.5a consists of columns having different gray tones. When the entire image is viewed, it seems that each column has no constant brightness along the horizontal direction. However, the intensity of each column is constant, as shown in Figure 3.2.5b. This is clearly seen, if we watch each column independently, by occluding artificially all other columns. Mach phenomenon is explained by the fact that the eye tries to increase the contrast between columns. Thus, we perceive the image intensity as shown in Figure 3.2.5c. The perceived image has clearly higher frequencies along the horizontal direction, since the image intensity discontinuities increased around image edges. Larger image in-

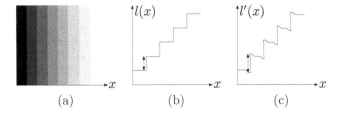

Figure 3.2.5: a) Mach phenomenon, b) true image intensities along the horizontal direction, c) perceived image intensities.

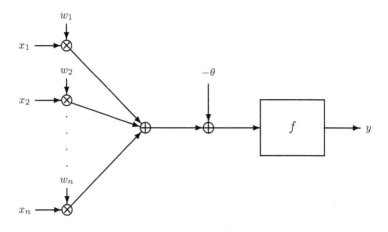

Figure 3.2.6: McCullogh-Pitts nerve model.

tensity discontinuities indicate the presence of higher image frequencies. Due to Mach phenomenon, the eye is sensitive to high spatial frequency information, e.g., image details, lines, contours or high-contrast image regions.

Several human eye functionalities can be explained by the physiology of the neurons in the retina. The *McCullogh-Pitts* model of such a neuron is shown in Figure 3.2.6. Neurons are excited by other neurons through the corresponding *synapses*. This way, the optical signals are transported by the optic nerve to the *visual cortex* in the brain. Essentially, the output of each neuron is a non-linear transform $f$ of the weighted sum of its inputs $x_1, \ldots, x_n$ coming from preceding neurons along the optical nerve. The weights $w_1, \ldots, w_n$ depend on the type of the synapsis and may be excitatory (i.e., they increase the neuron output) or inhibitory (i.e., they decrease the output). This model is used to derive a simple mathematical human vision model shown in Figure 3.2.7. The first part of the model describes the optical system of the eye, consisting primarily of its lens. This system is passive and has homogeneous low-pass features, i.e., it blurs the input image. Such a blur can be severe, in cases of eye diseases or disorders, such as *myopia* or *presbyopia*, and must be corrected by extra lenses. In principal, this system does not differ much from the model of an artificial lens. The logarithmic function used in the model explains certain phenomena, such as Weber law and contrast sensitivity. Other nonlinearities of the form $x^\gamma$ have been also proposed. The third part of the system is a high-pass filter, which enhances image details and explains the Mach phenomenon. Without this part, our vision would be more blurred, as shown in Figure 3.2.8.

Figure 3.2.7: Simple human vision model.

If we ignore the logarithm in Figure 3.2.7, we see that human vision has band-pass characteristics, i.e., it cuts off both low- and high-frequency content. It was found that the impulse response of the first part of the human visual system is similar to that of a *Laplacian-of-Gaussian* (LoG) function, which has the shape of a Mexican sombrero, due to positive synaptic weights to the nearby visual neuron cells, but negative synaptic weights to distant neuron cells. The LoG has band-pass frequency characteristics. This modeling is related to the operation of visual neurons: the positive synaptic coefficients provide image smoothing, while the negative ones improve edge sharpness. In short, the human visual system is sensitive to contrast and high-frequency information, when observing static images. This fact should be taken into account, when we process images

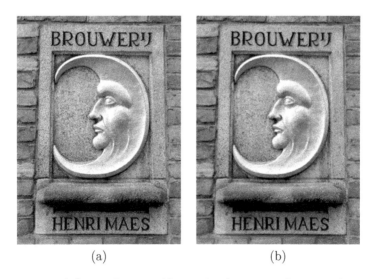

       (a)                          (b)

Figure 3.2.8: a) Original image, b) perceived image without employing the high-pass characteristics of HVS.

to increase their visual quality.

The described eye model is very simple and static and does not describe video understanding, since video is spatiotemporal signal. For spatiotemporal human vision modeling, complicated dynamic neural models of neurons must be used, as opposed to the static model of McCullogh-Pitts. Dynamic neuron modeling is particularly difficult. Furthermore, it is important to take into account the fact that the eye is itself a dynamical system: a) pupil diameter changes with light intensity, b) the human eye can rotate, because of the muscles attached to its exterior and can perform smooth pursuit movements. Because of these difficulties, the spatiotemporal modeling of human vision is performed through experiments, as described in Section 3.5.

## 3.3 Color theory

The visible light is an electromagnetic wave with wavelength $\lambda$ varying in the range 380 - 780 $nm$, where the human eye is sensitive. The perceived color depends on the spectral content of the light. Thus, a light signal, whose energy is concentrated around 700 nm, appears red. Similarly, if the light energy is evenly distributed across the visual spectrum, the light appears to be white. In this sense, the light with a narrow spectral content is called *monochromatic* (single-wavelength). Usually a source emits light at various wavelengths, e.g., the sun emits light in all wavelengths (*white light*).

The perceived color of a light source depends on its emitted energy at various wavelengths. The additive rule is followed: the perceived color from various mixed light sources depends on the sum of the source spectra. The reflective surfaces reflect light, as already described in Chapter 2. When the light is reflected, its energy at some wavelengths is absorbed. The perceived reflected light corresponds to energy at wavelengths which are not absorbed. The percentage of the absorbed energy at various wavelengths $\lambda$ depends on the *reflection coefficient* $r(\lambda)$. Then the *subtraction rule* is followed: the perceived color after reflection depends on the non-absorbed light wavelengths. The light intensity that is reflected from the objects of a scene is recorded as an image by the human eye or a camera.

Color perception by humans is due to the retina cones in the human eye. There are three types of cones, sensitive in the red, green, blue part of the light spectrum, as shown in Figure 3.3.1. The combination of these three sensor types enables the human eye to perceive any color. This implies that the perceived color depends only on three numbers $C_r, C_g, C_b$ rather than on the entire visible light spectrum $f(\lambda)$. This theory is known

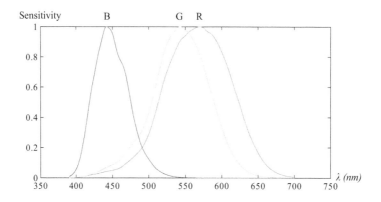

Figure 3.3.1: Cone sensitivity at different wavelengths.

as *trichromatic color vision*. Thus, while the world is *panchromatic*, it is perceived by humans as a trichromatic one. Similarly, artificial optical sensors (e.g., CCDs) have three types of cells that are sensitive to red, green and blue color, respectively. Therefore, cameras having such sensors perform a trichromatic imaging of the world.

There are two color image properties that describe the color sense in humans: *brightness* and *chromaticity*. Brightness refers to the light intensity and is proportional to the total energy in the optical band. The chromaticity respectively refers to perceived light hue and saturation. Brightness and chromaticity are essentially the perceived luminance and chrominance of a color image. Experiments have shown that there is a second processing stage in human visual system, which converts the three cone outputs in three new values. The first one is proportional to brightness and the other two are responsible for chromaticity perception. Human vision processes color signals in an antagonistic manner: red versus green, blue versus yellow and white versus black, since one such color produces excitatory and its opponent color inhibitory effects. This is known as the *opponent color model* of the human visual system. The result of this model is that the same amount of energy at different frequencies causes a different sense of brightness. The green wavelengths contribute more to the feeling of brightness, followed by red and blue.

The visual sense of color images is richer than that of black and white images. Therefore, color pictures or color videos are preferred in many applications. Thus, digital color image acquisition, processing and visualization is very important for a variety of applications, from printing industry to high-definition television (HDTV). Color representation is based on the theory of T. Young (1802), which argues that any color can be produced by mixing three basic colors $C_1, C_2, C_3$ in appropriate proportions:

$C = aC_1 + bC_2 + cC_3$. This theory is consistent with the fact that the human eye has three different types of cones in the retina. Therefore, each color image pixel can be represented by a triplet (vector) $(a, b, c)$ in the color space $(C_1, C_2, C_3)$.

Various color coordinate systems were proposed in the past. The *Commission Internationale de l'Eclairage* (CIE) proposed the fundamental spectral system RGB to match the monochromatic fundamental color sources $R_{CIE}$ (red 700 nm), $G_{CIE}$ (green 546.1 nm) and $B_{CIE}$ (blue 435.8nm). The white color reference is defined by $R_{CIE} = G_{CIE} = B_{CIE} = 1$. The CIE RGB fundamental spectral system can not describe all reproducible colors. For this reason, CIE proposed the XYZ color system having hypothetical (non real) coordinates $X, Y, Z$. The XYZ coordinates are linearly associated with the RGB coordinates, as follows:

$$X = 0.49R_{CIE} + 0.31G_{CIE} + 0.2B_{CIE} \tag{3.3.1}$$

$$Y = 0.177R_{CIE} + 0.813G_{CIE} + 0.011B_{CIE} \tag{3.3.2}$$

$$Z = 0.01G_{CIE} + 0.99B_{CIE}. \tag{3.3.3}$$

The white reference is represented by $X = Y = Z = 1$. The color coordinates:

$$x = \frac{X}{X + Y + Z}, \qquad y = \frac{Y}{X + Y + Z} \tag{3.3.4}$$

can be used to produce the color diagram shown in Figure 3.3.2. The ellipses shown in this diagram correspond to colors which are indistinguishable in human vision. The color differences within such an ellipse can not be seen by the human eye. It is clear that ellipse orientation and size vary. Thus, color differences can not be defined in a uniform manner in the $(x, y)$ domain. To this end, several color systems have been proposed, notably the $UCS$, $U^*V^*\,W^*$, $L^*a^*b^*$ and $L^*u^*v^*$ systems, to measure color differences.

All the above transformations can be easily calculated digitally, but they require fairly complex floating point operations. Therefore, simpler color systems have been proposed for television. It has been proven by experiments that the human visual system is less sensitive to color than to luminance. In the RGB color space, the three colors are considered to be equally important and they are all usually saved at the same bit resolution. However, it is possible to represent a color image more efficiently in a luminance-chrominance domain, by allocating higher spatial resolution

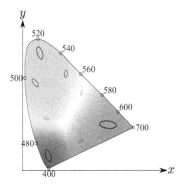

Figure 3.3.2: Chromaticity diagram in the $x, y$ color coordinates.

to luminance than to chrominance channels. To this end, the YIQ color system was used for NTSC TV broadcasting. The transformation from NTSC RGB to YIQ is given in the following equation:

$$Y = 0.299R + 0.587B + 0.114G \qquad (3.3.5)$$

$$I = 0.596R - 0.274B - 0.322G \qquad (3.3.6)$$

$$Q = 0.211R - 0.523B + 0.312G. \qquad (3.3.7)$$

The brightness is represented by the component $Y$. The components $I, Q$ encode image chromaticity. All the above transformations can be coded very easily. The main advantage of the YIQ system was that it guaranteed backward compatibility with monochrome television, when transmitting only the luminance $Y$ channel. Furthermore, the chrominance signals $I, Q$ were sent using much less bandwidth than the luminance $Y$ signal.

The $YC_bC_r$ color space and its varieties is a popular method for an efficient representation of color images in analog (PAL, SECAM) and digital TV. $Y$ is the luminance channel, which can be calculated as a weighted average (3.3.5) of the $R, G, B$ channels. As previously mentioned, the green color plays a bigger role in the definition of luminance. Blue is the least significant color, in terms of its influence on luminance. The chrominance information can be represented as color difference, where each color component is proportional to the difference between $R$ or $B$ and luminance $Y$:

$$C_b = B - Y, \qquad C_r = R - Y. \qquad (3.3.8)$$

BT.601 recommendation proposes a $YC_bC_r$ version, where the coefficients $Y, C_b, C_r$ result from scaling the factor $Y, U, V$ components, so as to take values in $[0, \ldots, 255]$:

$$Y = 0.257R + 0.504G + 0.098B + 16 \tag{3.3.9}$$
$$C_b = 0.148R - 0.291G + 0.439B + 128 \tag{3.3.10}$$
$$C_r = 0.439R - 0.368G - 0.071B + 128. \tag{3.3.11}$$

The main advantage of the $YC_bC_r$ system, in relation to $RGB$, is that the chromaticity $C_b, C_r$ components can be represented with less resolution, because the human visual system is less sensitive to chrominance than to luminance. This reduces the amount of data required to represent color information, without significant perceived visual difference to the viewer. Typically, for compression, we subsample the $C_bC_r$ chrominance components in relation to luminance $Y$. The best known subsampling systems existing in BT.601 and presented in Figure 1.3.1, are the 4:2:0, 4:2:2 systems described in Chapter 1.

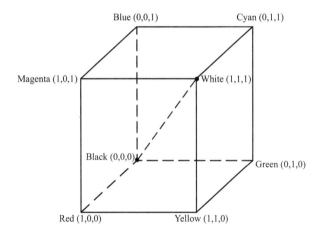

Figure 3.3.3: RGB chromatic cube.

Alternatively, a color image can be represented by the *subtractive* color primaries *cyan*, *magenta* and *yellow*, which are complementary of the red, green and blue primary colors $C = 1 - R$, $M = 1 - G$, $Y = 1 - B$, as shown in the RGB chromatic cube in Figure 3.3.3. Three cube vertices are the primary colors R(1,0,0), G(0,1,0) and B(0,0,1). Vertices (0,0,0) and (1,1,1) represent the black and white colors, respectively, while the rest of the vertices represent the subtractive CMY colors. The *CMY* color system

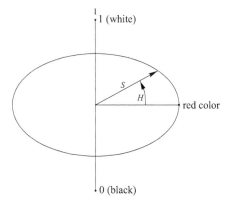

Figure 3.3.4: Definition color hue, saturation and brightness.

is mainly used in printing color images. Because if color ink imperfections, it can not reproduce well the black color. Therefore, it is complemented by the black coordinate $K = min(C, M, Y)$ to form the classical four-color (ink) $CMYK$ printing system.

All previously described color models have been designed to address either hardware issues (RGB, YIQ) or colorimetric ones (XYZ, $L^*a^*b^*$, UCS, $U^*V^*W^*$, $L^*U^*V^*$). Such systems can not approximate well the human visual intuition, notably the artistic one. Human color perception usually involves three properties known as hue, saturation and brightness. *Hue* describes color similarity to reference color stimuli (e.g., red, yellow, blue). Essentially, it determines the 'redness', 'greenness' or 'blueness' of a color. If the light source is monochromatic, hue is an indicator of the light wavelength. Color *saturation* describes the percentage of white light

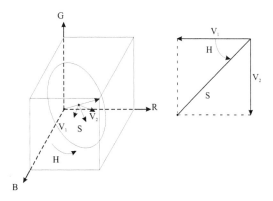

Figure 3.3.5: HSI color space.

added to a pure color. For example, pure red is a very saturated color, while pink is a less saturated one. Color *brightness* indicates the perceived amount of light reflected or emitted by an object. The coordinates of hue, saturation and brightness of a color are shown in Figure 3.3.4. They form a cylindrical coordinate system. Brightness varies from zero (pure black) to one (pure white color). Saturation ranges from zero (pure gray color) to highly saturation values. Hue is the angle between the actual color vector and a reference color vector (e.g., the one referring to red color).

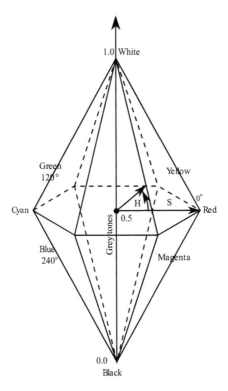

Figure 3.3.6: HLS color space.

Various color models have been developed, in order to represent color hue, saturation and brightness. Such a system is the *HSI* (Hue, Saturation, Intensity) color model. It is a cylindrical coordinate system, whose axis is determined by the line $R = G = B$ in the RGB cube, as shown in Figure 3.3.5. The colors that can be displayed in a cylindrical coordinate HSI system are those included in the RGB cube. For this reason, the allowable saturation range is very small for very bright or very dark images. Another color system based on human color perception is the *HLS* (Hue, Lightness, Saturation) color model. It is defined as a double hexcone in a cylindrical color coordinates system, as shown in Figure 3.3.6. Color hue is defined by an angle, whose value is zero for red color. When the HLS color space is traversed counter-clockwise, the colors appear in the following sequence: red, yellow, green, cyan, blue and magenta. The saturation of the gray light is $S = 0$. Maximum saturation appears in colors having $S = 1$ and $L = 0.5$. Another color system based on human color perception is *HSV* (Hue, Saturation, Value), also called *HSB* (Hue, Saturation, Brightness) system.

## 3.4   Stereopsis

Human vision provides descriptions of the 3D world we live in, obtained from images acquired through our eyes. In order to infer the 3D character-istics of the world objects, we possess *stereo vision* using two eyes. That is, our brain is equipped with the ability to process two (left, right) images at the same time (i.e., one from each eye) and acquire 3D information of the scene we are looking at. This ability is called stereo vision or *stereopsis*. Figure 3.4.1 depicts the so-called *binocular visual field*. Furthermore, it

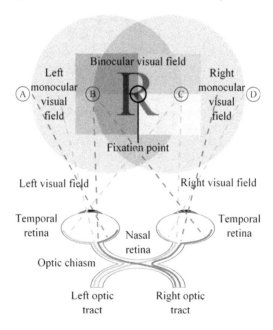

Figure 3.4.1: Binocular visual field and optic chiasm.

shows the projection of the binocular field of view onto the two retinas and its relation to the optical nerve crossing at the *optic chiasm*. Points in the binocular portion of the left visual field (*B*) fall on the nasal retina of the left eye and the temporal retina of the right eye. Points in the binocular portion of the right visual field (*C*) fall on the nasal retina of the right eye and the temporal retina of the left eye. Points that lie in the *monocular* portions of the left and right visual fields (*A* and *D*) fall on the left and right *nasal retinas*, respectively. The axons of neural cells in the nasal retina cross in the optic chiasm, whereas those from the temporal retina do not. As a result, information from the left visual field is carried in the right optic tract and information from the right visual field is carried in the left optic tract.

### 3.4.1  Human stereo image perception

In the case of stereo displays, we project two (left/right images) on the video screen for depth perception, as shown in Figure 3.4.2. Actually, we trick our eyes and our mind into thinking that there is depth, where there is none. This trick works better and produces a serious deception, if depth perception is an active process that involves eye muscles and movement. If this process is not smooth, we can have *visual discomfort*. The most relevant factors in contributing to this effect are excessive accommodation-convergence conflict, excessive binocular disparity and binocular crosstalk.

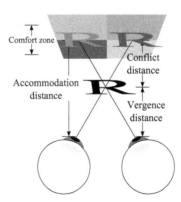

Figure 3.4.2: Accommodation and vergence conflict.

In human stereopsis, accommodation and vergence are two *oculomotor mechanisms*, which are usually hard to separate. *Accommodation* has to do with the change in ocular focus. It can be either a reflex or a consciously controlled action. The ability of accommodation declines with age. At a young age, the human eye can focus to distances as close as 7cm from the eye, in 350 ms. *Vergence* is the change in ocular alignment and is caused by the simultaneous movement of both eyes in opposite directions, in order to maintain single binocular vision, as shown in Figure 3.4.2. When we try to look closer at an object, the eyes rotate towards each other *(convergence)*. The opposite phenomenon is called *divergence*.

In a natural environment, the distance at which our eyes converge is the same to the distance at which our eyes focus. Let us assume that we project a 3D object meant to appear to be in front of the screen. Our left/right eye turns to look at the left/right image of the object. Put together, our eyes converge (vergence), as if the object exists in front of the screen, as can be seen in Figure 3.4.2. As our eyes converge, our brain sends instructions to the eyes to focus the way they normally would for a real object that is located at that convergence distance (accommodation). But in 3D movies, the "object" is in focus on the screen, which is behind this convergence point. This creates the so-called *vergence-accommodation conflict*. Therefore, it is best if the 3D object is displayed in a *comfort zone* that is close to the screen, as shown in Figure 3.4.2.

Left and right images have certain differences, due to view point change. Left and right image landmarks are linked through *disparity*. Binocular disparity must be kept within some limits. Excessive binocular disparity can lead to *diplopia* (double vision). In order to avoid it, the brain can, sometimes, ignore the image from one eye. This is obviously a very tiring process for the brain.

Another source of viewing discomfort is *crosstalk*. Ideally, the left-/right-eye image should be seen only by the left/right eye, respectively, without crossview (crosstalk). Crosstalk produces ghosting or maybe blurring and is a potential cause of eye strain and headaches. Typically, these issues are confronted during 3DTV content production/post-production to prevent visual discomfort, as described in Chapter 6. Without proper solutions, some viewers may experience discomfort, while viewing 3DTV content, such as dizziness, nausea and headaches.

Another issue related to stereopsis is *binocular rivalry*. When discrepant monocular images are presented to the two eyes, they rival for perceptual dominance. Therefore, only one monocular image is perceived at a time, while the other is suppressed from awareness. Binocular rivalry effects, which can be extremely disturbing, occur when the dominant image alternates from one eye to the other. Binocular rivalry depends on factors such as image size, sharpness and brightness differences. It can be exploited in stereo TV coding, where only the dominant image is coded in big detail.

# 3.5    Spatiotemporal sensitivity of the human

# visual system

Almost every video processing and display system ultimately addresses human viewers. It is, therefore, extremely important to understand how the human visual system perceives a video signal, so that the video display requirements are specified. In this section, we shall focus on our perception of spatial and temporal variations in image luminance. As will be shown below, the sensitivity of the human visual system to an optical pattern depends on its spatial and temporal frequencies. The HVS optical sensitivity is highest in some intermediate spatiotemporal frequencies. It decreases rapidly with either spatial or temporal frequency increase and it practically vanishes beyond some cutoff frequencies. Spatiotemporal video content variations beyond these cut-off frequencies are invisible to the human eye. Knowledge of the frequency response of the human visual system is very important in designing a video system. For example, the spatial and temporal cutoff frequencies are the basis for determining the scanning mode (progressive/interlaced), frame rate and spatial resolution, when displaying video either in TV or in cinema.

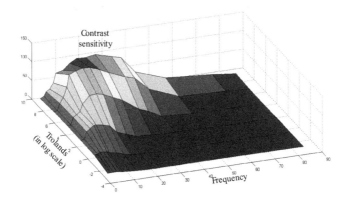

Figure 3.5.1: Contrast sensitivity of the human visual system.

The *temporal frequency response* (sensitivity) of the human visual system refers its sensitivity to temporal video content variations. Many experiments were conducted in the '60s by Kelly to determine the temporal frequency response of the human visual system, in order to study display *flicker* and to determine the necessary frame rate for television and cinema. *Contrast sensitivity* is a function of the temporal video frequency $F_t$ and average screen luminance $C$ (measured in trolands) is shown in Figure 3.5.1. *Troland* is a unit used to describe the light intensity entering the eye retina. It can be observed that the time response of the human visual system is similar to that of a band-pass filter, peaking at some intermediate temporal frequencies and then reducing sharply after a cutoff frequency approximately equal to 4.5 times the peak frequency. Peak frequency increases with the average image brightness.

The smallest display frequency, where the human eye can not perceive flickering is called *critical flicker frequency*. It ranges between 20 and 80 Hz, depending on screen brightness. Video must be displayed at rates above the critical flicker frequency. Since the cinema screens are rather dark, the frame rate in cinema displays is chosen to be only 24 fps. If the cinema display rate falls below 15 fps, intense image flickering occurs. On the other hand, higher frame rates (50 or 60 fields per second in PAL/NSTC systems, respectively) are chosen for video display on TV, since, in this case, the average screen brightness is bigger. In the case of computers, an even higher display rate (also called *refresh rate*) is used (at least 70 Hz), since the user is close to the computer screen and the perceived screen brightness is even bigger.

One reason that the eye has low sensitivity to high temporal frequencies is that it can retain the sense of an image (called *afterimage*) for a short time, even after the visual stimulus has been removed. This phenomenon is known as *vision persistence* and is caused by the temporal integration of the incoming light energy. Block's law states that the integration period is inversely proportional to that of the light intensity. The brighter the source is, the shorter is the integration period. Therefore, contrast sensitivity increases with screen brightness.

The *spatial frequency response* of the human visual system refers to its visual sensitivity, when viewing a static spatial pattern at different spatial frequencies, describing the level of image detail. Assuming that the spatial sensitivity is isotropic with respect to the orientation of the spatial variations, the spatial frequency response can be measured in relation to an arbitrary spatial axis. Typically the horizontal or vertical axes are used, despite the fact that it is known that our spatial sensitivity is higher along these axes, than along any other axis. In order to normalize viewing distance, the so-called *angular spatial frequency*, described in Chapter 4, measured in cycles per degree (cpd) of view angle, can be employed. Many experiments were made by Kelly to assess the spatial frequency response. It was found by experimentations that the spatial frequency response of the human visual system is similar to that of a band-pass filter. Figure 3.5.2 illustrates the spatial frequency response of the human visual system. The peak response is observed at about 2-5 cpd. The cut-off spatial frequency is

30 cpd. Figure 3.5.2 shows two sets of measurements, one for unconstrained eye motion and one for a stabilized eye that cannot move. Eye motion influences its spatial sensitivity. It is known that *saccadic eye movement* (from one fixation point to another) greatly increases its spatial sensitivity, but reduces the peak frequency from 5 cpd to approximately 2 cpd. The band-pass nature of the spatial frequency response can be explained by the HVS models presented earlier in this Chapter.

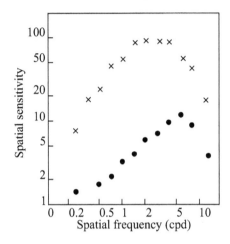

Figure 3.5.2: Spatial frequency response of the human visual system with ( × ) and without ( • ) saccadic eye movement.

Video perception changes greatly, when the video content changes both spatially and temporally. The resulting contrast sensitivity is visualized in Figure 3.5.3 as a function of the spatial $F_x$ and temporal $F_t$ video frequencies for unconstrained eye motion. We can observe that, when the temporal (spatial) frequencies are close to zero, the spatial (temporal) frequency response has band-pass characteristics, respectively. At higher temporal (spatial) frequencies, the spatial (temporal) frequency response is more of a low-pass nature with its peak response frequency reducing, when the temporal (spatial) frequency increases. This reveals that, when an image pattern moves very quickly, the eye will not be able to distinguish its very high spatial frequencies (image details). The eye can discern image details much better, when the image pattern is stationary.

One implication of this inverse relationship between spatial and temporal sensitivity is that we can "swap" spatial video resolution with temporal one and vice versa, as was wisely done in interlaced scanning in analog television systems. In interlaced scanning, fast moving scenes can be visualized well by virtually doubling the display rate using two temporally adjacent fields, each having half the number of frame lines. On the other

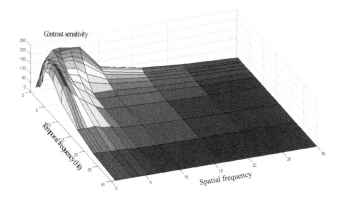

Figure 3.5.3: Spatiotemporal frequency response of the human visual system.

hand, when the visualized scene is static, the lines in two consecutive fields are perceived as one high spatial resolution video frame, thus allowing the perception of higher spatial frequencies (image details) in static scenes.

The inverse relationship between spatial and temporal responses also explains why we see flickering when watching TV at close range. In this case, the perceived angular spatial frequency is low. At low angular spatial frequencies, the human eye has higher temporal sensitivity and, therefore, can more easily perceive flicker.

The spatiotemporal frequency response of the human eye suggests that we have limited spatial sensitivity for fast moving objects. In fact, the human eye can see clearly the details in a fast moving object, when the eye follows the object trajectory. This is called *smooth pursuit eye movement*. For example, when we follow the trajectory of an airplane flying at high altitude, we can distinguish some of its details. This is because the relative object (airplane) motion on the retina becomes small or even zero, when the eye tracks the object.

## 3.6   Video Quality Estimation

In recent years, there has been an explosion in video applications, ranging from digital TV to videoconferencing, streaming and social media. In most cases, humans are the final users of such applications. Therefore, there is a need for *Video Quality Assessment* (VQA), i.e., to quantify video quality, as perceived by a human. The relevant algorithms play a key role in almost every aspect of video processing and display. Video quality is influenced by several factors, such as compression, noise, transmission errors and delays. Video quality assessment can help to meet the quality requirements for video storage and transmission. The quality of videos created by recording devices (e.g., digital camcorders) and video processing algorithms (e.g., video codecs, filters) can be evaluated automatically using quality assessment algorithms, aiming at optimizing video acquisition and processing systems.

The only reliable method for video assessment is to ask human observers to watch the video and assess its quality in a numerical or quantitative scale. This method is known as *subjective video quality assessment*. However, such subjective quality surveys are labor intensive and expensive to run. They may require a large number of viewers to cover human quality assessment variability and to provide a statistical certainty on the actual video quality. In such a case, the assessment depends on various factors, such as the video display screen size, the viewing distance from the screen, the video content, viewer familiarity with video processing, etc. Furthermore, it is impossible to subjectively assess all videos before broadcasting or delivery. Subjective assessment is useful in providing a benchmark reference to evaluate objective or automated VQA methods.

*Objective video quality assessment* methods (without using human observers) are divided into three categories. The *full reference VQA* algorithms operate on distorted video, while employing the original video reference for comparison purposes. The vast majority of quality assessment algorithms fall into this category, because of the simplicity of comparing original videos with their distorted versions. The *Mean Square Error* (MSE) and the *Peak Signal to Noise Ratio* (PSNR), measured in *decibel* (dB), calculated between the reference video and the distorted video are two video similarity metrics. They have been widely used to measure video quality, mainly because of their simplicity and mathematical convenience. The smaller the MSE is, the larger the PSNR (in *dB*) is and the smaller the distortion is. However, it is known that these two video quality measures correlate only very roughly with subjective visual quality. The main reason of their failure is that they do not take into account the characteristics of the human visual system.

The *reduced reference VQA* algorithms work without using the original reference video, but only some original video information. They do use the distorted video though. These algorithms can use, e.g., local spatiotemporal activity information or edge locations on the reference video. Other VQA algorithms in this class use knowledge about the video distortion process, e.g., the distortion introduced by video compression of filtering, such as image blur characteristics.

The *blind VQA* algorithms (without reference) attempt to assess video quality resorting only on the distorted video. In this view, no prior knowledge is known, neither about video distortion nor the reference video. In practice, this process has proven extremely difficult. Nevertheless, the fact that the average viewer can estimate the video quality almost instantaneously, probably predisposes that there is room for future developments in this direction.

$$4$$

# VIDEO PROCESSING

## 4.1 Introduction

In video processing systems, both their input and output are video streams, possessing different characteristics, e.g., less noise and better video quality. In order to understand the functionality of such systems, we have to introduce the notion of the frequency domain and image video/transforms. Video quality is very important in many applications, particularly when a human viewer is involved. Video processing provides various tools for video quality enhancement, notably contrast enhancement and noise filtering. Several other topics fall in the general category of video processing. Format conversion is such an important issue, e.g., for converting legacy video from 480i (NTSC) to 576i (PAL/SECAM) or to 1080p HDTV video formats. A special case of format conversion is de-interlacing, when we want to change interlaced video to progressive one.

Video processing, overlaps in many respects with image processing, particularly when processing is done at intraframe level. Therefore, an exposure to image processing can greatly help understanding the video processing principles. Furthermore, video processing, particularly signal/-image/video transforms, are highly mathematical in nature. A special effort has been made to present an illustrative and simplified, yet accurate, description of these mathematical tools. Therefore, we concentrate primarily on their physical meaning, rather than on their mathematical description.

## 4.2    Signal, image and video transforms

### 4.2.1    1D signal transforms

The notion of *frequency* is fundamental in signal, image, and video processing and analysis. In the case of *one-dimensional* (1D) signals $x(t)$, where $t$ denotes time, e.g., in audio and music signals, the *Fourier transform* $X(\Omega)$ describes the signal in the frequency $F$ or $\Omega = 2\pi F$ domain. Frequency $F$ describes signal changes over time and is measured in cycles per second or *Hertz* (Hz). Sinusoids are typical periodic signals, whose frequency is measured in Hz. The Fourier transform $X(\Omega)$ essentially decomposes a signal in a sum of properly weighted periodic signals (typically complex exponential functions). It produces complex numbers $X(\Omega)$ having a magnitude $|X(\Omega)|$ and a phase $\phi(X(\Omega))$. Low-frequency (bass) audio signals have most of their energy concentrated in the low $F$ (and hence $\Omega$) frequencies (e.g., in the range of 0-120 Hz). High-frequency audio signals have most of their energy concentrated in the high frequencies, e.g., above 10 kHz. The *DC term*, or *DC frequency* $X(0)$ for $\Omega = 0$ is essentially the average signal energy. The Fourier transform $X(\Omega)$ of a digital signal $x(n)$ having $N$ samples $x(0), ..., x(N-1)$ can be calculated via the *Discrete Fourier Transform* (DFT):

$$X(k) = \sum_{n=0}^{N-1} x(n) \exp\left(-i\frac{2\pi nk}{N}\right) =$$

$$= \sum_{n=0}^{N-1} x(n) \left(\cos\left(-i\frac{2\pi nk}{N}\right) - \sin\left(-i\frac{2\pi nk}{N}\right)\right). \qquad (4.2.1)$$

where $\sum$ denotes summation. The $N$ DFT coefficients $X(k)$, $k = 1, \ldots, N$ are complex numbers. The DFT coefficient magnitude $|X(k)|$ form the periodogram, which is an estimation of the power spectrum $|X(\Omega)|$. An example of the periodogram of a short music piece is shown in Figure 4.2.1. The DFT coefficients $X(k)$ correspond to low frequencies for small $k$ values (around 0) and to high frequencies for large $k$ values (around $k = N/2$). The DFT coefficient $X(0)$ is the DC term. The DFT (4.2.1) can be easily calculated via the *Fast Fourier Transform* (FFT) algorithm, having computational complexity $O(N \log_2 N)$.

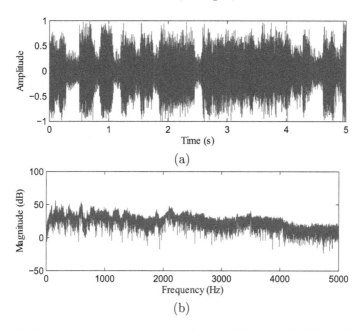

(a)

(b)

Figure 4.2.1: a) Short music piece in the time domain, b) its DFT magnitude.

## 4.2.2 Image transforms and frequency content

The notion of frequency domain can be gracefully extended to the case of images, which are *two-dimensional* (2D) signals $f(x,y)$, where $x$ and $y$ are the two spatial coordinates and $f(x,y)$ denotes image luminance at location $(x,y)$. The *2D Fourier transform* $F(\Omega_x, \Omega_y)$ describes the image in the frequency $(\Omega_x, \Omega_y)$ domain. Frequencies $(\Omega_x, \Omega_y)$ describe spatial image changes. Fast image content changes along the $x, y$ axes, e.g., image details, horizontal/vertical edges correspond to high frequencies $\Omega_x$ and/or

$\Omega_y$. Slow or no image content changes along the $x, y$ axes, i.e., homogeneous image regions, correspond to low frequencies $\Omega_x, \Omega_y$. The DC term $F(0,0)$ describes the average image intensity. The 2D Fourier transform $F(\Omega_x, \Omega_y)$ essentially decomposes an image in a sum of periodic signals (complex exponential functions). It is a complex transform, i.e., it produces complex numbers having magnitude $|F(\Omega_x, \Omega_y)|$ and phase $\phi(F(\Omega_x, \Omega_y))$. The 2D Fourier transform $F(\Omega_x, \Omega_y)$ of a digital image $f(n_1, n_2)$ having $N_1 \times N_2$ pixels can be calculated via the *2D Discrete Fourier Transform* (DFT):

$$F(k_1, k_2) = \sum_{n_1=0}^{N_1-1} \sum_{n_2=0}^{N_2-1} f(n_1, n_2) \exp\left(-i\frac{2\pi n_1 k_1}{N_1} - i\frac{2\pi n_2 k_2}{N_2}\right). \quad (4.2.2)$$

The 2D DFT coefficients $F(k_1, k_2)$ correspond to low frequencies for small $k_1, k_2$ values and to high frequencies for large $k_1, k_2$ values. The DFT coefficient $F(0,0)$ is the DC term. It must be noted that we have $N_1 \times N_2$ DFT coefficients $F(k_1, k_2)$, $k_1 = 0, .., N_1 - 1$, $k_2 = 0, .., N_2 - 1$. The DFT (4.2.2) can be easily calculated via the *2D Fast Fourier Transform* (FFT) algorithm. The 2D DFT coefficient magnitudes $|F(k_1, k_2)|$ of a digital image are shown in Figure 4.2.2. The DC term $F(0,0)$ is shown at the image center. Low frequencies are shown around the image center. It is clearly seen that most image energy is concentrated around the DC term in the low- and mid-frequency DCT coefficients. This fact is exploited in *transform-based image coding*: we discard or heavily quantize high-frequency transform coefficients, since they carry little information. This fact greatly compresses digital images. Two directional images having horizontal and vertical edges, respectively, are shown in Figure 4.2.3.

(a)                                      (b)

Figure 4.2.2: a) Digital image, b) its DFT coefficient magnitude.

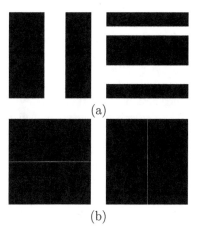

(a)

(b)

Figure 4.2.3: a) Directional images, b) their DFT coefficient magnitude.

Their corresponding 2D DFT spectra are directional as well. They have non-zero DFT coefficients only along directions that are perpendicular to their edges.

The 2D spatial frequencies $F_x, F_y$ ($\Omega_x = 2\pi F_x$, $\Omega_y = 2\pi F_y$) are a measure of how quickly the image luminance changes on the image plane. We can measure the spatial frequency along different orthogonal axes than $(x, y)$. The spatial frequency along a given axis is measured in cycles per unit length. In the metric measure system, we use *cycles per meter* (cpm). For example, a sinusoidal spatial pattern of $f(x, y) = \sin(12\pi y)$ has a frequency (0,6), which means that this image changes at 6 cycles per unit length along the vertical direction, while it remains constant along the horizontal direction. On the other hand an image $f(x, y) = \sin(20\pi x + 8\pi y)$ has frequency (10,4), that corresponds to ten and four cycles per unit length along horizontal and vertical direction, respectively. These sinusoidal patterns are shown in Figure 4.2.4.

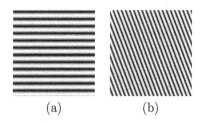

(a)                    (b)

Figure 4.2.4: Two dimensional sinusoidal images: a) $(F_x, F_y) = (0, 6)$, b) $(F_x, F_y) = (10, 4)$.

The spatial frequencies $F_x, F_y$ determine the luminance changes along directions $x, y$. This is not always useful, as the observed image frequency content depends on the observation distance and screen size. For example, an image, when viewed from close range appears to have lower frequency content, than when it is viewed from further apart. When displaying images, a more useful measure of spatial frequency is the *angular spatial frequency* measured in *cycles per degree* (cpd) of viewing angle. As shown in Figure 4.2.5, if a display screen has a height $H$ and is observed from distance $D$, the vertical observation angle is $\theta$. If there are $F_y$ cycles per unit picture height, then the number of observed cycles per degree (vertical angular spatial frequency) can be easily found. A similar procedure can define the horizontal angular spatial frequency. For a fixed observation distance, a bigger screen height $H$ lowers the angular spatial frequency. These results fit well to our intuition: the same image appears to change more rapidly, when the observer moves away from the image screen and changes more slowly if the image is viewed on a larger screen.

Since DFT is a complex transform and, furthermore, does not provide very good energy compaction, other transforms, notably the *Discrete Cosine Transform* (DCT), have been proposed for image compression. The following definition of the $N_1 \times N_2$ DCT can be used:

$$C(k_1, k_2) = \sum_{n_1=0}^{N_1-1} \sum_{n_2=0}^{N_2-1} 4f(n_1, n_2) \cos \frac{(2n_1 + 1)k_1\pi}{2N_1} \cos \frac{(2n_2 + 1)k_2\pi}{2N_2},$$

$$(4.2.3)$$

for $0 \leq k_1 \leq N_1 - 1$, $0 \leq k_2 \leq N_2 - 1$. DCT coefficients are real (not complex) numbers. An example of a 2D DCT transform can be seen in Figure 4.2.6.

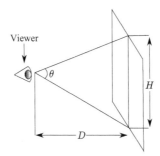

Figure 4.2.5: Relation between viewing angle and observation distance.

(a) (b)

Figure 4.2.6: a) Digital image, b) its DCT coefficients.

The 2D DCT essentially decomposes an image in a sum of properly weighted cosine functions. We still use the term 'frequencies' for describing DCT coefficients, though this term must be attributed to Fourier transform coefficients. The DC term $C(0,0)$ corresponds to the average image intensity and is displayed in the upper left image corner in Figure 4.2.6b. Most image energy is concentrated in the low- and mid-frequency range, close to the DC term, as shown in Figure 4.2.6. This fact is exploited in transform-based image coding: we discard or heavily quantize high-frequency DCT coefficients, since they carry little information. This procedure greatly compresses digital images and is routinely used in JPEG image compression and in MPEG-1/2/4 video compression standards.

### 4.2.3 Spatiotemporal frequencies in a video signal

The notions of frequency and transforms can be easily extended to cover video, which is a *three-dimensional* (3D) signal $f(x, y, t)$, where $x, y$ are the spatial image coordinates and $t$ denotes time. The *3D Fourier transform* $F(\Omega_x, \Omega_y, \Omega_t)$ describes the video in the 3D spatiotemporal frequency domain $(\Omega_x, \Omega_y, \Omega_t)$. Frequencies $(\Omega_x, \Omega_y)$ describe spatial video changes, e.g., image details and edges, whereas frequencies $\Omega_t$ describe temporal video changes, e.g., object motion. Fast video content changes along the $x, y$ axes, e.g., image details, horizontal/vertical edges correspond to high spatial frequencies $(\Omega_x, \Omega_y)$. Slow or no image content changes along the $x, y$ axes, i.e., homogeneous video frame regions, correspond to low spatial frequencies $(\Omega_x, \Omega_y)$. Fast object motion corresponds to high temporal frequencies $\Omega_t$. Slow object motion or almost still-picture video corresponds to low temporal frequencies $\Omega_t$. The DC term $F(0, 0, 0)$ describes the average video intensity. The 3D Fourier transform $F(\Omega_x, \Omega_y, \Omega_t)$ essentially decomposes a video in a sum of periodic signals (complex exponential functions). It has a magnitude $|F(\Omega_x, \Omega_y, \Omega_t)|$ and a phase. The 3D Fourier transform $F(\Omega_x, \Omega_y, \Omega_t)$ of a digital video $f(n_1, n_2, n_t)$ having $N_1 \times N_2 \times N_3$ pixels can be calculated via a *3D Discrete Fourier Transform*, which is a simple extension of equation (4.2.2).

In an one-dimensional temporal function $f(t)$, the meaning of temporal frequency $F(\Omega_t)$ is clear: it counts the number of signal alterations over time, in Hz. In the video signal, which consists of two-dimensional video frames changing over time, the temporal frequency depends on the spatiotemporal video content location $(x, y, t)$, i.e., on object motion. In general, when the video content is moving, either because of camera motion, or due to object motion, or due to a combination of both, the temporal frequencies depend on this motion. Frequently, there may be several scene objects having different motion patterns. Therefore, it is not easy to relate directly video content motion and temporal frequency. However, few qualitative observations can be easily made:

1) When a video frame shows only an object region having uniform luminance, then no temporal video content variation can be observed, regardless of the object motion.

2) The temporal frequency is zero $\Omega_t = 0$, if the local motion vector $(v_x, v_y)$ is orthogonal to the spatial frequency vector $\mathbf{\Omega}$, as shown in Figure 4.2.7. If we have an infinite-sized sheet of paper at a diagonal orientation, the vector $\mathbf{\Omega}$ is perpendicular to the paper edge. If the paper moves along the edge, the motion is not observable and does not produce temporal frequencies, because the motion vector $\mathbf{v}$ is perpendicular to vector $\mathbf{\Omega}$. Conversely, if the sheet moves with velocity $\mathbf{v}'$ perpendicular to the edge, then the luminance changes over time are maximized and temporal frequencies are produced as well. If, finally, the sheet moves so that its white part covers the entire observed image, again we have no observable motion.

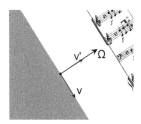

Figure 4.2.7: A moving infinite-sized sheet of paper.

# 4.3 Video filtering and enhancement

Videos are acquired by photoelectronic, e.g., CCD, sensors. Sensing devices tend to degrade the quality of the digital images by introducing noise, geometric deformation and/or blur, due to motion or camera misfocus, as already described in Chapter 2. One of the primary concerns in digital video processing is to increase image quality and to moderate the degradations introduced by the video acquisition devices. *Video restoration* techniques are concerned primarily with the reconstruction or recovery of a video that has been degraded, e.g., due to motion blur. A priori knowledge about the degradation phenomenon may be used for this purpose. *Digital video enhancement* techniques increase subjective image quality by sharpening certain image features (edges, details, boundaries), by increasing contrast and by reducing noise.

Digital enhancement and restoration operations can be performed using either one-dimensional (temporal) or two-dimensional (spatial) or three-dimensional (spatiotemporal) digital filters. When we operate on local temporal neighborhoods of one image pixel, we use one-dimensional filters. When we operate on each video frame independently, then we use two-dimensional digital filters. When we operate on each video frame, while employing information from neighboring video frames (e.g., from the previous/next frame), then we use three-dimensional digital filters. Filters can be distinguished in two big classes: *linear digital filters* and *nonlinear digital filters*. Linear digital image filters can be designed and/or implemented either in the spatial domain (*spatial operations*) or in the frequency domain (*transform operations*). Many digital restoration filters are linear ones and are usually implemented in the frequency domain. There are, of course, several nonlinear digital image restoration techniques as well. Spatial operations (linear or nonlinear) are primarily used for digital image enhancement. There are digital filters having *regions of support*, also called *filter windows* that consist of a single pixel (*point operations*) or a pixel neighborhood (*local operations*). Such neighborhoods can be spatial ones (residing within a video frame), spatiotemporal ones (covering parts of the current and neighboring video frames) and temporal ones, described by a pixel trajectory over time.

## 4.3.1 Linear and nonlinear video filtering

Since digital video acquisition and recording systems are not perfect, the recorded video may be noisy. Therefore, we have to filter the video to eliminate or reduce the recorded noise. In many cases, the noise is, or can be modeled as, additive and white one. Since it typically covers the high-frequency regions, while the image content covers the low- and mid-frequency regions, we use low-pass filters to remove such noise. In this section, we shall assume a simple additive noise model $f(n_1, n_2, t) = s(n_1, n_2, t) + w(n_1, n_2, t)$, where $f(n_1, n_2, t)$, $s(n_1, n_2, t)$, $w(n_1, n_2, t)$ denote the noisy video, the original (ideal) video and the recorded noise, respectively.

*Denoising* filters can be classified into temporal, spatial (intraframe) or spatiotemporal (interframe) ones. Generally speaking, when the video signal is filtered along one or two dimensions, we have reduced computational complexity and suboptimal filtering performance, because we can not take advantage of all possible degrees of freedom in filter design, as in the case of a true spatiotemporal filter. Yet, we do use temporal or spatial filters in video, due to their reduced computational complexity.

*Temporal filters* are one-dimensional, since they are applied only along the time $t$ coordinate. A simple temporal filter calculates the time-weighted average of successive video frames:

$$\hat{s}(n_1, n_2, t) = \sum_{l=-\nu}^{\nu} w(l) f(n_1, n_2, t - l) \tag{4.3.1}$$

where $w(l)$ are the filter coefficients (weights) for $2\nu + 1$ consecutive video frames. $\sum$ denotes summation. If all frames are equally important, the filter coefficients may be equal $\alpha(l) = \frac{1}{2\nu+1}$, resulting in an one-dimensional temporal *moving average* filter. Due to memory problems and computational complexity issues, in many cases, only the previous $f(n_1, n_2, t - 1)$ and the next $f(n_1, n_2, t + 1)$ video frames are used for filtering the current video frame $f(n_1, n_2, t)$, i.e., we choose $\nu = 1$. The following one-dimensional filter:

$$g(n_1, n_2, t) = \alpha g(n_1, n_2, t - 1) + (1 - \alpha) f(n_1, n_2, t) \tag{4.3.2}$$

can also be used for simple temporal video filtering.

Motion artifacts can be reduced significantly by using the filter (4.3.1) on pixels lying along motion trajectory. Then (4.3.1) becomes a *motion-compensated* temporal filter:

$$\hat{f}(n_1, n_2, t) = \sum_{l=-\nu}^{\nu} w(l) f(n_1 - dx, n_2 - dy, t - l), \tag{4.3.3}$$

where $(dx, dy)$ is the motion vector at pixel location $(n_1, n_2)$ calculated between the video frames $t$ and $t - l$. Such filters extending over very long time windows are used in removing noise from astronomical video observations. Noise reduction and motion estimation create competing demands, with respect to the temporal filter window length $2\nu + 1$. If the filter length increases, noise reduction performance increases as well. However, the same applies to errors due to incorrect motion estimation between video frames lying further apart in time.

*Spatial (intraframe) filters* operate on two-dimensional windows within a video frame. Since they do not defer at all from classical still image filters, we do not expand on this issue.

*Spatiotemporal (interframe) video filters* operate on spatiotemporal windows, typically extending at least to the previous, current and next video frame. Such a $3 \times 3 \times 3$ window is shown in Figure 4.3.1. A very simple three-dimensional low-pass filter is the 3D $L_1 \times L_2 \times L_3$ *moving average* filter. If the 3D window sizes are odd numbers $L_i = 2\nu_i + 1$, $i = 1, 2, 3$, then the filter is defined as follows:

$$g(n_1, n_2, n_3) = \frac{1}{L_1 L_2 L_3} \sum_{k_1=-\nu_1}^{\nu_1} \sum_{k_2=-\nu_2}^{\nu_2} \sum_{k_3=-\nu_3}^{\nu_3} f(n_1 - k_1, n_2 - k_2, n_3 - k_3).$$

$$(4.3.4)$$

The moving average filter is low-pass one and is widely used in in video processing and three-dimensional image processing, e.g., for medical imaging. A three dimensional nonlinear filter is the 3D $L_1 \times L_2 \times L_3$ *moving*

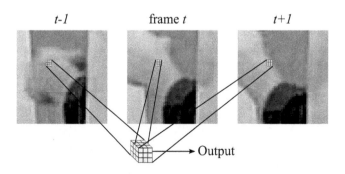

Figure 4.3.1: A spatiotemporal $3 \times 3 \times 3$ filter window.

*median* filter:

$$g(n_1, n_2, n_3) = \underset{k_1,k_2,k_3}{med} \{f(n_1 - k_1, n_2 - k_2, n_3 - k_3)\}, \qquad (4.3.5)$$

where $(k_1, k_2, k_3) \in [-\nu_1, \nu_1] \times [-\nu_2, \nu_2] \times [-\nu_3, \nu_3]$ and *med* is the pixel median value in the local filter window. The $L_1 \times L_2 \times L_3$ pixels in the median filter window are sorted and their median is chosen as the current output pixel. The three-dimensional median filter is widely used in video noise filtering and has the ability to retain spatiotemporal image edges. On the contrary, the moving average filter tends to blur such edges.

Moving average filters remove well additive noise and have best performance in additive Gaussian noise removal. Unfortunately, they tend to smooth spatiotemporal edges, creating spatial and temporal blur on still or moving object boundaries. The 3D median filters remove very well impulse noise, preserve spatiotemporal object boundaries, but tend to destroy spatiotemporal video details. For this reason, it is desirable to use *adaptive spatiotemporal* filters, which change the spatial windows, so that they are different on each video frame, depending on the local luminance distribution. They can also change the number of used frames before and after the current frame, so that the filter adapts to local spatiotemporal video luminance characteristics.

Based on the assumption that luminance changes along any motion trajectory are mainly due to noise, we can use *motion compensation* for noise reduction. The structure of such *motion compensated filters* varies according to:

- the motion estimation method,

- the filter window (temporal versus spatiotemporal) and

- the filter structure, e.g., adaptive versus non-adaptive.

Let us suppose that we want to filter the $t - th$ video frame of an image sequence using $N$ video frames $t - \nu, ..., t, ..., t + \nu$, where $N = 2\nu + 1$. The first step is to evaluate the distinct motion trajectory $\mathbf{d}(n_1, n_2, t, l,$ $l = t - \nu, ..., t, ..., t - \nu$ for each pixel $(n_1, n_2)$ at frame $t$. This is done using motion estimation, as detailed in Chapter 5. The estimated motion vectors show the displacement between the pixel $(n_1, n_2)$ at frame $t$ and the corresponding pixel at frame $l$. Figure 4.3.2 displays such a motion trajectory for N= 5 frames ($\nu = 2$). The window of the motion compensated spatiotemporal filter uses all local spatial neighborhoods (e.g., of size $3 \times 3$ pixels) that are centered on the motion trajectory positions.

Various filtering techniques can be used on such a filter window using motion compensation. For example, two-dimensional moving average

Figure 4.3.2: Motion trajectory along five successive video frames (*courtesy of the i3DPost FP7 project*).

or median filters can be used for denoising, as reported in previous paragraphs. Filter (4.3.3) is a special case of one-dimensional temporal motion compensated filter, where the spatial neighborhood at each video frame $t - \nu, ..., t, ..., t + \nu$ contains only single pixel. When motion estimation is perfect, the arithmetic mean of the image luminance along the motion trajectory provides effective noise reduction. However, if motion estimation fails, the arithmetic mean may produce video blur. In the case of spatiotemporal filtering, there may be spatial changes in the filter window along the motion trajectory, i.e., the spatial neighborhoods may vary in each frame $t - l$, $l = -\nu, ..., \nu$, depending on the image content around the position $(n_1 - dx, n_2 - dy, t - l)$. For example, the filter window can grow when we have spatially homogeneous image luminance locally around the location $(n_1 - dx, n_2 - dy, t - l)$ that is not very different from $f(n_1, n_2, t)$. For this reason, it is preferable to combine motion compensation and adaptive filter structures.

Legacy video content may suffer from color fade or shift, dust, scratches and tears that resulted from digitizing degraded films. In such cases, advanced spatiotemporal video filtering can be used for movie restoration. For example, color can be corrected, contrast can be enhanced, scratches and tears can be filled/eliminated. The video frame jitter due to small film frame misalignments can be reduced. Finally, film grain noise can be filtered out.

## 4.4   Video format conversion

Format conversion is an important issue, e.g., for converting legacy video from 480i (NTSC) to 576i (PAL/SECAM) video formats. *Frame rate conversion* falls in this category as well. A special case of format conversion is de-interlacing, when we want to change interlaced video to progressive one.

*Temporal interpolation*, or *frame rate upconversion*, refers to the in-

crease of video frame rate, e.g., from 24 frames/second to 50 or 60 frames/
second, helping us to achieve better motion visualization or to reduce flicker
in video displays. The simplest technique to increase frame rate is to perform temporal resampling independently at each pixel location. Linear
interpolation filters can be used, if we want to change the temporal video
sampling period from $\Delta t_1$ to $\Delta t_2$. The interpolated pixel can be calculated
by using a sinc kernel or other interpolation kernels, especially of polynomial form, e.g., zero-order, first-order (linear), or *spline* kernels. Generally speaking, high-order polynomial interpolation provides very good
interpolation performance, but it is not frequently used, due to increased
computational complexity. In most cases, we use simple low-order polynomial interpolation kernels, e.g., zero-order and linear interpolation kernels.
Generally speaking, simple interpolation kernels achieve good performance,
when minimal or no motion at all is present. If the motion level increases,
they can result in video blur. Finally, *frame rate downconversion* is performed, when we have to drop video frames to reduce excessive video rate,
in case we cannot sustain it during video acquisition, transmission or display.

Each digital video format has its own sampling grid $\Lambda$, defining the
sampling (pixel) locations in the spatiotemporal domain $(x, y, t)$, as shown
in Figure 2.4.2. *Spatiotemporal video interpolation* provides video sampling conversion from one three-dimensional spatiotemporal sampling grid
to another one, e.g., from 480i to 1080p. A system for sampling grid conversion from an initial grid $\Lambda_1$ to a final grid $\Lambda_2$ is as shown in Figure 4.4.1.
Initially, the input video is oversampled (upsampled) on the grid $\Lambda_1 \cup \Lambda_2$
having grid points coming from either the input $\Lambda_1$ or the output final
grid $\Lambda_2$. The unknown pixel values are zero-padded. After appropriate
interpolation filtering, the video is downsampled to the output grid $\Lambda_2$.

*Video deinterlacing* refers to video conversion from an interlaced sampling grid (input) to a progressive grid (output), shown in Figures 2.4.2a
and 2.4.2b, respectively. Progressive sampling has double the density of the
interlaced one, when the progressive video frame rate equals the interlaced
video field rate. Thus, we have to perform a spatiotemporal interpolation
by a factor of 2. The interpolation can be achieved by padding the interlaced video grid with zeros, followed by a low-pass interpolation filtering.
The easiest way to perform deinterlacing from 2:1 interlaced video to progressive one, is to pad the missing odd/even lines in each video frame with

Figure 4.4.1: Sampling grid conversion.

the ones from the closest video field. *Field weaving* is essentially a zero-order interpolation. Alternatively, consecutive *field blending* (averaging) can be used to produce video frames.

Generally speaking, simple interpolation kernels produce good deinterlacing results, when small or no motion is present. If the motion level increases, then severe deinterlacing artifacts are produced. Field weaving suffers from *combing*, as shown in Figure 4.4.2. Various alternatives can be used in such cases, primarily using motion estimation and compensation to improve deinterlacing performance.

Figure 4.4.2: Combing artifact during deinterlacing.

## 4.5  Contrast enhancement

Image contrast is an important video quality issue. Therefore, *contrast enhancement* can be performed, in case the image contrast is low, i.e., when the image/video is too dark or too bright. The empirical probability distribution of image intensities $f(i,j)$, called image *histogram*, carries important information on image contrast. Let us assume that the digital image has $L$ discrete gray levels (usually from 0 to 255) and that $n_k$, $k = 0, \ldots, L-1$, is the number of pixels having intensity $k$. The histogram is the relative pixel luminance frequency $\hat{p}_f(f_k) = n_k/n$, $k = 0, 1, \ldots, L-1$, where $n$ is the total number of image pixels. The image histogram can be calculated very easily. A histogram can be calculated either at video frame level or at video segment level.

Important information concerning the image content can be extracted from the image histogram. Images that are 'dark' have their pixel value concentrated in the low image intensities part of the histogram, as can be

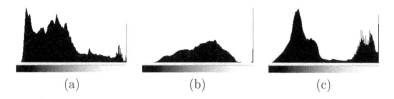

(a)                    (b)                    (c)

Figure 4.5.1: a) Histogram of a dark image, b) histogram of a bright image, c) histogram of an image containing two regions with different distributions.

seen in Figure 4.5.1a. A 'bright' image, on the other hand, has a histogram that tends to reside in the high image intensities, as shown in Figure 4.5.1b. The histogram of Figure 4.5.1c can be interpreted as originating from an image that contains two objects with different intensities (or even a single object in clear contrast to the background).

If the image histogram is concentrated on a small intensity region, the image contrast is poor and the subjective image quality is low. Image quality can be enhanced by modifying its histogram. This can be performed by *histogram equalization*. This algorithm has been applied to an image shown in Figure 4.5.2a, which has a very poor contrast. The equalized image has a much better contrast, as can be seen in Figure 4.5.2b.

In certain cases, histogram modification rather than histogram equalization is desired. For example, sometimes, we have to match the contrast between the right and left video channels in a 3DTV video. In such cases, the image $f$ having histogram $p_f(f)$ must be transformed to an image $g$ having a predefined histogram $p_g(g)$. This can be done in a two-step procedure, using an approach similar to that of histogram equalization.

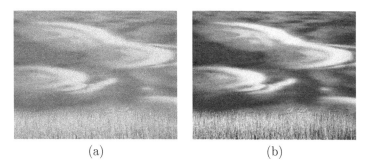

(a)                                    (b)

Figure 4.5.2: a) Poor contrast image, b) equalized image.

# 5

## VIDEO ANALYSIS

## 5.1 Introduction

Digital video analysis is an important task, since it can provide quantitative or semantic information on various moving image aspects, notably on object motion and camera motion. Motion estimation is a core task in video analysis. It provides motion fields that describe how objects and/or camera move. Motion estimation provides valuable information not only for video description, but also for video coding, since most video compression schemes use motion fields to reduce spatiotemporal redundancy by motion-compensated video frame prediction. Motion fields can also be used in motion compensated noise filtering, for improved noise reduction. Furthermore, motion-compensated de-interlacing and video format conversion also employ motion information.

Humans are an important semantic entity, since most videos contain

73

moving images of humans that describe their activities, status (e.g., their affect) or their interactions and behavior. Therefore, human detection and tracking in video is very useful in a variety of applications, ranging from human-centered interfaces to surveillance and to semantic video retrieval (e.g., find videos, where actor X speaks and smiles). Once human faces and/or bodies are detected and tracked, human identity can be detected, e.g., by face recognition. Furthermore, facial image analysis can lead to facial expression recognition and visible speech detection. With respect to the human body, we can detect body postures and we can recognize human actions or gestures. Human-centered video analysis can lead to the so-called *anthropocentric* video content description (from the Greek word *anthropos*, meaning human).

Object detection is another important video analysis task. It poses certain difficulties, since an object can have different appearance, when viewed from different view angles. Articulated and/or deformable object detection is, generally speaking, more difficult, than rigid object recognition. Human bodies or faces are particular types of objects that are both articulated and deformable. Object detection is coupled with spatial object localization. It is also related to region segmentation that, ideally, provides the spatial object *Region of Interest* (ROI). In case we perform moving region segmentation, we can get a spatiotemporal (moving) object ROI. An object can be tracked over time by tracking algorithms that provide the object trajectory (and moving ROI) over time. Object tracking is different from object detection, in the sense that it associates the detected object ROIs in successive video frames into video objects.

## 5.2   Motion estimation

Motion estimation is an important problem in digital video processing and analysis, which has been extensively studied by the scientific community. It has numerous applications not only in video analysis, but also in video compression and filtering. In this section, we first discuss the distinction between the two-dimensional and the three-dimensional motion. Then, there is a brief description of the displacement (motion) field models. Finally, we present block matching, which is one of the easiest ways to perform motion estimation.

The *two-dimensional motion*, also called *projected motion* is essentially the projection of the three-dimensional object motion on the image plane. The *three-dimensional motion* is described by the displacement of the 3D object points in three dimensions. Figure 5.2.1 illustrates the relation between the three-dimensional and the two-dimensional *displacement vectors*

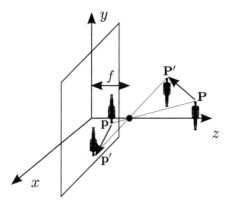

Figure 5.2.1: Two-dimensional and three-dimensional displacement vectors.

between time $t$ and time $t + \Delta t$. In this Figure, the object point **P** at time $t$ moves to point **P'** at time $t'$. On the image plane, the projected points **p**, **p'** define the two-dimensional displacement vector **d**. Such a displacement (or 2D motion) vector has two components $(dx, dy)$, showing the point **p** = $(x, y)$ displacement along the image plane axes $x$, $y$, respectively. When the video $f(x, y, t)$ shows a moving object, we can usually match the similar luminances $f(x, y, t)$ and $f(x', y', t')$ for a characteristic point moving on the image plane from the position $(x, y)$ at time $t$ to the new position $(x', y')$ at time $t'$. This *correspondence vector* provides an estimate of the displacement vector from the position $(x, y)$ on the video frame $t$ to the position $(x', y')$ at time $t'$. The correspondence or *optical flow* vectors determine the apparent motion. Sometimes, the optical flow field may be different from the two-dimensional displacement field. For example, when the light source (e.g., the sun) moves but the object stays still, we have apparent motion (optical flow) but no real motion, as shown in Figure 5.2.2. In other cases, if the object image has insufficient details, e.g., it is uniformly white, it may move, but this motion produces no optical flow.

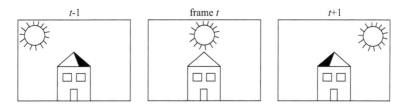

Figure 5.2.2: Optical flow generated by illumination changes.

## 5.2.1   Estimation of two-dimensional correspondence

### vectors

Motion estimation in digital video tries to find the two-dimensional displacement vectors, by estimating the correspondence vectors $\mathbf{d} = (dx, dy)$ of the pixels $(x, y)$ of video frames $t$ and $t+1$. In the case of digital video, $t$ denotes the frame number. The correspondence problem can be studied either as *forward motion estimation*, where the motion vector is defined from frame $t$ to $t+1$, or as *backward motion estimation*, where the motion vector is defined from frame $t$ to frame $t-1$, as shown in Figure 5.2.3. Backward motion estimation is more convenient than forward motion estimation for video compression with prediction, since, typically, only the previous video frames are available for predicting video frame $t$, via motion compensation.

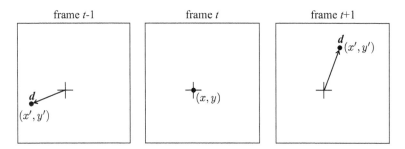

Figure 5.2.3: Forward and backward motion estimation.

Motion estimation suffers from many problems. The occlusion problem is due to the fact that no correspondence can be found between occluded and un-occluded object parts or background regions, due to object motion, as can be seen in Figure 5.2.4. The background regions that will be covered or will become visible in video frame $t+1$ cannot be matched to appropriate regions on video frame $t$, in order to find correspondence vectors.

The aperture problem is due to the fact that only local spatial information (within the camera aperture) can used for motion estimation, as shown in Figure 5.2.5. Suppose an object (sheet of paper) moves towards the top and left. If we estimate its motion based on the local window 'Aperture 1', it is not possible to determine the true object motion. Only the motion which is perpendicular to the object edge, called *normal optical flow* can be estimated. On the contrary, if 'Aperture 2' is used, we can estimate the correct motion vector.

We must find a way so as to measure the quality of the motion esti-

Figure 5.2.4: The occlusion problem: a) video frame $t$, b) frame $t + 1$, c) unoccluded (left) and occluded (right) regions (*courtesy of the i3DPost FP7 project*).

mator results. Such a metric is the *Peak Signal to Noise Ratio* (PSNR), which essentially measures the *Displaced Frame Difference* (DFD) between the target frame $t$ and the reference frame $t - 1$. PSNR is measured in $dB$. If the motion estimation is done correctly, the DFD is usually small and the PSNR has a large value. When using motion compensation in video compression, we are interested in having high PSNR, so that few bits are required to encode the DFD. Furthermore, we are interested in having smooth noiseless motion fields that can be easily compressed for transmission.

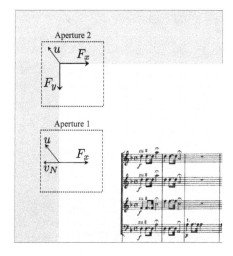

Figure 5.2.5: The aperture problem.

## 5.2.2  Block matching

We can assume that a video frame consists of moving blocks that are assigned to moving objects. First, we examine the simple case of two-dimensional block translation, where an $m \times m$ block in video frame $t$ can be described as a displaced version of a block of the same size in frame $t - 1$. The aim of block-based motion estimation is to find one displacement vector $\mathbf{d} = (dx, dy)$ per block $B$, so that the corresponding block difference is minimized over the entire block. Blocks in frame $t$ may be non-overlapping or overlapping, as shown in Figure 5.2.6a,b, respectively. When the blocks do not overlap, one motion vector corresponds to one block. When we have fully overlapping blocks, i.e., they overlap in all but one row/column, we can produce one motion vector per pixel (*dense motion field*).

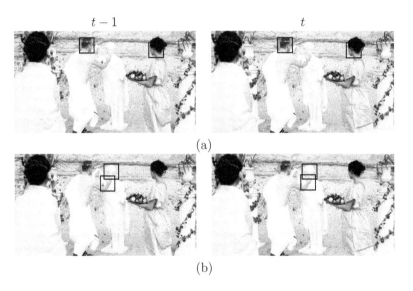

Figure 5.2.6: a) Non-overlapping, b) overlapping blocks (*courtesy of the i3DPost FP7 project*).

Block matching is done by exhaustive search of all candidate displacements $\mathbf{d}$. We can define a $m \times m$ pixel block centered at pixel $(x, y)$ in frame $t$. The search area on the previous video frame $t-1$ is a block having size $D \times D$ pixels, which is centered at pixel $(x, y)$. We search the entire $D \times D$ candidate block displacements, till we find the one that minimizes the displaced block difference. The result of motion estimation by block matching is shown in Figure 5.2.7.

If there are image edges within block $B$, we have a good motion esti-

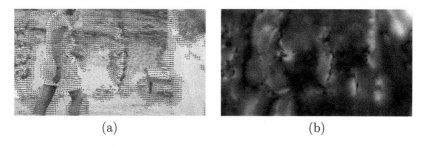

(a)                                    (b)

Figure 5.2.7: a) Motion field obtained by block matching, b) visualization of motion speed (*courtesy of the i3DPost FP7 project*).

mation. On the contrary, in homogeneous image regions, block matching may lead to a noisy motion field. During video compression, the estimated displacement vectors **d** are used to predict the pixel values of a picture block  for coding. Poor estimation of **d**s can lead to a large DFDs and, thus, in poor compression.

The advantage of the block-based motion estimation is that we can easily find displacement vectors minimizing the DFD. Another advantage of block-based motion estimation is that it can approximate fairly well complicated motion patterns of one or more objects, even at a cost of relatively big displaced frame difference. Block matching has several disadvantages. It may fail in motions due to zooming, rotation, as well as under some local image deformations. It tends to produce noisy motion fields. It has fairly large computational complexity.

Block-based motion estimation assumes that the displacement vector is constant within a two-dimensional image block. Problems occur when a block covers partially both a moving object and background or object regions moving in different directions, e.g., in the case of an articulated object. To moderate these problems, we can reduce the block size ($m \times m$ pixels).

Since block matching method by exhaustive search has a large computational complexity and, at times, poor performance, many motion estimation algorithms have appeared in the literature. Their review is beyond the scope of this book.

## 5.3   Use of motion information

Motion information is very important in video compression, processing, analysis and description. Its primary use is in video compression, as described in Chapter 7. Motion vectors can be used to predict current video frame blocks from blocks in previous/future reference frames. Then only the Displaced Frame Difference must be encoded and transmitted. Therefore, large compression ratios can be obtained by exploiting temporal video redundancy. Another use of motion fields is in *motion-compensated video filtering*. In this case, video filtering is performed only within the bounding boxes along motion trajectories, like the one shown in Figure 4.3.2.

A particular type of global motion appears in a video sequence, when the camera moves. Camera motion in a video can result from physical camera motion (e.g., camera pan/tilt, as described in Chapter 6), or by camera zoom in/out. Examples of such motion fields can be seen in Figure 5.3.1.

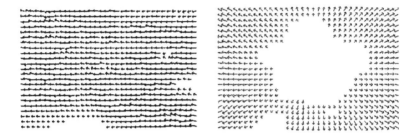

Figure 5.3.1: Optical flow generated by camera pan and zoom.

Motion fields also provide very useful video content descriptions. Strong motion fields typically denote action or sport shots. Moving object trajectories are very important in describing object motion direction (e.g., object moving to right/left, towards the frame center) or spatial object relations (e.g., persons approaching each other).

## 5.4   Human-centered video analysis

During the last two decades, an increasing research interest towards the so-called anthropocentric (human-centered) video analysis has been observed. The interest of the scientific community for anthropocentric video analysis stems from the fact that the extracted information (e.g., human presence, identity, body posture, emotional status, activities) can be utilized in various important applications. One such application domain is movie post-production, where anthropocentric video analysis results, such as human body segmentation, can be used in creating realistic computer generated imagery (CGI). Furthermore, it can be used in semantic video annotation tasks, for audiovisual content indexing and retrieval. In this way, we can, e.g., search for videos having two actors conversing with each other, while walking.

## 5.4.1 Face and person detection

Detecting people in a scene can be helpful in automating some of the post-production processes and in providing semantic information about the scene. There has been a significant amount of research in the field of human detection.

Human presence detection can be done through either face/head detection or through human body detection. The technology of human face detection has advanced significantly. A fast, high-performance face detection approach is a cascade of rejectors, that operate on *Haar-like* features, which essentially test whether a rectangle of an image is darker or brighter than the rest of the image. In order to facilitate the fast computation of Haar-like features, the algorithm works on the *integral image* representation of a picture. An integral image is a matrix $A$, whose elements measure the total brightness (sum of pixel luminance) of the image window that is above and to the left of the element. Haar-like features are fast and easy to compute. The cascade of rejectors approach to classification uses simple classifiers that have high acceptance and false positive rates. It builds a hierarchical structure of weak classifiers, so that the classifiers that reject most samples are placed higher in the hierarchy. In order for a sample to be accepted, it must be accepted by all classifiers. This way, images that are easy to reject are eliminated from the first few classifiers in the hierarchy. While many false positives may go through each weak classifier, one must go through all of them to be accepted and, therefore, the percentage of false positives decreases exponentially as the sample moves through the

Figure 5.4.1: Face detection (*courtesy of the i3DPost FP7 project and CVSSP, University of Surrey, UK*).

classifiers. A skin color detector can be used, in order to further reject false positives. An example for face detection is shown in Figure 5.4.1. Today, commercial digital cameras contain embedded face detectors.

For human body or upper body detection, *Histograms of Oriented Gradients* (HOG) have proven to be a powerful descriptor and provide good results in combination with state of the art classifiers. The image is split into square, non-overlapping *cells*. In every cell, the angle of the edge gradients is calculated and the value of the gradient is added to the appropriate quantized bin of the histogram. The cells are collected into square, overlapping blocks, which are then normalized to a sum of unity. The feature vector of an image window is the vector resulting from the concatenation of the blocks that are inside this window. This feature vector is then classified by a *Support Vector Machine* (SVM). This approach was originally proposed for pedestrian and upper human body detection, as shown in Figure 5.4.2.

Figure 5.4.2: Human body detection (*courtesy of the i3DPost FP7 project and CVSSP, University of Surrey, UK*).

An extension of the above method uses shape matching first, in order to find a silhouette template that matches the image. Only the blocks along the silhouette are concatenated into the feature vector. This way, the variance of appearance of the inside of a human body or upper body is rendered irrelevant to the classifier, leading to improved performance.

## 5.4.2   Face recognition

After a person has been detected in a video frame, then the next logical step is to attempt to identify that person. Face recognition is a well researched area. Several approaches have been proposed so far. They include the utilization of subspace methods, such as *Principal Component Analysis* (PCA), *Linear Discriminant Analysis* (LDA), or *Nonnegative Matrix*

*Factorization* (NMF). These methods project the image data into a lower dimensionality feature space, which can be described in terms of *basis images*. Basis images capture basic facial image characteristics, as shown in Figure 5.4.3. Few, e.g., $K$ basis images are enough to capture facial information. These basis images can be learned from training facial images. They are called *eigenfaces* (in the case of PCA) and *Fisherfaces* (in the case of LDA). Typically, the number of necessary basis images is much less than the facial image dimensions of $N \times M$ pixels, i.e., $K << NM$. Therefore, they form a very low dimensionality space, where facial images are projected. Basically, we decompose the facial images in a weighted sum of basis images. In the low-dimensionality space, the faces can be represented, e.g., by the decomposition weights. In this space, facial images belonging to one person can be more easily distinguished from images belonging to other persons. When a new facial image must be recognized, it is projected on the basis images and, then, the recognition task is performed using a high-performance classifier, such as a Support Vector Machine (SVM). Subspace techniques for face recognition perform very well, if the training and test images are perfectly aligned, so that their facial feature (e.g., eye) positions coincide.

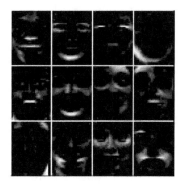

Figure 5.4.3: Basis images in an NMF variant (*courtesy of the MOBISERV FP7 project*).

Another approach for face recognition is based on *Elastic Graph Matching* (EGM). A facial image is represented by a deformable graph, as shown in Figure 5.4.4. Grid nodes contain local image information in the so-called *jet vector*. If we want to check whether a reference facial image and a new (test) image belong to the same person, we cast the reference facial image grid on the test image and we start deforming it. If, after deformation, both the reference and test jet vectors match well and the grid is not overly deformed, we declare a facial image match. Otherwise, facial recognition fails. EGM methods are very powerful and are widely

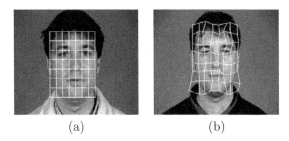

Figure 5.4.4: Elastic Graph Matching: a) original grid, b) facial grid after deformation (from the M2VTS multimodal face database).

used in security systems. However, they are computationally demanding, since grid deformation and matching is an expensive iterative operation.

*Facial image clustering* is a different task than facial image recognition: in this case, the aim is to cluster all images belonging to Actor X in one cluster, rather than to find actor identity. To do so, we can use clustering methods, e.g., fuzzy clustering. Alternatively, we can use similarity measures for image pairs, e.g., the *mutual information*. Therefore, facial images can be linked in a *similarity graph*. Graph clustering techniques, e.g., *N-cuts* can be used for facial image clustering. The resulting facial image clusters can be seen in Figure 5.4.5. Face recognition can follow face clustering, by assigning one label to each facial image cluster.

### 5.4.3   Facial expression recognition

Facial expression recognition is a very important task in affective computing and human centered interfaces. For example, smile detection can be used to assist novices, while taking pictures. In video search and re-

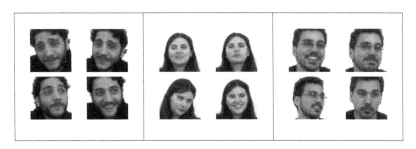

Figure 5.4.5: Three facial image clusters (*courtesy of the IMP·ART FP7 project*).

trieval, nice looking, e.g., smiling actor or politician images are desirable. The approach to facial recognition is to use deformable facial models, since facial expressions are due to facial muscle deformations. For example in *head and shoulder* scenes, we may use the *Candide* face model, shown in Figure 5.4.6. We can (hopefully automatically) fit this face model to the facial image of a person using horizontal scaling of the face model to fit the distance between the eyes and vertical scaling to fit the distance between the mouth and the eyes. This step can be followed by model deformation, so that it fits well to all important facial features. Then the model nodes can track the fiducial face landmarks (e.g., end of mouth, jaw) during facial expression formation. By analyzing these tracked face landmark positions, we can perform facial expression recognition.

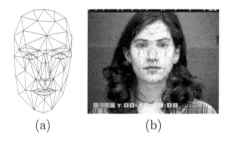

(a)                    (b)

Figure 5.4.6: a) Candide generic facial model, b) model fit to a facial image (from the Cohn-Kanade AU-Coded Facial Expression Database).

Specifically for face models, *Action Units* (AU) have been proposed, which describe facial expressions. Examples of AU-coded facial expressions are shown in Figure 5.4.7. The action units result from a *Facial Action Coding System* (FACS), which has been developed by psychologists. The system was developed to discern all possible visually distinguishable facial deformations. The FACS system combines facial deformations, due to more than one muscle contractions, in the formation of AUs for describing facial appearance changes. There are 46 AUs which describe facial expression changes and 12 AUs which describe gaze direction and head pose. If we can automatically recognize the AUs in facial images or videos, we can use them for facial expression recognition.

Other techniques, which employ *subspace image representations*, e.g., PCA LDA or NMF, have been used for facial expression recognition. They do not employ grid deformations, are very fast, but can suffer from facial image misalignment during recognition. Therefore, proper facial image registration has to be performed, before facial expression recognition.

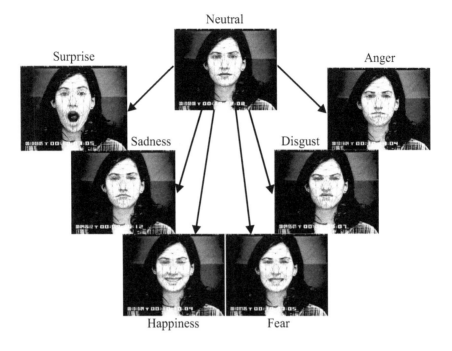

Figure 5.4.7: Facial expressions (from the Cohn-Kanade AU-Coded Facial Expression Database).

### 5.4.3.1 Other human body and face representations.

While the FACS system is based on human physiology, other face modeling approaches define characteristic facial features (landmarks), called *Facial Definition Parameters* (FDP), which can move dynamically, using the so-called *Facial Animation Parameters* (FAP). The FDPs are related to the Candide grid nodes. Figure 5.4.8 shows the points that can be used to define the head shape and the facial landmarks, which can move dynamically. The 68 FAPs used in MPEG-4 encoding are closely related to both muscle deformations and AUs. FAP facial motion parameters represent a complete set of basic head motions, including face, tongue, eye and mouth motions. Thus, they allow for the representation of natural facial expressions. Similar parameters have been defined in MPEG-4 for human body geometry (*Body Definition Parameters*, BDP) and motion (*Body Animation Parameters*, BAP) description. Generally, FDP localization in a facial image is not easy. If, however, it is done correctly and the FAP parameters describing their motion are estimated correctly, then we can encode very efficiently facial geometry and motion, including facial expressions. The same applies to BDP and BAP estimation for body geometry, posture and activity description.

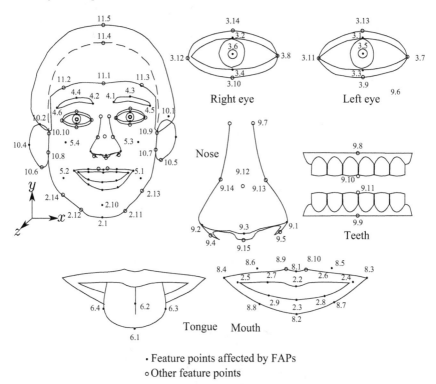

Figure 5.4.8: Facial definition parameters.

## 5.4.4   Human activity recognition

Human action recognition has been actively researched in recent years. Most work has been carried out in segmented foreground/background images, where the person appears isolated from the background, as shown in Figure 5.4.9. Activity recognition usually depends on a training stage and the existence of relevant training data. There is a limited set of possible actions that a classifier must choose from, when a new action sequence is tested.

In one approach, a database of training image silhouettes, like the ones shown in Figure 5.4.9, are organized into representative poses, called *Dynemes*. Each dyneme can be considered as the average of body postures

Figure 5.4.9:  Binary body silhouettes (*courtesy of the i3DPost FP7 project*).

that are similar in appearance. Such dynemes are shown in Figure 5.4.10. After the computation of the dyneme vectors in the training phase, every body silhouette is expressed through its distance from the various dynemes. Therefore, a body silhouette results in a so-called *dyneme space* representation. The distance of an input image from these dynemes is calculated and then used as a feature vector for classification purposes.

In the recognition phase, test binary body silhouettes are pre-processed in the same manner with the one used in the training phase, namely their representation in the dyneme space is found. Finally, the minimum distance between the new representation and existing action representations in the dyneme space is performed. The new test action is labeled accord-

Figure 5.4.10: Dynemes (*courtesy of the i3DPost FP7 project*).

ing to its closest action class in the dyneme space. The obtained results are good, provided that we know the position of the camera vs the human body, which should remain unaltered in the experiments. If this is not the case, then we have to resort to multiview or view-independent action recognition approaches.

## 5.5   Video Object Segmentation

An important step in video analysis is the segmentation (or *matting*) of a video frame into different regions that belong to the various scene elements. A basic distinction is between *foreground* and *background*, so that a CGI background can be seamlessly inserted into the video frame. Further foreground segmentation can be made, e.g., in various actors and props, so that occlusions can be preserved in case a synthetic actor is placed in front of something or someone. Video object segmentation is also a necessary step for the 3D actor reconstruction.

The most popular and simple method for background segmentation is shooting the scene in a monochrome background and using chroma-keying to determine the background pixels. Though any color can work, blue or green background are the most popular choices. *Chroma-keying* essentially labels every "too blue" or "too green" pixel as belonging to the background. The advantage of the blue screen vs the green screen is that every color naturally present on humans has a low blue component in it. On the contrary, blonde hair has a relatively high green component, thus increasing the chance that some foreground pixels will be mislabeled as background. Of course, if parts of the foreground have to be blue, then a green screen is preferred. It is important that the illumination of a scene filmed using a blue or green screen is carefully planned, in order to avoid or minimize the *spill*, i.e., the reflection of the background color on the foreground subjects.

Several more advanced image segmentation algorithms have been developed, in order to determine the background pixels in non-monochrome, cluttered backgrounds. They require various degrees of human interaction, in order to work well. Fully automatic methods sample the background color distribution around the outer border of an image, sample the foreground color distribution from the central image regions and then classify pixels to foreground/background based on their position, color and neigborhood. Other methods employ user initialization. For example, a user is requested to create a crude outline of the foreground subjects, or to roughly mark their interior. An example of video object segmentation from an experimental production of the king Midas story, filmed as part

 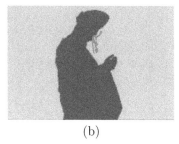

(a)                                              (b)

Figure 5.5.1: Video object segmentation: a) original image, b) segmented image (*courtesy of the i3DPost FP7 project*).

of the i3DPost R&D project in the UK, can be seen in Figure 5.5.1. The post-production aim was to use CGI to show the queen turning into a gold statue. Since the movie making industry, however, has extremely high quality standards, it is unlikely that an automated segmentation technique will perform perfectly. Therefore, some user supervision or interaction is required.

Sometimes, moving object segmentation is desired, e.g., in video coding. In this case, moving objects can be described by VideoObjects, which basically are object silhouettes in consecutive video frames. Moving object segmentation can be performed using both texture/color similarity within a VideoObject, but also object shape and location continuity over time.

## 5.6   Object Tracking

In many cases, we are only interested in the motion of one object or person, rather than in the overall motion field over the entire video frame. This can be achieved by using various 2D or 3D *object tracking* techniques. In this context, object means either a person or a scene prop. In the case of using 2D tracking, the 3D information can be extrapolated from the 2D tracking results in each camera. By definition, an object tracking algorithm requires some initialization, in order to start tracking. The initialization can be done manually or through an object or person or face detector.

*Window tracking* is the simplest approach in tracking. Given an initial object ROI position (window) on the first video frame for initialization, window tracking algorithms search every subsequent frame for windows that yield the highest similarity score with either the initial window or the last tracking result. This similarity can be measured in many different ways, the most common being cross-correlation or sum of squared differ-

Figure 5.6.1: Face detection and tracking (*courtesy of the MOBISERV FP7 project*).

ences. The search space for a new frame can also be limited to an area around the previous result. A tracking example is shown in Figure 5.6.1.

*Feature point tracking* uses geometric image features, such as edge lines, corners, SIFT points, ellipses and so on. These features can then be grouped to form a representation of the tracked object. By calculating these features in a video frame and matching each feature to a corresponding feature in the next frame, we can find a grouping of the new features to capture the position of the tracked object in the next frame.

If prior knowledge of the tracked object is available, then the object can be represented by a set of textures. Tracking can be performed by rotating and distorting the appropriate texture, then matching it against the video frame, e.g., through cross-correlation.

It is also possible to track the contour of an object, or actor, using snakes. In this method, a contour (*snake*) is initialized around the object. In subsequent frames, the snake deforms according to the edge map of the new video frame, while remaining under some elasticity and rigidness constraints. The task can be carried out in a similar fashion by B-splines. Finally, another option is to use deformable templates. However, in this case, the object must modeled by the templates beforehand.

A limiting issue for most tracking algorithms is error accumulation. Since every tracking result is not perfect, non-object features or regions may be included in the tracking window and degenerate the tracker over time, to the point where it may track the background or a different object. Thus, the concept of object detection and association is gaining ground. Instead of traditionally tracking the object across video frames, an object detection algorithm can be used on every frame. The detection windows of the latest frame are then matched to the windows of the previous frame. The advantages of this approach is that windows that cannot be associated with previous or subsequent frames can be dropped, reducing the amount of the detector false positives. Furthermore, missing detections can be interpolated from associated detections on previous and subsequent frames, making up for the detector false negatives.

In offline tracking tasks, like in the case of post-production, entire video sequences are available. Therefore, we can use both *forward* and *backward* tracking, in order to establish detection associations. Furthermore, in the case of multiview video, detections in various views can be associated to improve detection performance.

If the object to be tracked is articulated, as in the case of a human body, it is convenient to use *model-based tracking*. An articulated 2D or 3D model of a human body is built, usually having a head, torso, two upper arms, two forearms, two upper legs and two lower legs, as shown in Figure 5.6.2. These body components are connected in the way human anatomy dictates. The points, where two limbs are connected, are allowed to be disjoint within a small margin, when posing the model. It is then used to determine the 3D pose of the human body. When a new video frame is to be tested for human body tracking, several possible poses are generated, by changing the configuration of the current model by rotating and stretching the limbs. The resulting 3D poses are matched against the image, after being projected on the image plane. Such a matching can involve edges, background/foreground segmentation, color distribution, to name a few examples. It is also possible to apply some further constraints on the 3D pose, in order to avoid common model-based tracking pitfalls, which include cases where the two arms or the two legs end up grouped together into one actual human limb. This can be handled by incorporating the 3D pose prior probability, by introducing symmetry constraints or by adding a repulsive property to the limbs that pushes away the opposite limb. A faster, but less refined, approach is to create a database of shape templates for various human poses, organize them into a tree-like data structure and use template matching techniques to estimate the object pose.

Figure 5.6.2: Articulated human body model.

There are several 3D tracking methods and, depending on the task, one of appropriate complexity can be chosen. In order to track an actor head, it suffices to look for a cubic volume in the 3D reconstruction that is filled and surrounded by a second, larger and, otherwise, empty cubic volume, whose bottom side is on the same plane as the first volume. Tracking the actor head and 3D pose is useful, when a virtual actor character is to speak with a real actor and must look at the real actor's head, to make the rendered scene convincing. In order to track body parts in the voxel reconstruction space, one option is to build a skeleton of the human body. The model is then posed in a way that it matches the 3D voxel blobs of the reconstruction.

## 5.7   Object detection and recognition

Object detection (e.g., scene objects and props) can be approached in a fashion similar to face and human detection, by using a cascade of rejectors based on Haar-like features or classifiers based on HOG descriptors. However, object recognition is quite unlike most other tasks in computer vision, for example face recognition, human detection, or emotion recognition. This is because a class of objects may encompass a vast variety of different entities, both ontologically and visually, as can be seen in Figure 5.7.1. Moreover, in the case of objects, the border between recognition ('which one') and categorization ('what type of') is very blurry. This is due to the fact that, unlike humans, objects do not have a distinct identity and many objects can have multiple nearly identical copies (e.g., cars of the same model). Another characteristic of object recognition is that, with the exception of a few classes of radially symmetric objects, most objects exhibit a high visual variety from different views.

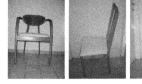

training set                    test image

Figure 5.7.1: Images used for chair recognition (*courtesy of the i3DPost FP7 project*).

One approach to object recognition is the *bag of keypoints* algorithm, which is founded on current trends in computer vision. It uses local image feature points as object descriptors and, then, performs classification using a high performance classifier, such as a Support Vector Machine (SVM). The extraction of local feature points from all (labeled) images of a training set consists of two generally independent components, a feature point detector, and a feature point descriptor. A good combination is using a) the Harris affine detector, whose advantage is that it is especially robust to geometrical transformations, as feature point detector and b) the classic SIFT descriptor, which consists of a set of Gaussian derivatives computed at 8 orientation planes over a $4 \times 4$ image grid, as feature point descriptor. The local feature descriptors are then clustered into a number of classes. The clustering of local feature descriptors is done in order to abstract the probability distribution of the feature points. The feature that is used for the assignment of a specific feature point to a cluster is the SIFT descriptor. At the end of the clustering procedure, only the cluster centers are retained. A summary descriptor (feature vector) is computed for each image in the training set. A histogram representing the number of feature points that were assigned to each class center is used as feature vector.

The feature vectors of all images are used to train a classifier (e.g., a SVM). Depending on the separation of the training example images into classes, the classification can lead to object recognition, object class recognition, or object verification.

In order to decide which object is depicted in an image, a similar procedure is followed: Harris-affine feature points are detected and their SIFT descriptors are extracted. These descriptors are then assigned into the previously computed cluster centers and the number of feature points assigned to each center forms a histogram, which is then passed to the previously trained Support Vector Machine for classification.

# 6

# VIDEO PRODUCTION

## 6.1 Introduction

Movie and TV production has been a multi-million dollar industry for many decades now. Big production studios invest large amounts of money in the production and marketing of modern movies, expensive equipment and state of the art technology are used in the production and artists have to put in many man-hours worth of effort, in order for a movie to be up to the constantly rising standards for visual effects. In this Chapter, we shall describe the movie production process, with an added emphasis on its digital video aspects. On a smaller scale, due to the usually more restricted budget, the process is similar for television productions.

Before the actual production can start, there is an initial process, called development, during which the basic idea, story, characters and mood of the movie is determined. One or more screenwriters are hired by a pro-

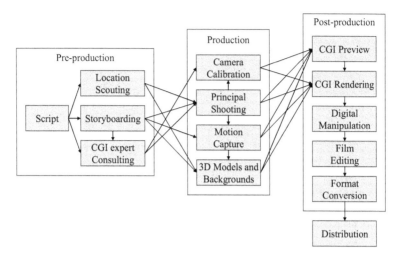

Figure 6.1.1: Movie production flow chart.

ducer to flesh out the story, which is then proposed, or 'pitched', to some financial backers. Once movie financing has been secured, or the movie gets 'green lighted', the production can start. There are three basic stages in the production process. In *pre-production*, the necessary preparations are made for the shooting to start. The *production* stage covers the principal shooting of the movie and the audio recordings for the dialogues, music and sound effects. Finally, in *post-production*, the shots to be used are further processed to add visual effects or otherwise improve their aesthetics and the final movie is put together by an editor. A general flow chart of the production process can be seen in Figure 6.1.1.

## 6.2 Pre-production

Pre-production is the planning stage, so that filming is carried out as smoothly as possible. A director is hired to bring the movie concept to life. He/she is given a budget for the production. The film crew is hired, which includes camera operators, a director of photography, a music composer, choreographers, costume designers and others. The script is storyboarded by artists, so that the director and the rest of the crew have a general idea of what they will be shooting. The *scenery sets* are built, if required. A casting director tries to find and hire suitable actors for each part in the movie. The filming locations are selected and the relative arrangements are made. The shooting schedule is determined to organize the production.

In the case where Computer Generated Imagery (CGI) will be involved in the production, further planning is required. A team of CGI experts is consulted, so that the crew can make sure that every measure is taken to ensure the easy and smooth insertion of CGI later, during the post-production stage. Modern CGI effects are rendered in high definition, which takes a lot of time and computational resources to be carried out. It is, therefore, important that the CGI sequences are planned way ahead, so that CGI experts can give some input and requirements to the filming crew, in order to make good, convincing CGI.

## 6.3 Production

Production, also called *shooting*, is the stage during which actors stand in the middle of a constructed set, in front of a blue screen, or on location and the cameras are recording. Unless there are budget constraints, or a choice for some artistic reason, more than one cameras are involved at any point during principal shooting. For example, there could be one camera pointed at each character with even more cameras covering different angles of the actors. While the live action footage of the movie is being recorded, it is possible for another production team to be dealing with the acquisition of motion capture data, for later use in video post-production. In the following, we concentrate on video production aspects.

### 6.3.1 Camera mounts

In professional productions, cameras are usually placed onto appropriate camera mounting equipment (*rigs*), according to the needs of the scene. However, on rare occasions, the camera is purely hand-held. The simplest camera mount is most likely a tripod that can keep the camera steady in place. Figure 6.3.1 shows several cameras mounted on tripods. Cameras can also be mounted onto vehicles. Wheeled camera mounts can be used to keep the camera height and vertical angle steady, while still allowing for movement and turns in the horizontal plane. These cameras are particularly popular in live television shows. When extreme precision in the camera movement is required, cameras can be mounted on wagons that run on railed tracks, as shown in Figure 6.3.2. In cases where vertical camera movement is required, cameras can be mounted on cranes. If the camera movement required for a scene is extremely complex, robotic arms with multiple articulation points can also be used to mount a camera. There is

Figure 6.3.1: Three cameras mounted on tripods at an outdoor filming location (*courtesy of the i3DPost FP7 project*).

also a variety of personal camera mounts. Simple examples of such mounts are helmet or shoulder mounts. More complex personal body mounts also exist, which usually consist of a vest that fixes an articulated arm to the operator's body, onto which a camera is mounted. Thus, the camera weight is on operator's torso, so that the arms do not get tired. Springs and gyros are also employed to provide better camera stability. Finally, there are wheeled robotic arm camera mounts that are manually operated.

Figure 6.3.2: A camera mounted on a railed wagon in a straight track (*courtesy of the i3DPost FP7 project*).

## 6.3.2 Camera movement and lenses

There are six degrees of freedom, in which a camera can move. Furthermore, various camera lens parameters can be modified to adjust the camera to the production needs. Cameramen have developed a terminology for the various camera movements shown in Figure 6.3.3 that are most frequently employed in their business. When the camera turns left or right in place, this movement is called camera *pan*. Moving the camera viewpoint up or down, without raising or lowering the actual camera, is called camera *tilt*. The, usually smooth, camera motion in a straight line on the horizontal plane is called camera *dolly*. Note that, during a dolly, the viewpoint of the camera is independent of the direction in which the camera is moving. Finally, when the camera moves in orbit around an actor, this movement is called camera *truck*.

Changes in the camera lenses will also affect the captured images. Modifying the camera zoom will change the magnification factor of the shot. Enlarging the image is called a *zoom-in*, while the opposite is called a *zoom-out*. Changes in the focal length of the camera affect the *focus* of the shot, which essentially determines the optimal distance from the camera that a subject must be, in order to be captured more crisply. Objects that are significantly closer or further away from the camera will appear blurry. Directors sometimes change the focus of the same shot from the foreground to the background or vice versa. It is also possible to combine camera movement with changes to the camera zoom, as in the so-called *dolly-zoom effect*. During this effect, the camera simultaneously dollys away, while zooming in on the subject or moves closer while zooming out. This results in the actor being depicted stationary in the shot, while the background seemingly enlarges or shrinks, respectively.

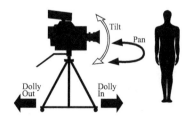

Figure 6.3.3: Camera pan/tilt/dolly.

### 6.3.3   Shot types

A *shot* is a video sequence resulting from an uninterrupted camera recording. If a shot is filmed multiple times, each individual instance of the same shot is called a *take*. Camera position, direction and lens parameters (e.g., focal length) determine the shot type.

While there are no strict rules on categorizing shots, they can generally fall into one of the following shot types. *Wide* shots, or *long* shots, include the entirety of the subject or subjects in the frame. *Medium* or *mid* shots include the upper body of the actors. *Close up* shots prominently feature a single actor head and shoulders. Reverse close up shots feature another actor head and shoulders. Alternating between close up and reverse close up shots is a standard way to present a conversation between two characters and the preferred method in television, due to time and budget constraints. *Extreme close ups* zoom further in, to highlight actor details. *Cut-in* shots show another part of the actor than head, for example to his/her hand, to draw attention to a hand gesture. *Cut-away* shots feature something other than the subject, to provide extra information about the scene to the audience. *Point-Of-View* (POV) shots are recorded from the perspective of the subject. *Over-the-shoulder* shots are recorded from behind and above the subjects. An example of a wide and a close up shot can be seen in Figure 6.3.4.

(a)                                        (b)

Figure 6.3.4: a) Wide shot, b) close-up shot (*courtesy of the i3DPost FP7 project*).

### 6.3.4   Lighting

The *lighting* (or *illumination*) conditions of the scene play an important part in both the artistic and the technical quality of the shots. Artistically, the lighting should most of the time be realistic, i.e., it should be coming from the logical light sources of the scene, without causing multiple contrasty shadows. In rare exceptions, more creative lighting setups can be used to convey mood and emotions to the audience. Technically, the cameras should be white-balanced before each shot, every time the lighting changes. This is because the color white can have varying temperatures, while still looking the same. For example, sunlight white is significantly hotter than the white produced by certain artificial light sources. Incorrect white balance can lead to the shot ending up either blueish or reddish, depending on which side the balancing error lies. Digital cameras can be automatically white-balanced, by being pointed at a white card under the desired lighting conditions and by using the appropriate white-balance control.

There are two basic kinds of lighting equipment: *spotlights* and *floodlights*. Spotlights provide a rather narrow beam of lighting through lenses or ellipsoid mirrors, while floodlights illuminate a wider volume of space. Spotlights are highly anisotropic and directional light sources. Floodlights have more than one lamps placed in a grid formation, in order to better diffuse the radiated light, so that it is not as directional, as the one provided by a spotlight. Floodlights can be employed to minimize the multiple shadows cast by a subject targeted by spotlights. They can provide, depending on their configuration, rather ambient illumination.

## 6.3.5 Motion capture

*Motion capture* (*Mocap*) is the process of acquiring animation data from real humans (actors), which can then be used as a basis for animating a virtual 3D actor or object model. This animation is typically done by CGI tools, during post-production. When trying to depict human or humanoid subjects using CGI, it is important that they move in a natural, human-like way. Animating these subjects by hand is very time consuming and may result in unnatural movements that will jar the audience. In such cases, motion capture is used to quickly and easily obtain natural articulated motion data. There are several methods for motion capture, requiring different equipment and involving varying degrees of user input. Mechanical, magnetic, ultrasonic or video trackers can be used. The actor usually wears a spandex suit and/or visual markers, as shown in Figure 6.3.5. The pieces of equipment are placed on or near the actor joints, as they contain the most relevant information, regarding the pose of the actor body. The actor performs the movement to be captured and the human pose data are mapped to a human body skeleton. This skeleton can then be fitted to a 3D CGI human body model, thus achieving human-like motion.

The quality of the captured data is judged on four factors: accuracy, jitter, drift and latency. *Accuracy* measures the overall deviation between the captured data and the actual motion data. *Jitter* measures the cap-

Figure 6.3.5: An actress having facial visual markers (*courtesy of the i3DPost FP7 project and CVSSP, University of Surrey, UK*).

tured data noise, or small fluctuations in the captured point coordinates, when, in fact, the actual point is stationary. *Drift* refers to the degradation of the motion data quality over time. *Latency* refers to the response time of the capturing system to actor's movement and to the speed of capture data updating.

*Mechanical trackers*, which, incidentally, were the first developed motion capture systems, use sensorized joints that connect two straight line rigid carriers. These sensorized joints directly measure the two angles that the two adjoined carriers form: their *bending angle* and their *twisting angle*. By knowing the length of the carriers and their relative angles, it is possible to hierarchically retrieve the captured human body pose. An actor wears an exoskeleton of rigid carriers along his/her limbs, chest and hips that are connected with the aforementioned sensorized joints, when performing their routine. Mechanical trackers are extremely accurate and have no issues related to visual occlusion. They are, however, cumbersome, compared to other trackers or markers and introduce some extra friction/inertia that interfere with actor movements.

Mechanical trackers also provide an interesting alternative to animating non-humanoid models in a computer program. It is possible to build a real life scaled model of the object with sensorized joints on every articulation point. The real life model can then be posed by hand, just like in the stop-motion method. Then, the joint angles can be retrieved from the sensors and used to make a non-humanoid skeleton animation.

Since the actor freedom of motion is quite important in motion capture, no-contact trackers that do not inhibit the actor body have been developed to replace the mechanical ones. *Magnetic trackers* calculate the relevant angles and positions, by having three orthogonal coils on a transmitter node and on two receiver nodes. These coils are used to measure the magnetic field fluctuations of the transmitter node coils at both receiver nodes. When properly calibrated, this system of nodes can infer the relative positions and angles from the magnetic field measurements. While magnetic trackers are not invasive, they are prone to interference from other magnetic fields. As an alternative, *ultrasonic trackers* use a static transmitter to infer the positions of moving receivers. The transmitter has three speakers, each on one vertex of a small, equilateral, triangle formation. Each receiver has three microphones in a similar, smaller triangle formation. The transmitter sends out three ultrasonic sound waves and these waves reach each microphone at the receiver at a different moment in time. The time lag of these receptions can be used to calculate a total of nine distances between the receiver microphones and the transmitter speakers. Through triangulation, these angles can be used to solve a system of equations that reveals the position of the receiver, relative to the position of the transmitter.

Any method utilizing visual markers requires multiple synchronized views of the motion capture actor from calibrated cameras. *Visual markers* can be either passive or active. In the passive case, several markers coated with retroreflective paint are placed on suitable points of the actor body, while bright lights are placed next to the cameras facing the capturing location. The actor performs the required movements, while recorded by the multiview camera setup. After the recording, correspondences of each marker to its different views on the various cameras are established. This can be done manually, or through a feature matching algorithm. Using the 2D location of a marker on multiple video frames and the camera calibration parameters, the 3D location of that marker can be computed through triangulation. More views produce more accurate results. The 3D markers are then mapped to a human skeleton model. Active markers work in a similar fashion, except that instead of reflecting light, they emit their own light. Then, the same procedure can be followed, as in the case of passive markers. Another alternative is to synchronize the active markers, so that only one of them is lit up at any time instance and each marker lights up in sequence. It is then trivial to associate the 2D position of the marker on each camera view, without human interaction and proceed as before. The camera frame rate must be high enough, so that the two consecutively captured positions of any given marker are spatially not too far apart.

In a similar fashion, it is possible to capture facial expressions from live actors and use the motion capture data to either directly generate the expression of a CGI human or as a basis for the expression of a non-human face. This can be done by a camera filming the actor face after markers have been placed on key points of the face. An example of such an image is illustrated in Figure 6.3.5.

Newer body feature point (landmark) trackers do not need the placement of visual markers on the human body and rely only on the detection and tracking of natural landmarks (e.g., mouth/eye end points). However, such trackers do suffer from feature point loss or tracking inaccuracies and have to be semi-automatically initialized from time to time.

## 6.3.6    Action and set recording

In the film era, movies were shot on film using one *principal camera*. Then, after 2000, this film was digitized to be edited in post-production. Starting 2010, digital video cameras are used for movie and TV recording. Furthermore, several other digital cameras, besides the principal camera, are used for action and set recording. Other instruments are used as well for capturing the visual texture and geometry of the set, its objects and actors, so that a complete 3D set and action modeling can be performed, aiming at a better blend of CGI and of visual effects, during post-production. Basically, nowadays the entire 4D (3D+time) world is expected to be captured. This is a large leap forward, compared to shot capture used only few years ago.

To start with, several movie cameras can be used instead of one principal camera for action recording. Furthermore, a number of high resolution *witness cameras* can be used for action recording from different view points. Stereo cameras can also be used for action recording, particularly if 3DTV or 3D movie content is produced. The aim is to perform a 3D reconstruction of action performance and/or of the set, its objects and its environment. *Depth cameras* can retrieve depth information and create depth maps (images) of actor bodies and/or set geometry. Kinect is a typical example of such a popular low-cost camera. *High-speed cameras* operating at 1000 fps are used to record slow-motion shots. Motion capture cameras or systems, described in a previous system, can be used to record and track actor's motion. In several cases, camera calibration/motion/lens information and lighting source information are also recorded.

High quality DSLR cameras are used to take thousands or even hundreds of thousands images of the 3D set to capture its geometry and visual texture, using uncalibrated 3D scene reconstruction approaches, to be described in a subsequent section. Such images can also be used to create *High Dynamic Range* (HDR) mosaics for backgrounds. HDR cameras offer a greater intensity range and can display better both the dark and the bright image regions than standard cameras. They can be used to make spherical ($360^o$ degrees) scans of the 3D set to capture real-world luminosity data. *Time-of-flight* (TOF) sensors can be used to get very detailed depth maps of the set. *3D laser scanners* can provide point clouds describing set geometry. *Light Detection And Ranging* (LIDAR) scanners illuminate the 3D set with laser light and record the backscattered light, creating 3D geometry information, as shown in Figure 6.3.6. 3D information coming from different sources, e.g., TOF sensors, 3D laser scanners, 3D geometry reconstruction from DSLR stills, 3D information from stereo disparity maps, can be registered to provide accurate 3D models of a set, its objects and its background.

Figure 6.3.6: 3D geometry reconstruction of the Guildford Cathedral from multiple LIDAR scans (*courtesy of the i3DPost FP7 project and CVSSP, University of Surrey, UK*).

The overall system used for action and set recording is shown in Figure 6.3.7. The entire action and set recording process is very complex, asynchronous and heterogeneous. It produces a tremendous volume of multimodal data (videos of varying resolutions, still images, trajectories, point clouds, depth maps, 3D surface models). It can easily produce hundreds of Terabytes of video for one movie shot. A two-hour movie may require shooting more than 2000 minutes per action at a rate of 20 min per day. A movie shoot with one principal camera and a number of witness cameras can produce several tens of Terabyte per hour. Compressed 4K video provides more than 40 MB/second. Eight HD witness cameras capturing 4:2:2 video generate 6 TB video per hour. A small experimental production in the framework of the European R&D project i3DPost, which employed a moving principal camera and a number of witness cameras, resulted in 60 TB of video in just 3 days of shooting. Such a huge data capture rate requires a large, high-speed and reliable storage system to be used on site. Furthermore, the captured data must be subsequently

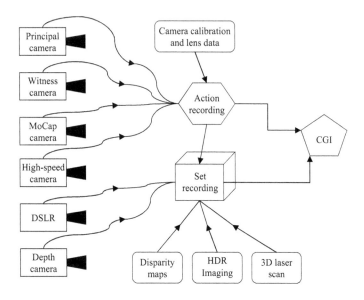

Figure 6.3.7: Action and set recording.

transferred to studios for post-production.

The existing *Media Asset Management* (MAM) systems can hardly cover the production needs, since they have not been designed to cover the multimodal nature of the produced data. All this amount of data cannot possibly be visualized during shooting. Therefore, synchronization or misalignment or other types of errors, to be detected later on during post-production, can destroy or deteriorate the quality of precious recorded data sets. Quality assurance mechanisms are very useful in the early detection and correction of such errors. The automatic extraction of relevant video metadata (e.g., actor identity and activity in a shot, video quality indicators) can help fast search of the captured video. This, in connection to fast video visualization/preview, with the aid of relevant video metadata, can greatly help the director and the production staff to check for shooting problems, before it is too late. The same type of metadata allows fast search and browsing of the recorded video content during post-production. Therefore, intelligent video content description, search, browsing, visualization is a very important R&D task. The European Union funded project IMP·ART addresses exactly these topics.

# 6.4 Post-production

Post-production is the final stage of the movie-making process that typically takes place after the principal shooting has been completed. Digital techniques are used to bring the movie in its final release form. Artists are employed to insert special effects into scenes or make new scenes completely on the computer and even correct some unwanted artifacts, like removing reflections of the camera crew or the wires used for acrobatics.

If a 35 mm celluloid film camera has been used in cinema production, the original camera negative has to be scanned and converted to digital video. Film scanners can perform this task directly from the film reel into a computer, without the need for intermediate printing of the film. The file format used for the scanned videos is the *Digital Picture Exchange* (DPX) format, as detailed in Chapter 12.

## 6.4.1 Computer generated imagery

*Computer generated imagery* (CGI) has been ever more prevalent in movie and television content production over the past decades. CGI is popular, because it offers many advantages. It can be used to compose scenes that would otherwise be too expensive or even impossible to shoot in real life, to manipulate the camera views in rather impossible ways and, generally, to bring a movie closer to the director's artistic vision, beyond real-life effects and set pieces. It also offers the convenience of shooting inside a studio and not having to deal with scouting for locations, transportation and harsh climate conditions.

Before the evolution of CGI into a usable form, movie makers had developed several other techniques to amaze their audiences. Spectacular backgrounds were actually matte paintings on glass, their obvious limitation being that they could have neither motion nor depth. Alien or monstrous creatures were portrayed by people in rubber suits or prosthetic make-up and even by animatronic puppets. Partial exposure of the film (shooting over the same roll of film with a different part of the camera lens covered on each take) could allow an actor to appear more than once in the same scene. Often in-scale miniature sets and props have been created to make a scene possible. Rotoscoping was used to properly overlay drawings on live action movies. *Stop motion* involved posing each prop of a scene for a single frame, then slightly changing the pose of each prop for the next frame and continuing to create an animated sequence. Sometimes, simply the clever use of the camera, like a *forced perspective shot*, left strong impressions on the audience.

The first feature film to use CGI is, most likely, Futureworld (1976), where CGI was used to depict a face and a hand. Since then, CGI technology was pioneered by many companies, such as Industrial Light & Magic, Digital Effects, Pacific Data Images, Digital Domain and software companies, such as Adobe, Autodesk and Wavefront. CGI has evolved from primitive vector graphics and textures to photorealistic models, with millions of polygons that cast shadows and reflect their surroundings.

Milestone movies in the development of CGI are Star Wars (1977), Tron (1982), Star Trek II: The Wrath of Khan (1982), Young Sherlock Holmes (1985), Willow (1988), The Abyss (1989), Total Recall (1990), Jurassic Park (1990), Terminator 2: Judgment Day (1991), The Lawnmower Man (1992), The Mask (1994), Toy Story (1995), The Matrix (1999), Final Fantasy: The Spirits Within (2001), the Lord of the Rings movies (2001-2003) and, recently, Avatar (2009). Toy Story was the first feature length film done entirely using CGI. Most of these movies have been nominated and even won Academy Awards for best visual effects in their respective year.

### 6.4.1.1    Stereo and multiview camera setups

Most post-production techniques discussed in this Chapter require information regarding the 3D structure of the filmed scene. While it is possible to get such information from a single monocular camera, stereo cameras or multiple camera (multiview) setups are often used, in order to acquire a better estimation of the relative parameters required to establish the correspondence between the real life world and the virtual computer world, where the rendering takes place.

A stereo camera is a single device with two or more lenses that each has its own sensor array for capturing images. Alternatively, two cameras on a stereo camera rig can produce stereo (left and right channel) video. The relative geometry of the lenses is known beforehand. If the camera parameters are known, the depth of each pixel can be calculated through disparity estimation. Thus, a depth map of the photographed subject can be extracted and a textured 3D mesh can be generated. Therefore, it is possible to make a 3D scene reconstruction out of individual left/right photograph pairs and the resulting depth maps.

In the case of multiple cameras, the digital cameras used can either be connected individually to one PC, or the first camera can be connected to a PC and every subsequent camera connected to the previous one, or a combination of both. The main issue that needs to be addressed in a multiview camera setup is *camera synchronization*. During shooting, every camera must capture a video frame at the same time with a sufficiently small margin for error. This can be accomplished by a hardware synchronization signal coming from the connecting cable.

Stereo video production has a particular importance for stereo TV (also called 3DTV). Its particularities come from the way humans perceive depth in 3DTV, as discussed later on in this Chapter.

### 6.4.1.2   Camera calibration

*Camera calibration* is the process of inferring the intrinsic and extrinsic parameters of a camera. The intrinsic (or internal) parameters are the camera focal length, aspect ratio, image plane center coordinates and lens distortion, while the extrinsic (or external) parameters are the camera rotation and translation parameters.

In a multiview setup, it is a very basic requirement that the cameras are calibrated, in order to establish a correspondence between the real world, where the scene is shot, and the virtual world, where the 3D CGI effects will be added. Otherwise the scale and position of the effects would have to be determined by hand, which takes much longer time. Mistakes in positioning, scale and perspective can be visually jarring to the audience.

Modern technology even allows directors to see a real time preview of how the virtual world will look like, as they move a camera around the set. It is also possible to see the CGI creatures that will be replacing the human actors in real time, as the actors move around.

### 6.4.1.3   3D scene reconstruction

In order for the shadows and reflections of the CGI to be correct and to avoid virtual object/actor collision with the real actors and props (often called *clipping*), it is essential that everything on screen also has an accurate 3D presence in the virtual world. The process of acquiring a 3D representation of a scene is called *3D scene reconstruction*. In order for the 3D reconstruction to be possible, there must be multiple synchronized views of the scene, captured from different cameras. The cameras can be initially uncalibrated. In such a case, the cameras should be calibrated, while performing the 3D reconstruction. However, it is always helpful, if they are calibrated beforehand. Some methods use photo-consistency measures in the reconstruction process or to refine the reconstruction results. Photo-consistency measures take into consideration the color appearance of a 3D voxel (volume pixel) projected into the 2D pixel of each camera frame that the voxel is visible from.

#### 6.4.1.4    Uncalibrated 3D scene reconstruction

When prior camera calibration is not available, it is possible for cameras to self calibrate, by using common reference points that are visible from a group of cameras or from different view points taken by a moving camera. A correspondence of reference points must be established between the views of two or more cameras. This can be done manually, but there are automated methods of selecting points and their correspondences. Typically, *Scale Invariant Feature Transform* (SIFT) points and cross-correlation can be used for feature point matching between views. At least 8 corresponding points must be defined, subject to the above restriction, in order to estimate the camera parameters. Each point must be visible by at least three cameras. After the camera parameters have been estimated, the coordinates of the 3D points in the point cloud reconstruction are computed through triangulation from their 2D coordinates in the camera frames. A 3D face reconstruction from three views can be found in Figure 6.4.1.

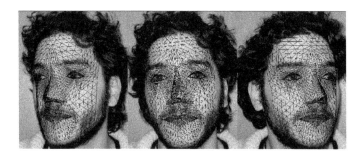

Figure 6.4.1: Reconstructed 3D face from three views.

#### 6.4.1.5    Calibrated 3D scene reconstruction

In most calibrated reconstruction algorithms, the frames from each camera must be segmented into foreground-background, before reconstruction. Algorithms for video object segmentation are covered in further detail in Chapter 5. The basic idea of the *volume carving* algorithm for 3D reconstruction is to start with an initial volume of voxels (volume pixels), then start eliminating voxels by drawing 3D lines through the volume. These lines are defined by the origin of a camera and a background pixel of the respective camera view. Since the pixel is background, there should be no object voxel in the resulting 3D line and, thus, every voxel that the line goes through is eliminated. At the end, the remaining voxels form the 3D

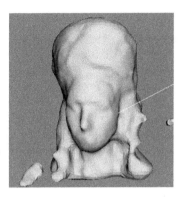

Figure 6.4.2: Voxel carving of a head (*courtesy of the i3DPost FP7 project and CVSSP, University of Surrey, UK*).

reconstruction of the scene. The result of a voxel carving method can be seen in Figure 6.4.2.

A more refined approach is to iteratively carve voxels from the volume. Starting from the entire volume and considering its outer hull as visible, at each step, the visible voxels are checked for photo-consistency. If a voxel is found to be photo-inconsistent, then that voxel is carved. Voxel visibility is recalculated, if voxels have been carved in an iteration. The process continues until no more voxels can be carved.

An obvious issue that arises is the choice of voxel resolution (voxel volume). The lower the resolution is, the faster the algorithm works. However, the 3D reconstructions obtained are blockier and less accurate. Another issue in volume carving is the way it handles concavities. It is likely that many more camera views will be required to properly capture concavities and, even then, the results can only be fair, at best. Finally, sometimes, artifacts of non-eliminated voxels stick out of the reconstructed scene objects and must be filtered out.

### 6.4.1.6 3D computer graphics animation

CGI effects come to life by using 3D computer graphics algorithms. A 3D model of each subject and the background is designed, then it is properly posed and positioned into the virtual scene, using information from the above processes. Then, the entire scene is rendered. There are several commercial and freeware programs of varying sophistication for the design and rendering of 3D objects and scenes.

The very basic elements of a 3D model are its polygons, the visual textures that are applied to each surface and the shading model used. This was all that was needed in the early days. However, technological advances in both software and hardware have made many more things possible. Models can cast realistic shadows. 3D object models can have an abrasive appearance, through the use of *bump mapping*. 3D object surfaces can be defined as reflective and have reflections recursively computed onto them. Several materials, such as metal and cloth, can have their properties modeled and then be accurately rendered. *Particle effects* have also evolved to the point, where they can realistically simulate smoke and explosions.

When rendering CGI, it is important to take the scene illumination into account. The same object can appear differently, under different ambient lighting in real life, hence the audience expects that CGI subjects are illuminated realistically in the environment they appear in. This means that the reflective surfaces of the virtual object must reflect the correct background and their color texture must be properly influenced by the scene illumination. If the background is computer-generated, then this process is automatic. However, if CGI is to be inserted into a scene filmed on a real location, then information regarding scene illumination must also be captured during shooting. This can be done by placing a clear, highly reflective grey sphere (called a *light probe*) in the center of the camera view and taking some shots. Due to the sphere shape, everything that is outside of the camera view is reflected onto the sphere, while the rest of the environment is in front of the camera. Properly calibrated software can then recreate the real-life illumination conditions in the 3D rendering program, using knowledge of spherical geometry and the pictures taken. It is a good idea to take another shot of the same sphere at the same place, but from a relative angle of 90 degrees, because the background reflection on the sphere perimeter gets too distorted. Taking more shots from a different perspective alleviates this problem.

An arising issue with CGI human models is the so-called *uncanny valley* hypothesis. It has been observed that as robots, or, in our case, virtual human models, become more humanoid, the reaction they provoke in real humans improves, but up to a certain point. After that point, the reaction quickly drops to negative and only improves again when the robot is extremely close in appearance and behavior to a real human. The likely explanation of this phenomenon is that, when something looks artificial, human-like characteristics make it more likeable. However, when something looks almost -but not quite- human, then its artificial characteristics begin to stand out and make the CGI model look like an odd, unnatural, or even sick human. Most people in the audience find it unsettling to look at. It is a current trend that CGI humans are designed to look somewhat cartoony, in order to avoid them falling into the uncanny valley.

## 6.4.2   Visual effects

*Visual Effects* (VFX) refer to image manipulations of the recorded video material that change the video content or its aesthetic value. They may or may not require 3D computer graphics.

There are also several CGI effects that do not require elaborate 3D graphics. Such a common effect is *background substitution*. When a scene is carefully filmed against a monochrome background, then it is easy to replace its background with a digital image of another location, or with a video shot in a different place without the actors, or even with stock footage. An example is shown in Figure 6.4.3. Illumination is crucial to the quality of such scenes, as improper lighting can result in the monochrome background color *spilling*, i.e., being reflected on the foreground actors and props.

(a)                                    (b)

Figure 6.4.3: a) An actor in front of a blue screen b) background insertion (*courtesy of the i3DPost FP7 project*).

It is also possible to digitally extend a limited background region to cover the camera view field. A 3D model of the terrain (or ground) can be extracted from at least two different pictures using stereo techniques. This digital terrain model can then be properly scaled and rotated, then placed under the actors.

*Crowd replication* is another popular effect. It is used to create scenes with innumerable people from footage of just a few live actors. The most common uses are populating a crowd or an army. Some actors are filmed at various distances from the camera, thus creating close, medium and far shots. Then they are copied and pasted on the scene, always taking scene perspective into account. The ground is scanned beginning from the farthest distance and moving towards the camera. Each horizontal line of the ground is filled by selecting people from the proper footage, close medium or far ones, then scaling them slightly and pasting them so that their feet appear to be on the current ground location.

*Retouching* can be helpful in removing movie artifacts that either went unnoticed, such as the reflection of the camera crew on the sunglasses worn by an actor, or the wires used for the scene stunt work. It is also possible to digitally remove actor tattoos that their character is not supposed to have, or to improve male actor physique and actress measurements.

Other digital image manipulation techniques that can improve the overall look of the movie are tonal range editing and color grading. *Tonal range* refers to the pixel intensity distribution. The lower intensities are called *image shadows*, while the higher intensities are called *image highlights*. Everything in-between is called *mid-tone*. By editing the tonal range through non-uniform histogram scaling, the darker or lighter parts of the image are emphasized, thus enhancing the image contrast. *Color grading (color correction)* can be used to correct the colors that either did not come off correctly due to illumination problems, or because the movie would simply look better, if some or all colors had a slightly different hue, saturation or intensity, as shown in Figure 6.4.4. Of course, there is no formal definition of what "looks better" and, so, the matter largely rests on artistic insight. The primary color correction affects all colors, while the secondary color correction is optional and only affects a certain color spectrum range. It is also possible to color grade a scene actually recorded in day light, in order to create the impression that it takes place at night.

There are also several image filters that can be applied to the video frames of a shot. The most common ones are the *blurring* and *sharpening* filters, while other filters can change the frame *transparency*, for the purpose of blending it with another video frame. Artificial Gaussian or other

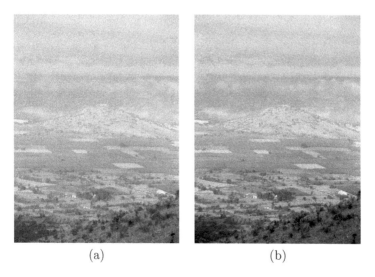

(a)                              (b)

Figure 6.4.4: a) Original image, b) color corrected image.

noise types can be added on the frame. Other artifacts can be added on the video frame to emulate the movie being projected by an old projector. There is even a *sepia toning* filter, which makes the frame look like it was captured using World War I era equipment.

In an interesting and amusing fact, a *lens flare* is the result of excessive light being refracted and reflected inside the lens; it is essentially the product of a flawed lens. Lens flares would show up, when an extremely bright object, such as the sun, would be in view of the camera. The effect is much less pronounced in modern lenses and can be completely avoided in CGI. However, the audience has grown so accustomed to seeing a lens flare, when a bright object comes into view that they will protest its absence. Movie makers will thus intentionally insert CGI lens flares into the appropriate scenes to make them look more "real", or for artistic reasons.

Practical effects are still in use. However, they are much less prevalent with the current state of CGI being so advanced. *Rotoscoping* is the act of projecting a frame onto a screen and having an artist draw effects on a transparent sheet of plastic on top of the screen, using the frame underneath as reference. It has been traditionally a practical effect, but, nowadays, it is done using computers. Sometimes, *pyrotechnics* are still used in the filming process, elaborate filming sets are constructed in real life, makeup artists are hired to attach prosthetics to actors and actors wear body suits to portray non-human characters. The use of practical effects is greatly appreciated by a good portion of movie-goers. However, CGI proves to be too attractive for most movie-makers. The dolly-zoom is still popular, however. Its the in-camera special effect that is achieved by moving the camera away from the actor while zooming in. The size and position of the actor remain roughly the same. However, the viewing angle of the camera is wider, when it is close to the actor and much narrower when it is far away. This causes the background to be seemingly growing larger and closer to the actor, thus invoking a unsettling feeling on the viewer. It is typically used to indicate that the character just had an epiphany, is shocked or otherwise disoriented.

## 6.4.3   Compositing of natural and synthetic scenes

*Scene compositing* is the movie post-production step, where everything comes together. The various parts of the composition, live actors, synthetic background, CGI characters, CGI effects, lie separately in layers. Each layer can have a matte to denote which part of the layer is active and must have a depth map, in order to determine which layer is in front of every other, on a per pixel basis, or how shadows will be cast. If the cameras are static and calibrated, the correspondence between the real camera and the virtual camera can be easily established. Then, the final compositing is a relatively straight forward process. However, there are some further issues to consider.

If a camera moves, then it is necessary that its motion parameters are known, so that the virtual camera can replicate the real camera movement. This can be done using hardware sensors to measure movement directly, or illumination markers on the filming set, which can then be used to infer the camera movement in a fashion similar to the camera calibration methods. There are also hardware setups that can be programmed to move a camera in a specific way and are capable of performing the exact same camera movement several times.

In both the static and moving camera cases, it is also good practice to film at least one empty sequence of the scene, without any actors or props, in case an actor or a prop is scheduled to disappear mid-scene, or some urgent reason dictates that a scene component needs to be erased.

Due to the huge amount of processing power that will be committed to rendering a full scene in high definition, it is possible and advisable to preview the CGI animation in the scene using wireframe or roughly shaded 3D models and making sure that no changes will be required before giving the final word to send the project to a computer graphics server farm for the time consuming rendering process.

## 6.4.4   Digital manipulation, video editing and format conversion

The last stage of post-production includes some digital manipulation of the footage that may be necessary, the *editing* of the finished shots into the final cut of the movie and the digital movie content conversion to an appropriate data format.

Video editing is the process of putting the final cut of the movie together. It is extremely important to the final movie quality. After the scenes have been filmed, the CGI has been rendered, the live action and CGI shots have been composited together and the digital manipulation has been complete, the scenes need to be combined in a way that their sequence tells a coherent story. This happens on most occasions, as incoherency may be part of the artistic vision. The editing must always result in a compelling story. Sometimes scenes that drag on must be cut to a shorter length, or dropped altogether, lest they bore the audience. The material on the screen must also closely match the musical score, though the latter is written with the relevant scenes in mind.

The transitions between scenes can mostly be either *cuts*, *fade in/outs*, or *dissolves*, depending on the circumstances. For example, a scene can start dark and blurry then steadily grow bright and clear to emulate the point of view of a character waking up (fade in). In another example, an action scene or a fight scene can have frantic cuts along different view angles to increase the intensity of the scene and possibly cover up shortcomings in choreography or action execution (abrupt cut). However, when taken to extremes, this approach can render the audience unable to follow the action and, thus, diffuse the tension. Finally, a shot can gradually blend in the next one (dissolve). An example of a dissolve can be found in Figure 6.4.5.

Figure 6.4.5: Video dissolve.

Modern video editing software programs provide many convenient tools to a movie editor. There is a main movie timeline and several video and audio streams. *Seeking* in the video streams is separate for each stream. The video and audio of the streams can be easily sped up or slowed down. The editor can easily choose through the user interface which streams go to the main timeline and how they combine with each other, thus giving the editor excellent control over what scene will be shown and what sounds will be played at any point in the movie. Most programs also provide cut and dissolve options for a scene from one stream to transition into the next scene from another stream.

Finally, after the final cut of the movie has been compiled by the editor, the end product is converted to an appropriate format, depending on the target medium. In order for a movie to be distributed to digital cinemas, a *Digital Source Master (DSM)* file is produced, containing all the video and audio clips used for the final cut and then converted to several *Digital Cinema Distribution Master* files, as described in Chapter 12. These files include the video streams (each frame following the JPEG 2000 encoding standard), the appropriate audio and subtitle streams for various languages and a composition playlist that dictates the order in which all these streams appear in the movie. For traditional cinemas that employ film projectors, the final cut of the movie is printed into rolls of celluloid film. For the DVD edition of the movie, the video is converted to the MPEG-2 format. MPEG-4 AVC format is used for HDTV broadcasting.

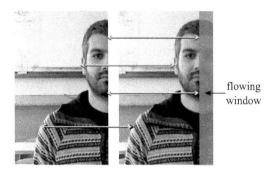

flowing
window

Figure 6.4.6: Right Stereoscopic Window Violation.

## 6.4.5   3DTV production and post-production

In 3DTV (stereo TV), a stereo camera rig is used to produce two syn-chronized videos, corresponding to the left and right view, respectively. Then, after post-production, the left and right video channels are projected on screen in such a way, so that each eye sees only the respective view, e.g., by using stereo glasses or autostereoscopic displays. Then the viewer has fake 3D depth perception based on stereo disparity. Disparity means that a feature in the left image is a horizontal shift of the corresponding feature in the right image and vice versa. Negative/zero/positive disparity denotes objects appearing in front/on/behind the screen, respectively.

Several issues arise, when using digital manipulation on frames from stereoscopic 3D productions. Most of them regard the fact that, while two manipulated video frames at the same time instance may look per-fectly fine on their own, inconsistencies between the manipulated pixels of each perspective will cause problems, when the frames are viewed as a stereoscopic pair. Moreover, a prolonged exposure to such phenomena can cause symptoms such as eye strain, headaches and visual fatigue. Such issues are the so-called stereoscopic window violations, UFO objects, bent window and depth jump cuts.

A *Stereoscopic Window Violation* (SWV) arises when part of an object is cut off at the left or right image border. SWV does not create any prob-lems, when it happens behind the screen (objects with positive disparity), because disparity and occlusion cues are in agreement, as they both say the object is behind the screen. However, when SWV involves objects that appear in front of the screen (i.e., when having negative disparity), the occlusion cue would be in conflict with the disparity. An example of the two types of stereoscopic window violation (left and right SWV) is shown in Figure 6.4.6. A strong cinematographic tool used by 3D movie makers to fix the SWVs is the so-called *floating window*. A floating window is

Left Image            Left Disparity Map

Figure 6.4.7: An example of UFO object.

created by adding black masks on the sides of the left or right images. Masking only one image does not reduce the frame size, but changes the perceived position of the screen window.

In 3D cinematography, a *UFO* is an object improperly displayed inside the theatre space. The cinematographic rule about UFOs states that an object reaching far inside the theatre space must be brought there in a specific way. This can be done either by smooth movement, i.e., a ball flying at a sustainable speed toward the audience or can be justified by the image construction, e.g., in the case of a ball held on a hand, with the respective arm getting out of the screen. If these rules are not met, the object is declared as a UFO. An example of a UFO object is shown in Figure 6.4.7. Such objects trouble the human visual system and cause discomfort and fatigue. Therefore, UFOs must be identified and treated during post-production to ensure proper stereo video quality.

A stereoscopic window violation can involve any screen boundary. Although the most distracting SWVs are those that occur at the left or right side of the screen, because they cause retinal rivalry, a violation can happen even on the top or bottom edges of the screen. Typically, top and bottom window violations cause less discomfort to human brain, but may ruin the 3D effect and change the way viewers perceive depth. Since they make the whole stereoscopic window look bent, they are called *bent windows*. An example of a tree trunk that causes a bent window effect is shown in Figure 6.4.8.

Left Image            Left Disparity Map

Figure 6.4.8: A tree trunk causing bent window effect.

Medium long Shot                Close-up Shot

Figure 6.4.9: A highly uncomfortable jump cut (*courtesy of the 3D4YOU FP7 project and the Hertz Heinrich Institute*).

During the editing process, which is part of the post-production phase, individually recorded segments are connected into a sequential order. This process is quite complex in 3D cinematography, because the editor has to take into consideration, besides other factors, the *depth continuity rule*. This rule states that one should not cut between two shots, if their depths do not match. Although there is no objective definition for the matching depth, a cut from a wide shot behind the screen to a close-up inside the room is a good example of an undesirable forward depth jump cut, as shown in Figure 6.4.9. A forward jump cut is much more disturbing than a backward one. In a forward jump cut, the incoming convergence point is closer to the audience. Thus the eye has to squint to restore stereopsis. On the contrary, in a backward jump cut, the convergence point is farther away from the previous one and the viewer has to relax its extraocular muscles.

# 7

# VIDEO COMPRESSION

## 7.1  Audiovisual content compression

Audiovisual content compression, also known as *source coding*, aims at attaining the highest possible bit rate reduction (in *Megabits per second* or *Mbps*) that is needed for storing or broadcasting digital video of a specific spatiotemporal resolution (and the relevant audio channels) at the minimal possible quality degradation, as it is perceived by the viewer. It is a very important topic in digital TV, since uncompressed video cannot be broadcasted, due to the required extremely high bit rate.

In general, audiovisual data compression algorithms take advantage of the following characteristics:

- *Spatial redundancy* of moving and still images, which refers to the correlation between spatially neighboring image pixels, having similar color and luminance, as shown in Figure 7.1.1.

- *Temporal redundancy* between consecutive video frames of the same scene, in the case of video sequences. It is high, when the scene content remains unchanged or changes only a little between consecutive video frames, as shown in Figure 7.1.1.

- Human visual perception characteristics, like the reduced human eye sensitivity in small image details in fast moving pictures.

- Human auditory perception characteristics that render certain audio artifacts inaudible.

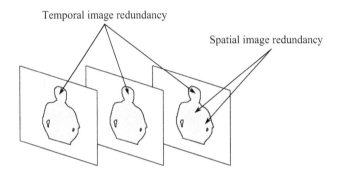

Figure 7.1.1: Spatial and temporal redundancy in video.

Compression can be *lossless*, when audio or video can be decompressed without errors and *lossy*, when the decompressed audio/video do contain (hopefully) imperceivable errors. Lossy compression typically offers much higher compression ratio than lossless compression. Lossless compression techniques, e.g., *LZW compression* used in *ZIP* compression, are typically suited for data (rather than media) compression. Certain lossless compression techniques, e.g., *Huffman coding*, are used as building blocks in media compression standards, such as JPEG or MPEG-2.

Video compression has been extensively studied and several standards have been developed, primarily by the *Moving Picture Experts Group* (MPEG), notably MPEG-1, MPEG-2 and MPEG-4. In the following, we shall describe the two prevailing video compression standards, namely MPEG-2 and MPEG-4. Other video compression methods have been developed as well, such as the H.26x family of standards (notably H.263 and H.264) by the *ITV-T Video Coding Experts Group* (VCEG) for videoconferencing.

## 7.2   Transform-based video compression

In general, we use the inherent spatiotemporal video redundancy to achieve high video compression. If we compress each video frame separately, as if it were a still image, we employ only the spatial redundancy within the video frame. In order to exploit the temporal video redundancy, we try to predict blocks of frame $f(x, y, t)$ from blocks of previous (or even future) reference frames $f(x, y, t - l)$ and compress only the *Displaced Frame Difference* (DFD), which is assumed to be small. A general system for video compression using image transforms is presented in Figure 7.2.1.

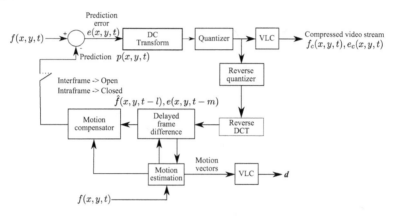

Figure 7.2.1: A general system for transform video compression.

This system supports two operation modes: the *intra-frame* and the *inter-frame* ones. Intra-frame coding of frame $f(x, y, t)$ does not take any input from other frames. The frame $f(x, y, t)$ is transformed using the *Discrete Cosine Transform* (DCT). The DCT coefficients are quantized and then encoded by a *variable-length encoder* (VLC). Finally, the compressed video frame $f_c(x, y, t)$ is transmitted to and eventually received by the decoder. The receiver decodes the compressed frame $f_c(x, y, t)$ producing the reconstructed video frame $\hat{f}(x, y, t)$.

In inter-frame coding, a feedback loop is used to produce a prediction error between the current frame $f(x, y, t)$ and the prediction $p(x, y, t)$. The motion vectors $\mathbf{d}_t$ and previously decompressed and reconstructed video frames $\hat{f}(x, y, t - l)$ produce this prediction. In the simplest case, the previous reconstructed video frame $\hat{f}(x, y, t - 1)$ or a linear combination of previous and subsequent reconstructed frames are used for prediction. During inter-frame coding, the current forecast $p(x, y, t)$ is subtracted from the current video frame $f(x, y, t)$ to form the current DFD $e(x, y, t)$, also called *prediction error*. The prediction error is DCT transformed. Its DCT coefficients are quantized, VLC encoded and transmitted to the receiver, along with the VLC encoded motion vectors $\mathbf{d}_t$. The decoder can reconstruct the current frame $\hat{f}(x, y, t)$ using the reconstructed prediction $\hat{p}(x, y, t)$ from the previous reconstructed frames $\hat{f}(x, y, t - l)$ (which are stored in the decoder) and the respective motion vectors. The encoded prediction error $e_c(x, y, t)$ is decoded to produce the reconstructed prediction error $\hat{e}(x, y, t)$, which is added to the prediction $\hat{p}(x, y, t)$ to produce the current frame $\hat{f}(x, y, t)$.

As there may be errors during transmission that will affect the reconstructed video, we periodically use the intra-frame coding, in which an entire current frame is spatially encoded without outside reference, to ensure that transmission errors will not spread over too many video frames, during decompression. Intra-frame coding can also be used when interframe coding does not achieve good compression, because the frame content prediction is poor.

The DCT has the ability to allocate the largest part of the image energy to a small number of transform coefficients. It is usually applied to rather small frame blocks (e.g., having size of $16 \times 16$ or $8 \times 8$ pixels), to take advantage of the high correlation of neighboring pixels. A *quantizer* is applied to the DCT coefficients, resulting in a lossy compression that can significantly reduce the required bit number. The allocated bit number per coefficient differs, according to the power of this coefficient and/or the properties of the human visual system. Typically, more bits are assigned to low-frequency coefficients, than to the high frequency ones, because most image power resides in low frequencies. The VLC coder is applied to the quantizer output to optimize compression. Inverse quantization and inverse DCT transform are applied to the encoded video frames $f_c(x, y, t)$ or encoded prediction errors $e_c(x, y, t)$ for the decompression of the coded frames. The *delayed frame memory* retains the current and previous frames or prediction errors necessary for the reconstruction of the prediction error $p(x, y, t)$. The number of previous frames stored in memory depends on the decoding algorithm requirements.

# 7.3   MPEG-2 standard

## 7.3.1   Introduction

Experts from different digital media and broadcasting sectors created an expert group in 1990, named Moving Pictures Experts Group (MPEG), aiming at storing and reproducing moving pictures and audio in digital form. The first standard created by this team was MPEG-1 in 1992, which aimed at storing live video and stereo sound in a CD-ROM at a bitrate of 1.5 Mbps. After that, MPEG-2 appeared, which offers much higher bitrates, ranging from 1.5 Mbps to 15 Mbps. It is the source encoding format, which is used in several digital television systems, notably in the European DVB and the American ATSC systems.

The main characteristics of MPEG-2 are the following :

- video compression is backward compatible to MPEG-1,

- MPEG-2 supports both interlaced and progressive video,

- it offers improved audio compression (high quality audio and support of mono and stereo sound),

- it supports multiplexed transmissions, combining different MPEG-2 streams in a single transmission stream,

- it offers other media services, e.g., graphical user interaction and encrypted data transmissions.

The major and most complex MPEG-2 functionality is video compression using motion estimation and compensation. Considering the strong temporal redundancy between consecutive video frames, the information needed for video storage and transmission can be greatly reduced using motion compensation. Motion-compensated compression techniques draw as much as possible information for the current video frame from previous (and/or subsequent) reference video frames and compress only the DFD between the current video frame and the reference one. During video decoding, the decoded frame difference is added to the (already decoded) reference frame to create the current frame. Motion estimation is needed only for video encoding and not for video decoding.

## 7.3.2 Basic MPEG-2 characteristics

MPEG-2 is widely used as a digital television compression format, for terrestrial, satellite and cable broadcasting, as well as for distributing movies and other audiovisual material on DVDs. Therefore, digital television receivers, DVD and other audiovisual playback devices must be compatible with this format. It consists of four parts:

**Part 1:** This MPEG-2 system part specifies the coding layer. It defines a multiplexing structure for audio and video data, as well as a temporal information representation, which is needed for the synchronized audiovisual stream playback in real time. This part defines two container formats:

the *transport stream*, which is designed for sound and video transfer over lossy media channels and the *program stream*, which is designed for reliable media channels, e.g., hard and optical disks.

**Part 2:** It defines encoded video data representation and video decoding. This part provides interlaced video support, which is traditionally used in analog television. All MPEG-2 decoders are capable of reproducing MPEG-1 video streams as well.

**Part 3:** It defines audio encoding/decoding. It supports encoding of more than two audio channels, including stereo sound. It is backwards compatible, allowing MPEG-audio decoders to decode the first two compressed audio streams.

**Part 4:** This part defines MPEG-2 compliance with its specifications.

### 7.3.3   MPEG-2 video stream hierarchy

Figures 7.3.1, 7.3.2 present the MPEG-2 digital video stream hierarchy and its basic elements. It begins with a header, includes one or more groups of pictures and ends with an end code. The video stream hierarchy basically consists of five layers: *Group Of Pictures* (GOP), Pictures, Slices, Macroblocks, Blocks. A GOP consists of a header and a series of one or more pictures. A *Picture* is the basic coding unit in a video sequence, consisting of three matrices (buffers), representing picture luminance $Y$ and chrominance $C_b$, $C_r$ channels, respectively. The $Y$ buffer has an even number of lines and columns. The $C_b$ and $C_r$ buffers can frequently have half the size of the $Y$ buffer along each dimension (horizontal and vertical ones), for compression reasons, since the human eye is more sensitive to luminance, rather than chrominance information. One picture *Slice*

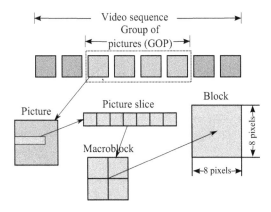

Figure 7.3.1: Video stream hierarchy in MPEG-2.

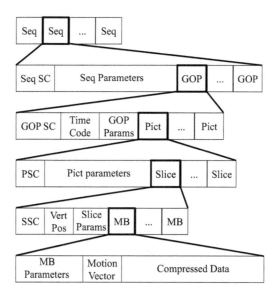

Figure 7.3.2: Video stream hierarchy.

consists of one or more Macroblocks. Macroblocks in a picture Slice are scanned in a row-wise manner: left to right and then top to bottom. Picture Slices are important for proper error management in video decoding. If the video bit stream contains an error, the decoder can detect it, skip the relevant picture Slice and continue with the next one. The existence of many picture Slices offers better error concealment. *Macroblocks* are the basic coding unit in the MPEG-2 algorithm. Motion estimation is done at a Macroblock level and, then, it is used in its constituent Blocks. One Macroblock contains $16 \times 16$ pixels in a video frame. Since the $C_b$ and $C_r$ channels are subsampled, compared to the luminance channel $Y$, one Macroblock consists of four $Y$ Blocks, one $C_r$ Block and one $C_b$ Block. The *Block* is the smallest picture part, whose pixels are jointly encoded. It consists of $8 \times 8$ pixels and can contain either $Y$ luminance, or $C_b$ color or $C_r$ color information.

Due to block-based coding, MPEG-2 video compression suffers from blocking artifacts, particularly in cases of very strong compression. Furthermore, MPEG-2 compression is video content ignorant, as it employs blocks, rather than objects, as its basic compression entity.

## 7.3.4 Picture types in MPEG-2

There are three picture (video frame) types in MPEG-2.

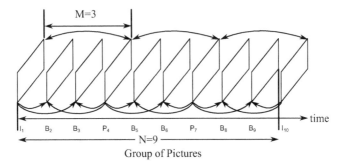

Figure 7.3.3: Picture coding types MPEG.

- *I-pictures* (Intra pictures). These pictures are independently encoded, without depending on any other video picture. They are the main access point in a compressed video stream, e.g., for video browsing and can be used as a reference for coding other video frames. Since no temporal redundancy is exploited in intra picture coding, their compression ratio is rather low.

- *P-pictures* (Predicted pictures). These pictures are encoded using prediction from previous I- or other P-pictures. A P-picture can be used to predict a subsequent P-picture. Since temporal redundancy is exploited, their compression ratio is higher than the one of I- pictures.

- *B-pictures* (Bi-directionally predicted pictures). They are encoded with bi-directional interpolation between the I- or P-pictures, which precede or follow the B-picture. They have the highest compression ratio.

Figure 7.3.3 depicts a MPEG group of pictures. $M = 3$ is the frame distance between two consecutive P-pictures and $N = 9$ is the frame distance between two consecutive I-pictures. The bit stream which is produced by the video or sound decoder is termed as an *Elementary Stream (ES)*.

MPEG-2 format supports progressive and interlaced video encoding, as shown in Figure 7.3.4. Thus, backward compatibility is ensured with

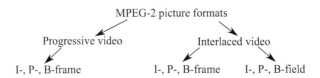

Figure 7.3.4: Progressive and interlaced MPEG-2 video encoding.

NTSC or PAL/SECAM video that has already been digitized ($480i$ or $576i$ formats).

### 7.3.5 I-picture encoding

The MPEG-2 compression algorithm for I-pictures contains the following steps, as shown in Figure 7.3.5:

- Discrete cosine transform (DCT),

- quantization,

- run-length encoding,

- Huffman encoding.

Picture blocks have a high spatial redundancy, i.e., their neighboring pixels have similar luminance/chrominance. The MPEG-2 standard employs the Discrete Cosine Transform (DCT), in order to transform the picture Blocks of size $8 \times 8$ pixels from the spatial domain $(x, y)$ to a 'frequency' domain, to reduce this redundancy. The DCT components consist of the *DC term (coefficient)*, which is equal to the average luminance of the Block and the *AC terms (coefficients)*. The signal power is concentrated on a few DCT components that usually lie near the DC term. They are quantized and represented with more bits. A quantization coefficient table, containing $8 \times 8$ quantization coefficients, is presented in Table 7.3.1. The low frequencies are near the top left corner of the $8 \times 8$ DCT coefficient table. Most of the picture information is concentrated in this area. For this reason, we use low quantization coefficients (i.e., more bits) near the DC

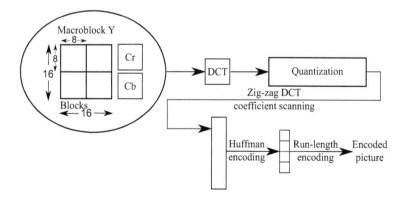

Figure 7.3.5: : I-picture Encoding.

Table 7.3.1: DCT quantization coefficient table.

| 8 | 16 | 19 | 22 | 26 | 27 | 29 | 34 |
|---|----|----|----|----|----|----|----|
| 16 | 16 | 22 | 24 | 27 | 29 | 34 | 37 |
| 19 | 22 | 26 | 27 | 29 | 34 | 34 | 38 |
| 22 | 22 | 26 | 27 | 29 | 34 | 37 | 40 |
| 22 | 26 | 27 | 29 | 32 | 35 | 40 | 48 |
| 26 | 27 | 29 | 32 | 35 | 40 | 48 | 58 |
| 26 | 27 | 29 | 34 | 38 | 46 | 56 | 69 |
| 27 | 29 | 35 | 38 | 46 | 56 | 69 | 83 |

term. We observe that the high frequency DCT coefficients are strongly quantized. The combination of DCT and coefficient quantization results in many zero-valued DCT coefficients, especially at high spatial frequencies, as shown in Figure 7.3.6. Thus, the quantized DCT coefficients are scanned in a *zig-zag* manner, so that they produce long zero runs. Then these DCT coefficients can be represented by a pair of numbers, where the first number shows the number of zero-valued coefficients and the second number is the value of the next non-zero DCT coefficient. These pairs are encoded with a variable length code (Huffman coding) that uses shorter codewords for frequently occurring number pairs and longer codewords for rarely occurring number pairs.

Some picture Blocks must be encoded with better accuracy than other ones. For instance, Blocks with smooth luminance must be coded fairly accurately, so that pseudo-contour artifacts are avoided. High-detail Blocks must be coded accurately as well, when we want to preserve image details. MPEG-2 addresses this problem by allowing different quantization coefficients for every Macroblock. This mechanism can also be used to provide smooth encoding adjustment to specific transfer bit rates.

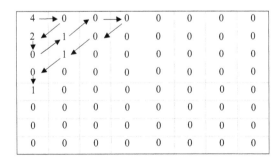

Figure 7.3.6: Zig-zag scan of the quantized DCT coefficients.

## 7.3.6  P-picture encoding

A P-picture is encoded taking into account a previous reference picture, which is of I- or P-type. As shown in Figure 7.3.7, the highlighted block in the target picture (the one to be encoded) is similar to that in the reference picture, pointed by a properly chosen motion vector found by motion estimation. Most changes between the two consecutive video frames can be approximated by displacements of such small image blocks. For this reason, image prediction combined with motion compensation is used for P-picture coding.

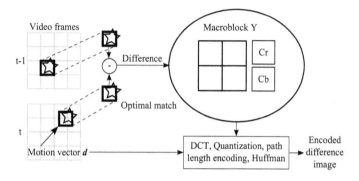

Figure 7.3.7: P-picture encoding.

This prediction takes advantage of the temporal redundancy in video content. In consecutive video frames, a rather precise prediction of target frame blocks is possible, based on the reference picture data, provided that block displacements (motion vectors) have been correctly estimated, by employing motion estimation algorithms (typically *block matching*). The prediction process leads to significant video content compression. In P-pictures, motion estimation is performed on every $16 \times 16$ Macroblock from a Macroblock of a previously encoded I- or P-picture. A search is executed in the reference frame, so that a Macroblock is found, which matches the Macroblock of the P-frame under examination. The difference between two matching blocks can be encoded in the DCT domain. The DCT of the prediction error leads to only few non-zero DCT coefficients which, after quantization, demand a very small bit number for their representation. Further compression is achieved using run-length Huffman encoding. The quantization tables used for prediction error Blocks are different from those used for intra block coding, because of their different spectral characteristics.

Horizontal $x$ and vertical $y$ displacements between the Macroblocks are described by motion vectors. Differential encoding of motion vectors reduces the required bit number, by transmitting only the difference between motion vectors of consecutive Macroblocks.

### 7.3.7    B-picture encoding

Some pictures (video frames) contain information, which can not be found in past reference pictures, e.g., when a new object enters the frame. Thus, B-pictures are encoded similarly to P-pictures, except that the motion vectors can be referred either to previous reference pictures, or to subsequent ones or both. Figure 7.3.8 illustrates B-picture encoding.

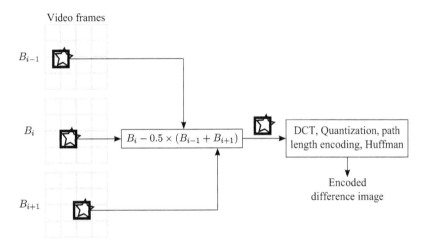

Figure 7.3.8: B-picture encoding.

If we use both a past and future reference picture, then the prediction error is produced by subtracting the average of the reference Blocks. Prediction error encoding is similar to the one of the P-picture encoding.

### 7.3.8    Interlaced video support in MPEG-2

MPEG-2 defines two new picture types for interlaced video:

1) *Frame pictures*, which are obtained by de-interlacing even- and odd-numbered fields, as shown in Figure 7.3.9. This can be of I-, P-, or B-type. De-interlacing produces artifacts in the presence of strong motion.

2) *Field pictures* that are simply the even- and the odd-numbered video fields considered as separate images. They may be of I-, P- or B-type.

Field pictures do not exploit well the spatial information redundancy, in the case of little or no motion.

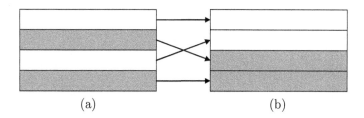

(a)                                    (b)

Figure 7.3.9: The luminance component of a) a frame picture, b) field pictures.

There are two options in interlaced MPEG-2 field encoding: a) each field block can be encoded independently (*field encoding*) or b) two fields can encoded together as a frame picture (*frame encoding*). Switching between field and frame encoding is permitted. Frame or field encoding are preferred for relatively stationary video content or in the presence of significant motion, respectively. MPEG-2 allows to choose DCT on a field or frame basis, at each Macroblock in a frame Picture, depending on the presence/absence of strong motion, respectively.

There are two main types of motion-compensated prediction for interlaced video: field or frame prediction, using data from one or more previously decoded fields/frames, respectively. In a field picture, only field predictions can be used, whereas in a frame picture, either frame prediction or field prediction can be used, depending on the presence/absence of strong motion in each Macroblock.

Regarding DCT coefficient VLC encoding, besides zig-zag scanning, MPEG-2 allows the optional *alternate scan*, shown in Figure 7.3.10. Alternate scanning is preferred for interlaced video, whose fields have relatively higher frequency content in the vertical direction. Thus, alternate scanning gives more weight to the higher vertical frequencies than to the horizontal ones.

## 7.3.9   Profiles and levels

MPEG-2 has been designed to support a wide range of applications and services of varying video quality. For many applications, the support of the entire MPEG-2 format is non-realistic and very expensive. Therefore, MPEG-2 supports *profiles* and *levels*, so that each application may support only a subset of MPEG-2 functionalities. Profiles define subsets

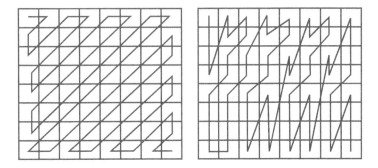

Figure 7.3.10: Zig-zag and alternate DCT coefficient scanning.

of MPEG-2 characteristics like, for instance, the compression algorithm, color analysis and scalability type. Levels define quantitative indices, like, for instance, maximal bit rate and image resolution. Then, a MPEG-2 compliant application defines the compression specifications in terms of profiles and levels. For instance, a DVD device may support only the main profile and main level (usually denoted by MP@ML). MPEG-2 profiles and levels are shown in Tables 7.3.2 and 7.3.3.

## 7.3.10  Scalability

*Scalability* refers to the capability of coding/decoding only a specific part of the video bit stream at a desirable spatiotemporal resolution or

Table 7.3.2: MPEG-2 profiles.

| Abbreviation | Name | Picture types | Color type | Aspect ratio | Scalability |
|---|---|---|---|---|---|
| SP | Simple profile | I, P | 4:2:0 | square pixels, 4:3, 16:9 | None |
| MP | Main profile | I, P, B | 4:2:0 | square pixels, 4:3, 16:9 | None |
| SNR | SNR scalable profile | I, P, B | 4:2:0 | square pixels, 4:3, 16:9 | SNR |
| Spatial | Spatially scalable profile | I, P, B | 4:2:0 | square pixels, 4:3, 16:9 | SNR or spatial |
| HP | High profile | I, P, B | 4:2:2 4:2:0 | square pixels, 4:3, 16:9 | SNR or spatial |

Table 7.3.3: MPEG-2 levels.

| Abbreviation | Name | Frame Rate (Hz) | Maximal Horizon- tal Analysis | Maximal Vertical Analysis | Maximal bit rate (Mbps) |
|---|---|---|---|---|---|
| LL | Low Level | 23.976, 24, 25, 29.97, 30 | 352 | 288 | 4 |
| ML | Main Level | 23.976, 24, 25, 29.97, 30 | 720 | 576 | 15 |
| H-14 | High 1440 | 23.976, 24, 25, 29.97, 30, 50, 59.94, 60 | 1440 | 1152 | 60 |
| HL | High Level | 23.976, 24, 25, 29.97, 30, 50, 59.94, 60 | 1920 | 1152 | 80 |

quality. Thus, MPEG-2 decoders having different complexities decode and display video at a different spatiotemporal resolution from the same compressed video bit stream. The minimal bit stream subset that can be decoded is called *base layer*. All other scalability layers are *enhancement layers*, which improve video resolution quality of the base layer. MPEG-2 syntax allows two or three video layers. There are four different scalability forms:

- *Spatial scalability* allows video decoding at various spatial resolutions, without prior decoding and subsampling of the entire video frames. The base layer provides a low spatial video resolution. The enhancement layers provide higher spatial frequency information. To this end, MPEG-2 uses a pyramid encoding approach. The input base layer is acquired by subsampling the initial video input. The enhancement layer is the difference of the original video frames and those of the interpolated base layer video.

- *SNR scalability* offers decoding options, using different quantization tables for the DCT coefficients. The base video layer is acquired employing a coarse DCT coefficient quantization at the same spatiotemporal resolution to the input video. The enhancement layer refers to the difference between the base layer and the original input video.

- *Temporal scalability* refers to video decoding at different frame rates, without the need to decode every video frame.

- *Hybrid scalability* refers to any combination of the above scalability types.

A significant benefit of scalability is that it provides better transmission error resilience, as the base video layer is usually transmitted with better error correction methods.

## 7.3.11   Audio coding

MPEG-2 provides several sound encoding techniques. These are:

- Low bit rate encoding for multichannel 5.1 surround sound. In total, five full bandwidth audio channels (left, right, central and rear left/right channels), as well as a *Low Frequency Effects* (LFE) channel, are supported. The LFE channel is used to power the subwoofer and carries only audio frequencies up to 120 Hz, or roughly one tenth of the bandwidth of the other five channels. Hence it is denoted as ".1" channel.

- MPEG-2 audio format expands MPEG-1 audio formats for better sound quality at bit rates lower than 64 Kbps per channel.

The Dolby AC-3 audio standard used in MPEG-2 coincides with the ATSC A/52 standard and was developed by Dolby. It is a high quality, low complexity multichannel audio codec. The Dolby AC-3 algorithm divides the audio spectrum of each channel into narrow frequency bands of different range that eliminate noise coding. Dolby AC-3 supports the standard 5.1 surround audio. The Dolby AC-3 bit rate ranges from 32 Kbps to 640 Kbps and has a sampling rate up to 48 kHz.

The audio compression standards MPEG-1 and MPEG-2 (Layer I and Layer II) are described in ISO/IEC 11172-3 and ISO/IEC 13818-3. MPEG-1 provides a single channel or two channels of audio (joint stereo or stereo). MPEG-2 audio is a compatible multichannel extension to MPEG-1 audio that provides 5.1 audio channels, such as Dolby AC-3. MPEG-1 Layer I works at a bit rate from 32 kbps up to 448 kbps and Layer II has a bit rate from 32 kbps up to 384 kbps. MPEG-2 audio streams can have a bit rate higher than 384 kbps (up to 682 kbps). The sampling rate for MPEG-1 or MPEG-2 (Layer I and Layer II) audio is from 16 kHz up to 48 kHz.

MPEG-2 Layer III audio format is widely known as *MP3 audio*. It has become a de facto standard for digital audio playback. It supports audio at various bit rates, ranging from 32 kbps to 160 kbps or even 320 kbps and at various sampling frequencies from 18 kHz up to 48 kHz.

MPEG-2 *Advanced Audio Coding* (AAC) is an ISO/IEC 13818-7 audio compression standard, which can support from 1 to 48 channels at sampling rates ranging from 8 to 96 kHz, with multichannel and multilingual support. AAC supports transmission rates from 8 kbps up to 160 kbps for very high quality encoding, which allows multiple encoding - decoding cycles. AAC was designed to become the successor of the widely used MP3 (MPEG-1 Audio Layer 3) format and can generally achieve better sound quality than any other audio standard.

## 7.4 MPEG-4 standard

MPEG-4 is an ISO/IEC format for audio, video and three-dimensional graphics compression, developed by MPEG. It became an international standard in 1999. MPEG-4 audiovisual data compression is used for digital TV broadcasting, media streaming, DVD distribution, video telephony and other video applications. MPEG-4 shares has many characteristics with the MPEG-1 and MPEG-2 standards and other related compression formats. It supports new features, like *Virtual Reality Modeling Language* (VRML), three-dimensional (3D) imaging, *Digital Rights Management* (DRM) and various types of user-content interaction. MPEG-4 supports multiple transmission rates and has been used in a variety of applications, ranging from digital terrestrial TV to video compression for Blu-ray optical discs or media streaming.

MPEG-4 consists of several parts. Most companies promoting MPEG-4 use some, but not necessarily all, parts. The most frequently used parts are MPEG-4 Part 2 (MPEG-4 SP/ASP), which includes codecs like DivX, Xvid, Nero Digital, 3ivx and QuickTime 6 and MPEG-4 Part 10 (MPEG-4 AVC/H.264), which is used in the latest versions of digital TV broadcasting systems, e.g., in DVB-T2 and ATSC. It is also used in Blu-ray video compression. The content providers can decide which MPEG-4 features will be implemented in a particular application or service. This means that there is probably no full implementation of the entire set of MPEG-4 features. To overcome this problem, MPEG-4 supports profiles and layers, allowing the determination of a specific set of feature options that are suitable for an application subset.

Initially, MPEG-4 was aimed primarily at low-rate video communications (e.g., Internet streaming). Its scope was later extended to become a general multimedia coding format. MPEG-4 is efficient in a variety of transmission rates, ranging from a few kbps to Mbps. MPEG-4 provides the following functionalities:

- improved coding efficiency,

- ability to encode various digital media modalities (video, audio, three-dimensional graphics),

- error resilience to allow proper digital media distribution,

- user interaction with the audiovisual scene generated at the receiver site.

## 7.4.1 Audio coding in MPEG-4

MPEG-4 does not support a unique audio coding algorithm. Since there is no encoding method to cover its wide application range, from encoding very low bit rate speech signals up to high-quality multichannel sound coding, MPEG-4 supports a set of audio coding algorithms to achieve optimal coding efficiency for each application. The scalable audio codecs can be divided into the following categories:

1) For lower transmission rates, a *text to speech* (TTS) synthesizer is supported, using an MPEG-4 TTS interface.

2) Low rate speech coding (3.1 kHz bandwidth) is based on *Harmonic Vector Excitation Coding* (HVXC) that encodes audio at a rate of 2-4 Kbps.

3) Telephone speech quality (8 kHz bandwidth) and wide-band speech (16 kHz bandwidth) are coded using the *Code Excited Linear Predictive* (CELP) encoder at rates in the range of 3.85-23.8 kbps. The CELP codec can create five layer scalable bit streams.

4) General sound sources are encoded in the range of 16 kbps to more than 64 kbps per channel, using a more efficient implementation of MPEG-2 Advanced Audio Coding (AAC) encoder, which can support high quality sound. In addition to audio encoding, audio MPEG-4 defines music composition at the receiver, using a series of structured audio tools to unify the world of algorithmic music composition. Finally, it implements scalability and the concept of audio/sound objects.

## 7.4.2 Basic video encoding

In MPEG-4, the spatiotemporal image of an object is designed to be an entity, called *Video Object* (VO), thus allowing content-based user interaction. Therefore, we can refer not only to video frames, but also to Video Objects. MPEG-4 encodes VOs independently, using their motion, texture and shape. In the decoder, different VOs compose the visual scene to be displayed. Appropriate syntactic structures should be developed to

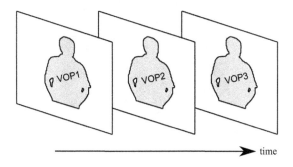

Figure 7.4.1: Video Object and its Video Object Planes.

support such an operation. A Video Scene, which is the highest syntactic structure, may consist of several VOs. A VO has three dimensions (two spatial dimensions and time). A time instance of a Video Object is called *Video Object Plane* (VOP), which is typically a spatial region in a video frame. A VO and its three VOPs are shown in Figure 7.4.1. A VOP can be fully described by color *texture* (luminance and chrominance values of its pixels) and its *shape*. In order to facilitate video object processing and random access, consecutive VOPS can be grouped into one *Group of Video Object Planes* (GVOP). VOP motion, texture and shape are encoded in I-, P- and B-modes, comparable to the respective MPEG-2 predictive coding

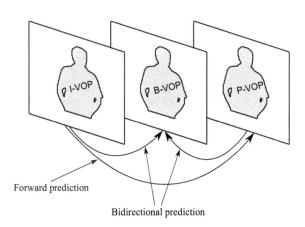

Figure 7.4.2: Various coding options for Video Object Planes (P-VOP, B-VOP).

Figure 7.4.3: Binary alpha table.

methods (I-, P- and B-frames). By extending the concepts of intra, predictive and bidirectional predictive frames of MPEG to VOPs, we obtain I-VOPs, P-VOPs and B-VOPs, as shown in Figure 7.4.2.

The shape of a VOP is described by using an *alpha map* (or *alpha plane* or *alpha mask*), which has the same spatial resolution with the VOP luminance signal. A binary alpha map defines the pixels belonging to the object, as shown in Figure 7.4.3. Grayscale alpha maps define object transparency, typically using 8 bits per pixel. Alpha maps may be associated to Macroblocks. A binary alpha table of a Macroblock is called *Binary Alpha Block* (BAB).

### 7.4.3   Video encoding based on objects

MPEG-2 is a block-based coding scheme. Therefore, it cannot provide video object functionalities. Furthermore, blocking artifacts are visible in case of strong compression. Such problems can be remedied by object-based video coding. MPEG-4 allows Video Object encoding, in order to provide object-based functionalities, e.g., for video editing. While MPEG-4 does not specify video object segmentation algorithms, it does specify shape encoding and decoding algorithms. Subsequently, we describe the individual tools used in object-based MPEG-4 video encoding.

**Shape coding.** An *arithmetic codec* is used to encode boundary object Blocks. A boundary Block contains pixels of both the object and the background. For a non-boundary Block, the codec marks only if it is part of the object or not. A sequence of alpha maps describing a Video Object may be encoded and transmitted, without using texture information. BABs are either intra- or inter-frame encoded. Motion compensation can be used in inter-frame coding. Object shape coding may use motion vectors for shape prediction.

**Texture coding.** A VOP is divided into Macroblocks having size

Figure 7.4.4: Pixel filling outside the object region.

16 × 16 pixels. They are in turn divided into four luminance blocks of 8 × 8 pixels and 2 chrominance Blocks of 8 × 8 pixels. Non-boundary blocks are DCT coded in approximately the same way as in MPEG-2. For boundary Blocks, MPEG-4 allows the use of certain transform coding tools for coding the object texture, within a shape described by a corresponding BAB. In this case, MPEG-4 may use tools like pixel filling outside the object regions, as shown in Figure 7.4.4, and, subsequently, the DCT transform for texture encoding. Alternatively, *Shape-Adaptive DCT* (SA-DCT) can be used for boundary Block coding. It offers higher compression, but has also higher computational complexity.

Generally speaking, object based video coding has not found many applications in practice, mainly because video segmentation in semantically meaningful entities (objects) is a very difficult task that should usually be performed either manually or semi-automatically. There are though some notable exceptions, e.g., when *chroma keying* is used in video production. Until now, object based coding has been primarily an interesting research topic.

### 7.4.4 Coding improvements in MPEG-4

Apart from the obvious changes, due to support of object-based coding, MPEG-4 adopted several methods to increase coding efficiency, compared to the MPEG-2 standard.

Some changes are related primarily to motion estimation and compensation:

- Four motion vectors are allowed for each Macroblock. The same approach is followed in the H.263 video compression standard.

- Arbitrary motion vectors are allowed. Compared to H.263, longer motion vectors can be used, covering a larger motion range.

- Large background images, called *sprites*, can be transmitted to the decoder. The encoder can transmit affine transform parameters that match a sprite region to screen for visualization. By changing these parameters, the decoder can zoom or pan to the right or left in the background image.

- *Global motion compensation* is allowed to compensate camera motion, camera zooming or large moving object motion. Global motion is compensated according to its eight parameter model. Such motion compensation is an important tool to improve image quality for scenes containing global motion. Such scenes are not suited for block-based coding. Unlike scenes containing random local motion, the human eye is capable of tracking image details in the case of global motion. Therefore, in such cases, global motion compensation helps to improve the perceived image quality.

- *Quarter pixel* (Qpel) motion compensation is supported. Its main objective is to increase accuracy at an extra computational cost, thus leading to more precise motion estimation/compression and, hence, to smaller prediction errors. Qpel motion compensation is applied only to pixel luminance. Chrominance information is compensated at half-pixel accuracy.

In MPEG-4, several changes concern DCT coefficient coding:

- *DC coefficient prediction* is improved compared to the provisions of MPEG-1/2. The current DC value is predicted either from the preceding Block or from the Block above the current Block.

- *AC coefficient prediction* is allowed. The Block, which was chosen to predict the DC coefficient, is also used to predict a line of AC coefficients. If the prediction is based on the previous Block, the AC coefficients of first column are used to predict the corresponding AC coefficients of the current Block. If the prediction is based on the Block of the previous Block line, it is also used to predict the AC coefficients of the first Block line. AC coefficient prediction does not work well for Blocks containing coarse texture or diagonal, horizontal or vertical edges. Switching AC prediction from active to inactive status at Block level is desirable, but very computationally expensive. Therefore, this decision is taken at Macroblock level.

- An *alternate horizontal scan* of DCT coefficients is allowed. This scan was added to the two scans foreseen in MPEG-2. The alternate

MPEG-2 scan is referred as an *alternate vertical scan* in MPEG-4. The alternate horizontal scan is formed by mirroring the vertical scan. The alternate scan mode is selected according to the AC prediction mode. In the case of AC prediction from the previous Block, the alternate vertical scan is selected. In the case of AC prediction from the previous line Block, the alternate horizontal scan is chosen. If AC prediction is off, zig-zag scanning is selected.

- Three-dimensional VLC coding supported. DCT coefficient coding is achieved in a manner similar to that of H.263 video compression format.

As already noted, some of these improvement are similar to those employed in the H.263 format. H.263 supports motion compensation of overlapping Blocks. This feature is not included in any MPEG-4 profile, because of its high computational complexity for large images and its limited improvement for high quality video.

Apart from the tools developed to increase coding efficiency, MPEG-4 contains tools for increasing transmission error resilience.

## 7.4.5 MPEG-4 parts and profiles

### 7.4.5.1 MPEG-4 part 2

MPEG-4 Part 2 is a video compression technology developed by MPEG. It belongs to MPEG-4 ISO/IEC format 14496-2 and provides compression schemes that are similar to the ones of previous formats, such as MPEG-1 and MPEG-2. Several popular video codecs, including DivX, Xvid and Nero Digital are implementations of this format.

In order to address the requirements of various market sectors ranging from low-quality, low-resolution video obtained from surveillance cameras to high definition television broadcasting and DVD, MPEG-4 supports groups of characteristics, which are divided into profiles and levels. The MPEG-4 Part 2 has 21 profiles, including *Simple, Advanced Simple, Main, Core, Advanced Coding, Advanced Real Time Simple* profiles, etc. The most commonly used profiles are the Advanced Simple profile and Simple profile, the second being a subset of the first one.

Most video compression systems specify bitstream format and, therefore, the decoder, but leave room for the encoder design to individual implementations. Therefore, specific profile implementations are identical, with respect to decoder characteristics, such as DivX or Nero Digital, which are implementations of the Advanced Simple Profile and Xvid, which implements two profiles.

Simple Profile is mainly used in cases of low-bitrate, low-resolution transmission, due to, e.g., bandwidth restrictions or display resolution. Examples are mobile phones, inexpensive video-conferencing and camera surveillance systems. The Advanced Simple Profile has remarkable technical characteristics:

- it provides quantization similar to that of MPEG-2,

- it supports interlaced videos,

- it supports B-picture encoding,

- it provides Qpel motion compensation,

- it supports global motion compensation.

In fact, the main MPEG-4 Part 2 encoder/decoder is similar to that of the H.263 standard. Quantization, interlaced video and B-picture support are similar to those of MPEG-2 Part 2. The support of Qpel motion compensation was innovative when adopted. Later, Qpel compensation was included (in somewhat different forms) in MPEG-4 part 10 (H.264) and VC-1. Some video compression formats do not support this option, because it has a significant negative impact on speed and is not always beneficial for compressed video quality. Global motion (e.g., zoom) compensation is not supported in most codec implementations, despite the official codec specifications. This is due to its adverse effect on speed and codec complexity, without significant compression benefits.

### 7.4.5.2   H.264/MPEG-4 part 10 format

H.264 is a video compression format that is equivalent to MPEG-4 Part 10, also called MPEG-4 AVC. Developed by the ITU-T Video Coding Experts Group (VCEG) together with ISO/IEC Moving Picture Experts Group (MPEG), it was the product of the Joint Video Team (JVT) working group. The ITU-T H.264 and ISO/IEC MPEG-4 Part 10 (formally, ISO/IEC 14496-10) formats are jointly maintained, so as to have the same technical content. The final draft of their first edition was completed in 2003. It is the latest block-based motion-compensated video coding format. MPEG-4 Part 10 contains a number of new features allowing very efficient video compression and enhanced flexibility for applications in a wide range of network environments. For these reasons, it has been highly successful in many applications.

The original intention of MPEG-4 Part 10 development team was to create a format capable to provide good video quality at lower transmission rates than previous formats (e.g., half or less the rate of MPEG-2,

H.263, or MPEG-2 Part 2), without excessive implementation cost. An additional aim was to provide sufficient flexibility for its application in a broad range of networks and systems, including low and high transmission rates, low and high video resolution, TV broadcasting, DVD storage, RTSP/IP packet networks and multimedia ITU-T telephony systems.

Finally, the MPEG-4 Part 10 AVC has led to a very wide range of applications, covering almost all compressed video forms, from video streaming on the Internet to HDTV, with very good quality/bit rate characteristics. For example, it has been used in digital satellite television at 1.5 Mbps, compared to 3.5 Mbps needed in MPEG-2 video. It is also used in Blu-ray optical discs, YouTube, iTunes Store video, satellite (DVB-S2) terrestrial (DVB-T2) television and real-time videoconferencing. Blu-Ray discs include MPEG-4 Part 10 AVC High Profile as one of the three mandatory video compression formats. Sony has also chosen this format for video storage on Memory Sticks.

MPEG-4 Part 10 AVC is in fact, a family of formats, whose members are the profiles described below. Each decoder can decode at least one profile. After the first version of MPEG-4 Part 10 AVC was released in 2003, the JVT group has developed extensions of the original model, known as the *Fidelity Range Extensions* (FRExt). These extensions support higher quality video coding, increased bit depth and higher spatial video resolution, including the BT.601 YUV 4:2:2 and YUV 4:4:4 video formats.

### 7.4.5.3   H.264/MPEG-4 part 10 profiles and levels

H.264/MPEG-4 Part 10 format contains 17 profiles. Each one covers a different application area. No profile contains the entire format. New released versions either correct or add profiles. Once, one profile has been removed. H.264/MPEG-4 Part 10 initially identified three profiles, each of them supporting a specific set of compatible encoder/decoder specifications. These profiles are:

- *Baseline profile.* It is widely used in low-cost applications, using limited computing resources, in videoconferencing and mobile telephony. It supports intra-coding and inter-coding, using I- and P-Slices. It supports entropy coding using *Context-Adaptive Variable-Length Coding* (CAVLC).

- *Main profile.* Originally, it was intended for mainstream consumers. Its importance waned, when High Profile was developed for the same applications. It supports interlaced video, intra-coding and inter-coding using B-Slices, weighted prediction and entropy coding using *Context-Based Arithmetic Coding* (CABAC).

- *Extended profile*. Intended for video streaming, it offers relatively high video compression and some additional robustness to packet loss. It supports neither interlaced video encoding nor CABAC coding. It offers new modes allowing for adequate switching between coded streams (SP-and SI-Slices). It has improved resilience to transmission errors (data partitioning).

Newer profiles are the following ones:

- *High Profile* (HiP). It is the main broadcasting and optical storage profile, particularly for HDTV. This profile is approved for use in the Blu-Ray format.

- *High 10 Profile* (Hi10P). Going beyond the current capabilities of consumer products, this profile builds on the High Profile, supporting color depths up to 10 bits per pixel.

- *High 4:2:2 Profile* (Hi422P). Primarily addressing professional applications using interlaced video, this profile builds on the High 10 Profile, providing support for 4:2:2 color subsampling and color depth of up to 10 bits per pixel.

- *High 4:4:4 Predictive Profile*. This profile extends the High 4:2:2 Profile, supporting color formats up to 4:4:4 and color depth up to 14 bits per pixel. It offers lossless region coding and independent color channel coding for each picture.

Apparently, these profiles address high end applications employing high-resolution and high quality video.

### 7.4.5.4   MP4 container format

*MP4* is a multimedia container file format that is formally defined as MPEG-4 Part 14. The respective file extension name is '.MP4'. It is frequently used for compressed audio or video file streaming. The video files are compressed using MPEG4 codecs (either Part 2 or Part 10). Digital audio is compressed using the AAC codec. Several media players can play MP4 files, such as QuickTime player, Windows Media Player and Flash player. Many hardware devices (MP3/MP4 players) support this format. Besides audiovisual streams, MP4 files can contain still images and/or subtitles.

## 7.5 HEVC video compression standard

*High Efficiency Video Coding* (HEVC) format, also informally known as H.265, is a draft video compression standard that is expected to become the successor of the highly successful H.264 (MPEG4 Part 10 AVC) video compression standard. Its first version was approved in 2013. It is jointly developed by ITU-T VCEG and ISO/IEC MPEG expert groups. It is expected to have superior performance than H.264. It can double video compression, while maintaining the same video quality. Inter- and intra-frame coding is used, as in previous video compression standards. Although the basic coding options are similar to previous standards (e.g., motion compensation, fractional motion vector support, VLC or arithmetic entropy transform coefficient coding), they are richer, more complex and more powerful. For example, picture regions of up to $64 \times 64$ replace the Macroblocks and up to 34 intra-prediction directions can be used.

HEVC can support new upcoming HDTV formats, such as 4K UHDTV (2160p), video having resolution of $3840 \times 2160$ pixels and 8K video (4320p), offering resolution of $7680 \times 4320$ pixels. Higher color depth (more than 24 bits per pixel) is well supported. HEVC is expected to have increased error robustness and better network support. Its Main Profile offers compatibility to H.264 High Profile.

# 8

# DIGITAL TELEVISION

# BROADCASTING

## 8.1   Overview of digital television

*Digital television* (DTV) appeared in the early '90s. Till then, many video compression algorithms have been developed, offering high compression ratios. This was the main technological advance that allowed the introduction of digital television, because it solved many digital video transmission problems, by greatly reducing the amount of the digital data that are necessary for DTV transmission. The first digital television channel began to broadcast in 1994 in the United States of America. In Europe, the discussion for the digital television broadcasting format began in 1991. The first digital broadcast was made in the United Kingdom in 1998. Since then, many countries abandoned the analog television step by step and introduced DTV broadcasting.

Digital television broadcasting system consists of four subsystems:

- audiovisual content compression,

- source multiplex and transport,

- channel coding,

- modulation.

At the receiver site, the inverse operations take place in an inverse order: demodulation, channel decoding, demultiplexing, audiovisual content decompression. Audiovisual content compression has been extensively covered in Chapter 7. Therefore, only the remaining three digital TV subsystems will be presented in detail in this chapter.

## 8.2    Source multiplexing and transport

The source multiplex and transport subsystem uses the digital audiovisual data *Packets of Elementary Streams* (PES) provided by the audio/video encoder, adds ancillary data for identifying each packet and multiplexes the packets of video, audio and ancillary data streams to form *Transport Stream* (TS) packets. They, in turn, can be multiplexed and transmitted. After multiplexing, the packetized data stream can be (optionally) scrambled. As a result, the DTV receiver will be able to demultiplex and decode the video streams, synchronize the video with the audio data and offer to the user a bouquet of channels to choose from. Furthermore, the transport mechanism should offer interoperability among terrestrial, cable and satellite distribution.

## 8.3    Channel coding

After source multiplexing, the transport stream consists of packages of certain byte size, e.g., having 188 bytes each. This signal is transmitted to users via a satellite or a terrestrial radio frequency transmitter or through a cable network. These communication channels are not error free. A compressed digital television signal, which is free of redundancies, can tolerate low or zero bit error rate. Thus, in order to detect and correct transmission errors at the receiver, we apply channel coding methods, before signal modulation. This procedure adds *redundancy bits* to the transported stream, so that data transmission is more tolerant to errors that occur in the transmission channel. *Channel coding* refers to procedures for error detection and correction and may also include data modulation. Error correction is achieved using *Forward Error Correction* (FEC) procedures. The basic blocks of channel coding for Forward Error Correction are shown in Figure 8.3.1. Energy dispersion randomizes the transmitted signal, so that low frequencies (DC term), which arise from long zero or one runs, are suppressed. At the receiver site, a reverse procedure is applied, using the same pseudo random number generator. *Reed-Solomon* (RS) and *Forney interleaving* aim to *burst error* correction, which may occur during transmission. They are applied independently on all packages, including the synchronization ones. *Convolutional coding* refers to the correction of other error types and is used only for satellite and terrestrial transmission.

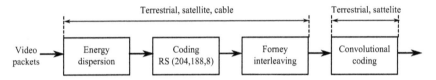

Figure 8.3.1: Channel coding in DVB.

## 8.4 Modulation

The modulation (or physical layer) exploits transmission channel and digital data stream information for the modulation of the transmitted DTV signal. The technical characteristics of transmission, as the signal to noise ratio and echo existence, depend on the nature of the transmission channel. Therefore, signal modulation techniques are different for each transmission type (terrestrial or satellite one), so that transmission performance is optimized for each channel type. Examples of modulation in terrestrial and satellite channels follow.

### 8.4.1 Modulation in terrestrial channels

Various difficulties exist in the terrestrial radio frequency reception, especially the mobile one using simple antennas, because of transmission echoes (due to multiple radio frequency signal paths, because of RF reflections) and possible signal interference. Channel bandwidth varies from 6 MHz (USA) to 7 or 8 MHz (Europe).

In the European terrestrial Digital Television Broadcasting (DVB-T) system, the modulation is based on the *Orthogonal Frequency Divided Multiplexing* (OFDM) having 2K or 8K carriers. Its principle is the high-bit rate stream distribution over a big number of orthogonal carriers (ranging from few hundreds to some thousands), each of them transmitting information at a low bit rate. Its main advantage is its excellent behavior in the case of multiple path reception. Carriers are modulated using *Quadrature Phase Shift Keying* (QPSK), or *Quadrature Amplitude Modulation* (16-QAM or 64-QAM). The transmitted data undergo a rather complicated interleaving procedure to increase system robustness to errors. *Fast Fourier Transform* (FFT) is used to move from the temporal domain to the frequency domain and vice-versa and to modulate the high number carriers. 8K modulation allows good reception, even in the presence of long duration echoes. This fact offers the possibility to create wide area networks, using everywhere the same channel. Such *Single Frequency Networks* (SFN) consist of transmitters, which can be tens of kilometers away from each other. 2K modulation offers simple demodulation, but cannot support SFNs. Furthermore, transmission robustness to impulsive noise is reduced. Such noise occurs, e.g., due to electric sparks produced by cars having gas engines or by some electrical household appliances.

### 8.4.2   Modulation in satellite transmission

At satellite reception, the *Carrier-to Noise Ratio* (CNR) can be very low (10 dB or lower). However, the signal is not affected at all by echoes. The channel bandwidth is generally between 27 and 36 MHz. In Europe, the satellite digital television specifications are in the DVB-S and DVB-S2 systems. The best spectral characteristics in satellite transmissions are provided by QPSK modulation (2 bits/symbol).

## 8.5   An overall system for digital television broadcasting

Figure 8.5.1 depicts all basic transmission and reception stages in digital television broadcasting. The sound and video signals of the TV programs to be broadcasted enter an MPEG-2 encoder, which delivers the packetized video and audio stream (PES) to source multiplexing (approximately four or eight TV programs for each channel frequency, depending on the chosen coding parameters). These PES are used by a source multiplexer to create packets of 188 bytes for scrambling and transmission. Channel coding raises the packet size to 204 bytes, by adding redundancy bits. In the case of satellite transmission, convolutional coding raises even further the transmission rate. Symbol mapping followed by signal filtering and D/A conversion to analog signal produces the analog signal to be broadcasted. The $I$ and $Q$ signals are modulated by QPSK (satellite) or COFDM (terrestrial) modulation to create an IF carrier of approximately 70 MHz. This IF carrier is up-converted to the appropriate radio frequency zone (depending on the transmission medium) for broadcasting to the end users. The final radiofrequency signal is amplified before transmission. In the case of satellite broadcasting, the frequency up-conversion will bring it to the uplink frequency of the satellite transmitter. At the satellite, the transmission frequency will be modified for end user reception in the KU zone (10.7-12.75 GHz).

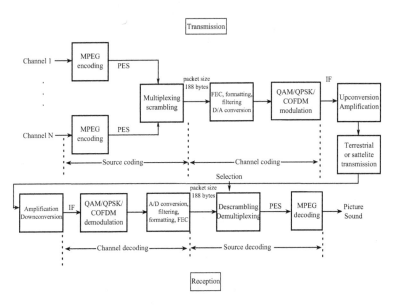

Figure 8.5.1: Transmission and reception in digital video broadcasting.

In the case of satellite transmission, the initial frequency down-conversion takes place after the antenna, at the *Low Noise Block Converter* (LNB or LNC), which down-converts the frequency in the range of 950-2150 MHz at the input of the set-top box (receiver-decoder). There, it is down-converted again to a frequency around 480 MHz. For terrestrial reception, there is only one frequency down-conversion from the VHF/UHF channel frequency range to an *Intermediate Frequency* (IF) carrier at 36.15 MHz (in Europe). The demodulation of this IF carrier produces an analog signal, which is A/D converted. Then, digital signal filtering and recovery of the $I$ and $Q$ signals takes place. Forward Error Correction retrieves the original 188 byte packets. Demultiplexing produces the PES, which corresponds to the user selected TV program. Descrambling may precede, when needed. MPEG-2 decoding reconstructs the synchronized video and audio streams of the desirable program to be viewed on the television screen.

# 8.6   Digital television broadcasting systems

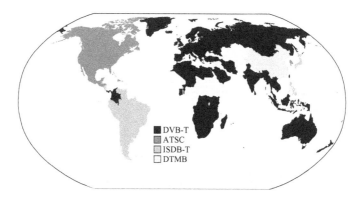

Figure 8.6.1: Geographical coverage of DTV systems.

The following digital TV broadcasting systems have been developed: *Digital Video Broadcasting* (DVB) format in Europe, *Advanced Television System Committee* (ATSC) format in USA, *Integrated Multimedia Broadcasting* (ISDB) system in Japan and *Digital Terrestial Multimedia Broadcast* (DTMB) in China. The current geographical coverage of these systems is shown in Figure 8.6.1. All these formats are based on the MPEG-2 standard. MPEG-4 is also supported in newer versions. ATSC uses the Dolby-Digital AC-3 audio codec and offers 5.1 sound format (five audio channels and one low frequency channel). ISDB HDTV broadcasts in Japan use the MPEG AAC audio format, which also supports 5.1 sound. The European DVB format allows both AC-3 and AAC audio codecs. DTMB supports Dolby AC-3 or MPEG-1 and MPEG-2 (Layer I and Layer II) audio. ATSC supports neither the hierarchical modulation nor SFNs. The ATSC signal is more sensitive to RF transmission changes. The main characteristics of ATSC, DVB, ISDB are shown in Table 8.6.1.

## 8.6.1   The DVB-T standard

The *Digital Video Broadcasting Terrestrial* (DVB-T) standard defines the specifications for digital terrestrial television broadcasting in Europe and other parts of the world. It was first published in 1997. This system transmits compressed digital audiovisual data based on the MPEG-2 or MPEG-4 standards, employing OFDM modulation having 2K or 8K carriers. The channel bandwidth varies from 7 to 8 MHz. FFT is used to move from the temporal domain to the frequency domain and vice-versa to perform modulation. 8K modulation allows good reception, even in the presence of long duration echoes. 2K modulation offers simple demodulation, but there is no possibility of creating SFNs.

## 8.6.2   The DVB-S standard

In Europe, the digital satellite television specifications are covered in the *Digital Video Broadcasting Satellite* (DVB-S) and *DVB-S2* systems. The best spectral characteristics in satellite transmission are provided by QPSK (92 bits/symbol), 16-QAM or 64-QAM modulation, because, at satellite reception, the carrier-to-noise ratio (CNR) can be very low (10 dB or lower) and the signal is not affected at all by echoes. The channel bandwidth is generally between 27 and 36 MHz.

In satellite broadcasting, the basic steps of transmission and reception are the same as in terrestrial broadcasting and they are illustrated in Figure 8.5.1. In satellite broadcasting, convolutional coding is employed after channel coding, as shown in Figure 8.3.1, which raises even further the transmission rate. The produced $I$ and $Q$ signals are modulated by QPSK modulation. The frequency up-conversion will bring the IF signal to the uplink frequency of the satellite transmitter. The frequency down-conversion takes place after the antenna, at the LNB (or LNC), which down-converts the frequency to the range of 950-2150 MHz, at the input of the receiver-decoder. There, it is down-converted again to a frequency around 480 MHz.

Table 8.6.1: Technical specifications of satellite TV.

| Digital TV systems | ATSC 8-VSB | DVB COFDM | ISDB BST-COFDM |
|---|---|---|---|
| Source coding | | | |
| Video | Main profile syntax of ISO/IEC 13818-2 (MPEG-2 video) | | |
| Audio | ATSC Standard A/52 (Dolby AC-3) | ISO/IEC 13818-2 (MPEG-2 layer II audio) and Dolby AC-3 | ISO/IEC 13818-7 (MPEG-2-AAC audio) |
| Transmission systems | | | |
| Channel coding | - | | |
| External coding | R-S (207, 188, t=10) | R-S (204, 188, t=8) | |
| External interleaver | 52 R-S block interleaver | 12 R-S block interleaver | |
| Internal coding | Rate 2/3 trellis code | Punctured convolution code: Rate 1/2, 2/3,3/4, 5/6, 7/8 Constraint length = 7, Polynomials (octal) = 171, 133 | |
| Internal interleaver | 12 to 1 trellis code interleaver | Bit-wise interleaving and frequency interleaving | Bit-wise interleaving, frequency interleaving and selectable time interleaving |
| Data randomization | 16-bit PRBS | | |
| Modulation | 8-VSB and 16-VSB | COFDM QPSK, 16QAM and 64QAM Hierarchical modulation: multi-resolution constellation (16QAM and 64 QAM) Guard interval: 1/32, 1/16, 1/8 & 1/4 of OFDM symbol 2 modes: 2k and 8k FFT | BST-COFDM with 13 frequency segments DQPSK, QPSK, 16QAM and 64QAM Hierarchical modulation: choice of three different modulations on each segment Guard interval: 1/32, 1/16, 1/8 & 1/4 of 3 modes: 2k, 4k and 8k FFT |

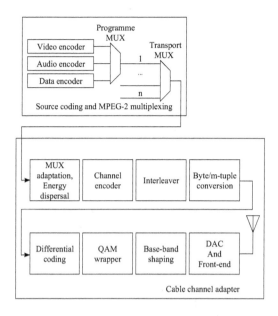

Figure 8.6.2: The DVB-C transmission system.

### 8.6.3 The DVB-C standard

*Digital Video Broadcasting - Cable* (DVB-C) is the European Standard for broadcasting digital TV over cable, first published in 1994 by ETSI. A block diagram of the DVB-C transmission system is shown in Figure 8.6.2. The audio-visual MPEG-2/MPEG-4 encoded streams are a multiplexed to produce PES. Several PES are joined together to form the Transport Stream (TS), which is then divided into packets of 188 bytes length. Energy dispersal follows, which decorrelates the sequence of bytes in the packets. Channel encoding (Forward Error Correction) is applied on the resulting packets, which consists of block coding and Reed-Solomon (204, 188) encoding. FEC achieves a maximum error correction rate of 8 wrong bytes per packet. Then, convolutional interleaving and byte/m-tuple conversion is applied to the stream. The two Most Significant Bits (MSBs) of each symbol enter a differential encoder, producing a rotation-invariant constellation. The resulting bit stream is modulated with one of the five available QAM modes: 16-QAM, 32-QAM, 64-QAM, 128-QAM, or 256-QAM. Then a raised-cosine shaped filter is applied, which eliminates any mutual signal interference at the receiver. Finally, the signal passes through a D/A converter and an RF front-end modulator.

In April 2010, a new standard for cable television broadcasting was published, called DVB-C2, which will gradually replace the current DVB-

Table 8.6.2: DVB-C and DVB-C2 specifications.

| | DVB-C | DVB-C2 |
|---|---|---|
| Input Interface | Single Transport Stream (TS) | Multiple Transport Stream and Generic Stream Encapsulation (GSE) |
| Modes | Constant Coding & Modulation | Variable Coding & Modulation and Adaptive Coding & Modulation |
| FEC | Read Solomon (RS) | LDPC+BCH |
| Interleaving | Bit-Interleaving | Bit-, Time- and Frequency-Interleaving |
| Modulation | Single Carrier QAM | COFDM |
| Pilots | Not Applicable | Scattered and Continual Pilots |
| Guard Interval | Not Applicable | 1/64 or 1/128 |
| Modulation Schemes | 16- to 256-QAM | 16- to 4096-QAM |

C specification. DVB-C2 employs improved modulation and coding techniques, which enhance the efficiency of the cable networks (increased capacity by at least 30%, multiple input protocol support, improved error performance). It finds applications in video-on-demand and HDTV broadcasting. A list of modes and features available in the two standards are shown in Table 8.6.2.

## 8.6.4 The ATSC-T standard

The American *Advanced Television Systems Committee* (ATSC) standard was developed in the early '90s by Grand Alliance. It is designed to transmit high quality video and audio over a single 6 MHz channel. For a terrestrial broadcasting channel, the achieved bit rate is 19 Mbps. It reaches 38 Mbps for a cable broadcasting channel. The transmission of a high quality video source, with resolution equal to five times that of a NTSC television channel, requires high video compression, which reduces the bit rate by a factor of 50. The ATSC system employs the MPEG-2 standard for data compression and multiplexing. Since 2008, ATSC also supports MPEG-4 Part 10 video compression.

ATSC offers two modulation methods: A terrestrial broadcast mode, the so-called *Vestigial SideBand* (VSB) modulation with 8 discrete amplitude levels (8-VSB) and a high data rate VSB method with 16 discrete amplitude levels (16-VSB). The 8-VSB modulation method consists of a required Main Service and combinations of additional options, called *Enhanced 8-VSB* (E8-VSB). It achieves higher immunity to channel impairments than the Main Service, at a lower bit rate transmission. The

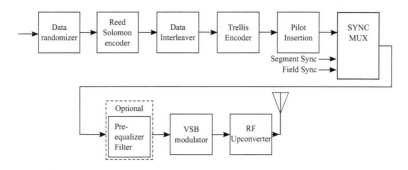

Figure 8.6.3: The block diagram of the ATSC-T Main Service.

16-VSB mode achieves high transmission robustness of 28.3 dB signal-to-noise threshold at a reduced data rate of 38.75 Mbps. The 16-VSB mode is very similar to the 8-VSB mode. The main difference between the two modes is the number of the discrete amplitude levels (16 instead of 8) and the use of the trellis encoder and NTSC interference rejection filters in the 8-VSB mode.

A block diagram of the Main Service is shown in Figure 8.6.3. First, the incoming data enter a randomizer and, then, FEC is performed, through the RS encoder, which adds 20 RS parity bytes to the TS packet. One-sixth data interleaving and two-thirds rate trellis encoding follow. The TS packet is then formatted into Data Frames and, finally, the Data Segment Sync and the Data Field Sync are multiplexed. Pilot insertion, VSB modulation and RF up-conversion follows.

## 8.6.5   The ATSC-C standard

The ATSC-C standard is designed to transmit digital video and audio using a 6 MHz cable channel. This system can be combined with data streams emanating from satellite channel distribution. The cable channel, including the optical fiber, is a linear channel of limited bandwidth, which suffers from white noise, interference and multi-path distortion. Therefore, Quadrature Amplitude Modulation (QAM), together with adaptive equalization and concatenated coding, is applied to the data stream. The data format input to the encoder and the modulator employs the MPEG transport framing, which consist of a continuous stream with 188 byte packets of fixed length. The first byte of each packet is a sync byte, having the hexadecimal value 47. This sync byte is used for packet delineation and error detection, independent of the FEC layer. The FEC system contains four layers: Reed-Solomon coding, interleaving, randomization and trellis coding. The FEC system achieves a low *Bit Error Rate* (BER) of one error event per 15 minutes. Finally, ATSC-C uses two modulation modes: QAM with 64 point signal constellation (64-QAM) and 256 signal constellation (256-QAM). These modes achieve symbol rates of 5.057 Mbps and one 5.361 Mbps, respectively.

### 8.6.6    The ISDB-T standard

The Japanese ISDB-T format employs the multiplexing system defined in MPEG-2, re-multiplexing several transport streams (TS) into a single TS. The resulting TS undergoes channel coding system and, finally, it is modulated using OFDM. Apart from fixed-reception service, ISDB-T also offers mobile reception service from the same television channel, through time interleaving. In ISDB-T, the signal is transmitted through hierarchical transmission, with a maximum of three layers. The bandwidth of a television broadcasting channel consists of 13 consecutive OFDM blocks, called OFDM segments. The bandwidth of each segment is equal to $\frac{1}{14}$ of the television broadcasting bandwidth. Each hierarchical layer contains one or more OFDM segments, a carrier modulation scheme, an inner-coder and a time interleaving scheme. ISDB-T offers three system modes, defined by three distinct spacings between the OFDM carrier frequencies. Mode 1 offers 4 kHz, mode 2 offers 2 kHz and mode 3 offers 1 kHz spacing. The three modes have different number of carriers, but the bit rate is common.

## 8.7    High definition digital television

### 8.7.1    Introduction

Digital TV broadcasting technology has already moved from *Standard Definition DTV* (SDTV) to *High Definition Television* (HDTV). The term *High Definition* (HD), which is used to describe the high-resolution television systems, is not new. It was used for the first time in Britain in 1936 and, later, in USA, USSR, Japan and Europe. In the past, some attempts were made to create analog HDTV (e.g., the HD-MAC system in Europe and the MUSE system in Japan). However, HDTV became available to consumers and profitable for TV content providers and television manufacturers only in early 2000, due to the transition from analog to digital television. Till now, HDTV provides the highest available digital television picture quality. It is a digital broadcasting system with much greater

Figure 8.7.1: Image quality comparison between standard resolution (left) and high resolution (right).

spatial resolution, compared to that of the traditional television systems, such as NTSC or PAL/SECAM or their digital equivalents (480i and 576i SDTV formats). HDTV images can have up to 5 times the information that a standard-definition image normally has. This quality improvement is especially noticeable, when the video is displayed on a 32 inch or larger screen.

HDTV is broadcasted digitally, because digital transmission requires a relatively small bandwidth, if proper video compression is used. It uses the same bandwidth as analog TV, with the exception that HDTV transfers about six times more information. HDTV color quality is far superior to that of a standard TV and its picture is much cleaner, as shown in Figure 8.7.1. HDTV sound follows the 5.1 audio format.

## 8.7.2 HDTV specifications

HDTV formats are extensions of the standard digital television ones, notably ATSC, DVB, ISDB and DTMB. In general, all HDTV standards have many technical similarities. They include coding and transmission of digital video and audio. The HDTV image specifications set the image resolution, scanning system, frame rate and aspect ratio, as shown in Table 8.7.1. Screen image resolution typically refers to the number of distinct pixels that can be displayed along each $x$, $y$ image dimension. When it comes to HDTV, however, only the number of pixels in a vertical line (vertical pixels) is enough for defining resolution (e.g., 1080p). The scanning system can be progressive or interlaced. The frame rate, also referred to as frame frequency, is expressed in frames per second (fps) or in Hertz (Hz), when it comes to screens. HDTV supports 16:9 aspect ratio, which provides better viewing experience than analog TV, which supports a 4:3 aspect ratio, as shown in Figure 8.7.2.

Table 8.7.1: Technical specifications for HDTV.

| Type | Horizontal pixels | Vertical pixels | Aspect ratio | Scanning System | Frame rate (Hz) |
|---|---|---|---|---|---|
| **ATSC** | | | | | |
| 1080 p | 1920 | 1080 | 16:9 | Progressive | 23.976, 24, 29.97, 30 |
| 1080 i | 1920 | 1080 | 16:9 | Interlaced | 29.97, 30 |
| 720 p | 1280 | 720 | 16:9 | Progressive | 23.976, 24, 29.97, 30, 59.94, 60 |
| **DVB, DIMB** | | | | | |
| 1152 i | 1440 | 1152 | 16:9 | Interlaced | 25 |
| 1080 p | 1920 | 1080 | 16:9 | Progressive | 23.976, 24, 29.97, 30 |
| 1080 i | 1920 | 1080 | 16:9 | Interlaced | 29.97, 30 |
| 1035 i | 1920 | 1035 | 16:9 | Interlaced | 25, 29.97, 30 |
| 720 p | 1280 | 720 | 16:9 | Progressive | 23.976, 24, 29.97, 30, 59.94, 60 |
| **ISDB** | | | | | |
| 1125 i | 1920 | 1080 | 16:9 | Interlaced | 29.97 |
| 1125 i | 1440 | 1080 | 16:9 | Interlaced | 29.97 |
| 750 p | 1280 | 720 | 16:9 | Progressive | 59.94 |

All HDTV standards use MPEG-2 for video compression. MPEG-2 is able to support much higher bit rate compared to MPEG-1. This rate is 12-20 Mbps for HDTV transmission. MPEG-4 Part 10 is also currently supported, e.g., in DVB-T2.

Recently, *Ultra High Definition TV* (UHDTV) formats have been standardized by ITU. 4K UHDTV supports 3840 × 2160 image resolution (2160p). 8K UHDTV offers 7680 × 4320 video (4320p). UHDTV offers

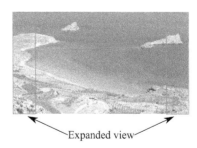

Expanded view

Figure 8.7.2: Comparison of image aspect ratios 4:3 and 16:9.

frame rates of 24, 25, 50, 60 and 120 fps, as well as top quality video and sound, rivaling the ones available by digital cinema and IMAX. Therefore, it attracted the attention of broadcasters, despite the difficulties in UHDTV video acquisition and compression (e.g., by the HEVC compression standard).

### 8.7.3 HDTV equipment

There are three ways to transmit HDTV signal: terrestrial, optical cable, or satellite transmission. A set-top box (tuner and decoder) with HDTV support is needed. In addition to that, a HDTV screen is required, having a minimum resolution of about 1080 vertical pixels (horizontal lines) with aspect ratio 16:9 that can display 1080p video. There are two general options for HDTV sets, as shown in Figure 8.7.3.

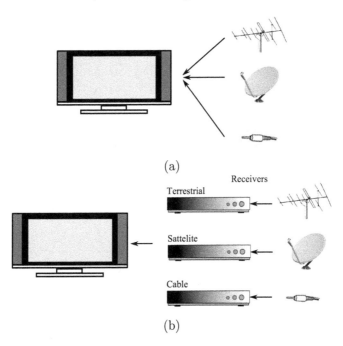

Figure 8.7.3: a) Integrated HDTV set, b) HDTV set using external receivers.

- *Integrated HDTV set.* This option is an "all in one" solution, which includes a HDTV screen and one or more tuners (terrestrial, satellite or cable).

- *Separate receivers.* This option offers the same picture quality as a built-in set, but requires external receivers, in order to receive and display terrestrial, cable or satellite HDTV programs. It is used when a high resolution and high quality monitor (e.g., a Plasma screen) does not have a decoder.

HDTV screens can have a Digital Visual Interface (DVI) video input, which provides a top quality, fully digital video connection and/or a High-Definition Multimedia Interface (HDMI) interface, which can handle both audio and video in one cable.

As far as the audio experience is concerned, a home theater system is required, in order to fully reap the benefits of multi-channel surround sound. Such a sound system has the following modules:

1) A digital audio connection (optical or coaxial), between the HDTV set or the HD set-top box and the audio system.

2) A digital audio processor that can handle Dolby AC-3 and / or other multichannel audio formats.

3) A multi-channel audio amplifier, which can amplify six or more audio channels (left, center, right, rear left, rear right channels and low-frequency channel).

4) Five or more full-range loudspeakers and a subwoofer to reproduce the six or more channels of the digital surround sound. They must be properly placed in the listening area, as shown in Figure 8.7.4.

Such a HDTV set can also be connected to other HD devices, such as Blu-ray DVD players, HD game consoles, or HD video cameras.

# 8.8   Mobile TV

Due to the unprecedented growth of mobile telephony, new technologies have been developed, giving viewers the opportunity to watch streaming media, e.g., digital TV on their mobile phone. The reception is no longer limited to a receiver at home or in a vehicle. This opens new horizons in TV program consumption at any place. The typical user environment for a handheld TV terminal is similar to that of the mobile radio. Multi-media mobile phones and PDAs can become handheld TV terminals. All these devices have a number of common characteristics: small size, light weight and limited battery power. These properties suggest some limitations in the transmission/reception system. Mobile devices usually have

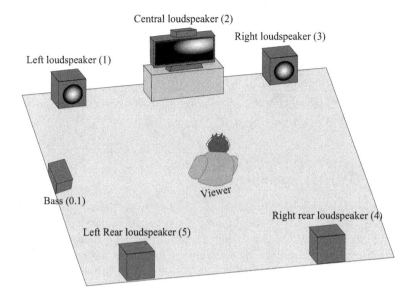

Figure 8.7.4: 6-channel 5.1 speaker system.

no external power supply and limited autonomy. Therefore, low power consumption is necessary. Portability is also a necessary characteristic, which means that service access should be available not only within or outside buildings, but also within fast moving vehicles. Mobile reception is hindered by the fact that the antennas of portable devices have small dimensions and can not focus on the transmitter, if the mobile terminal is moving. Furthermore, the transition from one transmission cell to another one should be seamless. Several mobile TV systems have been developed, notably as extensions to the DVB, DMB and ATSC standards to meet these specifications and provide wide geographical coverage.

## 8.8.1 Introduction to mobile TV format DVB-H

The development of *Digital Video Broadcasting to a Handheld* (DVB-H) format allows the reception of live television on a mobile device. DVB-H followed the extensive use of the DVB-T format, which is installed in millions of homes. Since DVB-H combines the functions of a mobile phone and television, it has encountered new deployment scenaria, e.g., TV content distribution using DVB-H by traditional TV broadcasters, mobile phone companies or a mixture of the two. In this spirit, new potential business models are examined that will allow collaboration between mobile telephony operators and television broadcasters to create new services. The

DVB-H format was formally adopted as ETSI EN 302 304 standard in 2004. In 2008, it was formally adopted by the European Union as the preferred technology for terrestrial mobile TV broadcasting. The main competitors of this technology are *Digital Multimedia Broadcasting* (DMB) and ATSC-M/H. DVB-SH (Satellite services to Handhelds) and DVB-H2 are possible developments of this technology, providing improved spectral efficiency and greater flexibility.

## 8.8.2   DVB-H specifications

The commercial specifications of DVB-H were defined in the DVB Project in 2002. DVB-H should provide video broadcasting services for portable and mobile use, including audio and video streaming at an acceptable quality. The data rate should be sufficient for mobile environments. DVB-H format specifies a data rate up to 10 Mbps for each video channel. The transmission channels will employ the UHF broadcast band. Alternatively, they can use the VHF III band. Other frequencies may be used as well, if they are available for transmission.

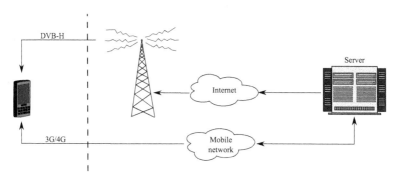

Figure 8.8.1: DVB-H mobile TV system.

A mobile TV system shown in Figure 8.8.1. DVB-H can offer a channel for downloading digital video at high data rates that can be used independently, or in combination with other mobile services, as shown in this Figure. Finally, the new system should be similar to the existing DVB-T system for digital terrestrial television. The structure of DVB-H and DVB-T networks should be compatible with one another, to allow reuse of the same broadcast equipment. DVB-H extends the DVB-T system, which was very successful for digital terrestrial television, with the necessary features, to cater to the requirements of portable, battery-powered devices. DVB-H can coexist with DVB-T in the same multiplexed stream. DVB-H

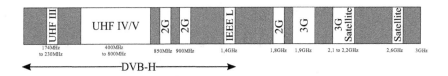

Figure 8.8.2: DVB-H and DVB-SH frequency spectra.

is designed to work in the following frequency bands, as shown in Figure 8.8.2:

- VHF-III (170-230 MHz). *Very High Frequencies* (VHF) is the frequency range from 30 MHz up to 300 MHz.

- UHF-IV/V (470-862 MHz). *Ultra High Frequencies* (UHF), cover the frequency range between 300 MHz to 3 GHz.

- IEEE L (1452-1492 MHz). *IEEE Band L* (20 cm radar long-band) is a part of the microwave band (ranging from 1 to 2 GHz). It is used by some communication satellites and in terrestrial digital audio broadcasting (DAB).

It is estimated that the DVB-SH and DVB-H2 will extend the supported bands beyond 2 GHz.

The *time slicing* technology, shown in Figure 8.8.3, is used to reduce power consumption for small handheld terminals. Data are transmitted as packets in small time slots. Each packet can include up to 2 Mbit of data (including parity bits). There are 64 parity bits for each 191 bits of data, protected by a Reed-Solomon code. The first part of the receiver turns on only during data transmission. In this short time slot, a high data volume is received and is stored in a buffer. This buffer can store parts of video streams to be reproduced later on screen. The achieved power savings depend on the ratio of on/off time durations. If there are ten or

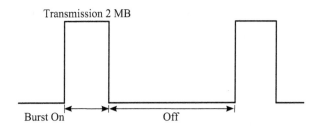

Figure 8.8.3: Time slicing.

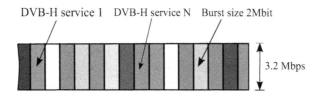

Figure 8.8.4: Time multiplexing in a DVB-H stream.

more channels in a DVB-H stream, the power savings in the first part of the receiver can be up to 90%.

DVB-H has the following advantages:

1) DVB-H allows the receiver to stop its operation during inactivity periods, resulting in power savings of up to 90%.

2) Time multiplexing of TV channels is allowed in a DVB-H stream, as shown in Figure 8.8.4.

3) DVB-H improves Forward Error Correction. The optional MPE-FEC multiplexer-level error correction technology renders DVB-H transmission more resilient to transmission errors.

4) DVB-H can coexist with DVB-T. For example, a provider may choose to send two DVB-T services alongside one DVB-H transmission to a multiplexed DVB-T stream. DVB-H can be used on channels of 6, 7 and 8 MHz. MPEG-2 video compression is used, as shown in Figure 8.8.5.

*Satellite DVB-H* (DVB-SH) is a media content and data transmission format to mobile terminals, such as mobile phones or computers, based on a hybrid satellite/terrestrial data downloading channel, supporting data transfer from satellite to terminal and, for example, a GPRS uploading

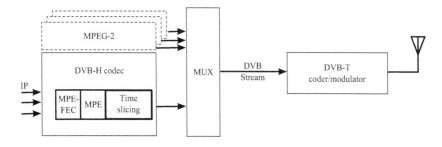

Figure 8.8.5: DVB-H encoder and transmitter.

channel transferring data from terminal to satellite. The DVB Project has adopted the DVB-SH format in 2007. The DVB-SH system was designed for frequencies up to 3 GHz, supporting UHF, L and S bands, as shown in Figure 8.8.2. It complements and enhances the DVB-H format. It provides better frequency use, measured in bits/Hz. It offers a combined satellite and terrestrial cover. DVB-SH has several improvements over the DVB-H:

- more frame rates are available,

- 64 QAM modulation is not supported,

- 1.7 MHz bandwidth and 1K FFT support,

- use of FEC Turbo coding,

- improved temporal interleaving,

- support of multiple antennas at terminals.

### 8.8.3 ATSC-mobile/handheld standard

The *ATSC Mobile/Handheld* (ATSC-M/H) service uses a portion of the 19.4 Mbps of the ATSC-TS Main Service RF channel. The M/H system performs stream delivery over IP transport. A graphical illustration of the ATSC-M/H broadcast system with TS Main and M/H services is depicted in Figure 8.8.6. The M/H system includes additions to the ATSC transmission physical layer, which can be decoded under high Doppler rate conditions. The enhanced stream reception is supported by additional FEC. The M/H system is compatible to the ATSC legacy receivers.

### 8.8.4 Technical specifications of ATSC-M/H

ATSC-M/H supports two types of files for transmission: content files, such as audio and video files, and parts of the Service Guide, which contains information for service protection, logos and SDP files.

M/H data are divided into *Ensembles*, each Ensemble containing one or more services. Ensembles utilize independent FEC structures called *Reed-Solomon Frames* (RS Frames), enabling them to be decoded in different error protection layers, according to the application. M/H data are forward error coded at packet and trellis level, inserting long training sequences and robust and reliable control data, which are handled by the M/H receivers. Furthermore, M/H receivers are energy saving, as they have the ability to cycle the power in the tuner and the demodulator, due to the increased transmission rate of the M/H data.

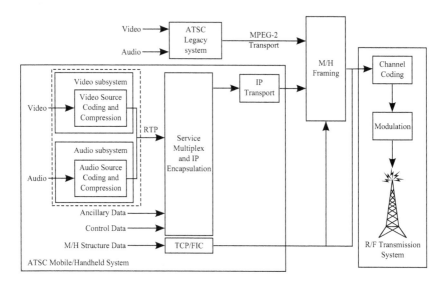

Figure 8.8.6: The overall ATSC broadcast system.

The M/H data share the same 8-VSB channel with the TS data on a time-slice basis. This enables increased reception rate of parts of the M/H data by the M/H receiver. The time interval of an M/H Frame is split into 5 sub-intervals of equal length, the so-called *M/H Subframes*. The M/H Subframes are divided into 4 *M/H Sub-divisions*, each one having length 48.4 ms. This is the required time for a VSB Frame transmission. Finally, the M/H Sub-divisions are divided into 4 *M/H Slots*, so that for each M/H Subframe there are 16 M/H Slots.

The transmitted M/H data are prior organized into M/H Ensembles, which are sets of consecutive RS Frames. The RS Frames are divided into *M/H Groups*, which, consequently, are grouped in multiples of 5, forming *M/H Parades*. M/H Parades consist of M/H Groups, either from a single RS Frame or from a primary and a secondary RS Frame. These M/H Groups go into M/H Slots, which are uniformly distributed among the M/H Subframes of the M/H Frame. RS Frames comprise the basic data delivery unit. The number and size of the RS Frames is determined by the M/H physical layer transmission mode. In the same M/H Parade, the primary RS Frames have a bigger size than the secondary RS Frames.

The M/H transport subsystem contains a *Fast Information Channel* (FIC), which is used for delivering essential information through the RS Frames, achieving rapid acquisition of the M/H Service. This information is related to binding the M/H Services with the corresponding M/H Ensembles, as well as to the M/H Service Signaling Channel.

*M/H Service* is a package of IP Streams which are transmitted through the M/H Multiplex. The M/H Service forms TV or audio programs which are controlled by the broadcaster. M/H Services are organized into M/H Ensembles.

## 8.8.5 Service issues in ATSC-M/H

The Announcement subsystem provides information about the services, which are available by the broadcaster, via a service guide. The service guide is an M/H Service, defined in the Service Signaling System. The M/H receiver accesses information about the available service Guides in the *Guide Access Table for M/H* (GAT-M/H). It contains information about the available service guides and their accessibility. The ATSC-M/H Service Guide is a constrained and extended version of an *Open Mobile Alliance Broadcast Services Enabler Suite* (OMA BCAST) Service Guide. It is delivered through a single or multiple IP streams. The *Announcement Channel* is transmitted through the Main Stream, along with zero or multiple streams containing the guide data. In the case of a single stream, the guide data are transmitted through the Announcement Channel Stream.

The M/H System targets the delivery of audio-visual services from a transmission site to portable or handheld devices. The broadcaster, except from the M/H audio-visual service, can also edit and send additional data concerning supplementary components, which can be utilized together with the service. This functionality is supported by the *Application Framework*. It enables the declaration of supplementary graphical components, the delivered service layout, the correspondence between the supplementary components and the service components. Furthermore, it gives to the broadcaster the ability to alter service presentation and to control its timeline. Moreover, the Application Framework supports various functionalities, like coherent rendering of the M/H service on different types of devices and user interaction with the delivered service, through action buttons and input fields.

*Service Protection* is a mechanism which controls the accessibility of a pay service and protects the content (i.e., files and streams) of the delivered service. The ATSC-M/H Service Protection System is based on the OMA BCAST DRM profile and contains key provisioning, Layer-1 registration, *Long-Term Key Message* (LTKM), *Short-Term Key Messages* (STKM) and traffic encryption. It is based on the *Advanced Encryption Standard* (AES), *Internet Protocol Security* (IPsec) and *Traffic Encryption Key* (TEK) encryption standards. The ATSC-M/H System supports an interactive mode and a broadcast-only mode for service protection. In the first mode, i.e., the interactive mode, the system contains an interaction channel, which enables the communication of the mobile receiver with the service provider for downloading service protection information. In the second mode, the interaction channel does not exist. In this case, service access is requested through other mechanisms, such as telephone calls or emails to the service provider.

# 8.9   Advantages and disadvantages of digital television

Digital television offers many benefits. It provides superior image quality (wide screen, with typical aspect ratio 16:9) and improved audio quality (Dolby 5.1 surround sound). It can support good reception on mobile devices, even for users on the more (e.g., in cars). It provides much better picture quality in remote areas that are not covered well by analog transmission, such as on islands. It displays beautiful vivid images, without shadows and interference artifacts. When a digital TV receiver receives two signals broadcasted from two transmitters, only one is eventually amplified and displayed, without interference from the other channel, as typically happens in analog television. Video and audio signal compression results in better exploitations of the transmission frequency, by requiring narrower bandwidth for each channel. Hence, a multitude of TV channels can be broadcasted at each transmission frequency. On the contrary, every VHF or UHF frequency supports only one analog television program. Thus, every television station can broadcast a bouquet of digital TV programs, rather than just one program. Digital television offers special functionalities, e.g., *Electronic Program Guides* (EPG), which are much better than the analog TV Teletext service and additional language support, by *dubbing* or *subtitling*. It can offer interactivity support that transforms a passive viewer to an active one. It offers services to people with special needs (improved subtitles, speech to text or text to speech support). For interactivity support, a return channel must feed action/reaction/comments/choices from the viewer. Such channels are typically Internet-based or mobile phone-based ones. Furthermore, the displayed commercials can be selected according to the viewer profile and interests. Pay-per-view or video-on-demand can be supported.

HDTV offers all the benefits of standard definition digital television and higher picture and sound quality. Pictures are comparable in quality to those of an analog movie film, with respect to resolution, contrast and special effects. HDTV also supports the 16:9 widescreen display, which, compared to the 4:3 aspect ratio of SDTV, offers an experience close to that of cinema. Finally, HDTV provides high sound quality, similar to that of a CD player and can support surround sound.

Mobile digital TV is another challenging technology that builds up on the success of both mobile telephony and digital TV. It can provide seamless TV broadcasting to commuters and people on the move, as well as wide geographical coverage. Several TV stations already provide mobile TV worldwide. However, its massive adoption is yet to be seen.

There are virtually no technical disadvantages in digital television, but only commercial ones, which depend on the business model used by the broadcaster or content provider, i.e., whether the content is encrypted or whether the user pays a subscription fee. Because of the superfluous offer of digital television channels, the viewer can easily be overwhelmed by the huge amount of offered information. User acceptance of interactive television is still unknown, since traditional users tend to associate TV with passive viewing. Since digital content can be easily copied, digital television confronts digital content piracy. Many significant research efforts have been made for copyrights protection, e.g., by employing encryption or watermarking of the audiovisual content. However, this problem is far from being solved.

# 9

# MEDIA STREAMING

## 9.1 Introduction to media streaming

Media (e.g., music or video) streaming is defined as the continuous transmission of media files over a local or wide area network. Instead of waiting to transfer an entire file, in order to start audio or video playback, streaming allows media reproduction during file transfer. Media data are transferred via the network (e.g., Internet), played back and then deleted. Furthermore, media streaming can provide user control over media file playback.

As in TV broadcasting, digital media streaming allows real-time or on-demand access to audio, video or other multimedia content of choice, while simultaneously offering certain copyright protection of the digital content. Furthermore, media streaming can allow user interaction. Unlike analog TV broadcasting, the digital nature of media streaming facilitates user-content interaction, by providing tools, such as chapterization, clickable hotspots on a video frame, choice of different URLs that automatically lead to certain WWW sites at specific times during media playback and smart indexing of multimedia content using keywords.

According to digital media market research, seven out of ten U.S. Internet users claim that WWW sites would be more pleasant, if they included audio and video content. The vast majority of Internet users have already heard audio or watched video on-line by streaming. Businesses also reap streaming benefits. Numerous Microsoft studies on websites show that many companies already earn remarkable profits by using media streaming technology. A typical case is Google's YouTube. Common professional uses of streaming are social media, corporate communications, sales, marketing and e-learning.

Media streaming attracts affluent consumers. Its power is evident in the development of electronic commerce. According to a study conducted in the U.S., Internet users exploiting streaming are more experienced and spend 50% more time on-line, than an average user. Furthermore, a new research in the U.S. indicates that the majority of young people from 18 to 35 years old watch television or video on-line at least once a week. People who watch TV or video on-line spend much more time on the web than other users of the same age and are twice as likely to see web advertisements and shop on-line.

Media streaming technology allows real-time or on-demand access of audio, video and multimedia content over the Internet. It enables almost real-time web transmission of events recorded on video and/or sound. This transmission form is called *webcasting*. Streaming technology also allows on-demand distribution of media content that has been pre-recorded and/or pre-processed. Streaming media are transmitted by means of a *media server* and are received, processed and played back by a client application, known as *media player*. The player can begin to playback streaming media directly after receiving sufficient data, without having to wait for the arrival of the entire file. As data are transferred to the client, they are stored in a buffer, until enough data have been accumulated for proper playback. Pseudostreaming techniques, such as *progressive downloading*, allow media playback, before the file transfer is completed. Therefore, the ability to start playback, before completing file transfer, is a characteristic of media streaming, but does not necessarily discriminate it from other technologies. Streaming media are received and played back, without retaining any content backup file on the receiving device. Hence, an important advantage of media streaming (unlike either traditional or progressive transfer) is that it provides certain copyright protection.

## 9.2 Streaming technology

### 9.2.1 File transfer/progressive download

Traditional media transfer keeps users on hold, since they must wait, until the entire file is transferred to the client end, before it can be played back. File transfer technology is preferable, if the end users would like to retain the digital content and play it back, whenever they want. If an artist or a publisher does not allow end users to store content, then this technology is problematic, since copyright can easily be infringed, through illegal distribution.

Unlike traditional file transfer types, progressive downloading, also known as *pseudostreaming* (in QuickTime terminology), or as *fast-start media streaming*, permits audio or video playback, before the media file is fully transferred. Unlike media streaming, progressive downloading saves a replica of the media file on the receiver hard disk. Despite the disadvantages of progressive downloading, it can be a good alternative, if media streaming is unavailable. Progressive downloading can be easier and less costly to implement than media streaming.

*Web server streaming*, also known as *HTTP streaming*, is a variant of the progressive transfer. It creates a locally-cached copy of the media file. Therefore, there is no way to prevent end users from copying it. However, an interesting HTTP stream advantage is its ability to transfer media stream files through firewalls, which often do not allow media streaming files to go through.

### 9.2.2 Media streaming technology

Media streaming is performed in real time and, thus, can support live radio or television broadcasting. This feature can not be supported by a media file transfer. Media Streaming servers offer stream control and interaction options to media users. The user can control audio or video playback in a conventional way, which is impossible, when transferring a file, until, of course, the entire file is transferred. Streaming allows the user to navigate through the content and move forward/backwards, in contrast to progressive transfer, which requires serial playback from start to end. Streaming also supports either content-on-demand or live webcasting in real time.

Streaming requires a specialized media server. Media files, which have been encoded in a streaming media format, can be distributed by a network server. Transferred media files, including those prepared for a progressive transfer, are usually served by a standard network server, which has no ability to regulate transfer in an uncontrolled environment having strong bit rate variations that are inherent on the Internet. Streaming technology exploits Internet transport protocols (e.g., TCP or UDP), as well as client-server technologies, to facilitate the continuous playback of synchronized audio and video in real time. Streaming media files are usually encoded in different versions, each optimized for different transmission rates. A streaming media server delivers the appropriate media version, either selected by the user, or suggested by the default browser settings. In some cases, the server can automatically select the best version, based on available information regarding the network platform and connection speed. Depending on the media server and the built-in intelligence in the media player, media streaming can be dynamically adapted to variations in the available bandwidth. The use of a specialized media stream server allows more efficient exploitation of the available network bandwidth, better audio and video quality to clients, support of a large number of concurrent users and adequate content copyright protection.

Since audio and video are time-dependent media, their information packets must arrive on time and in good condition at the media player end, so that they are seamlessly played back. However, Internet inherently provides asynchronous communication and offers no guarantee on the order of the received packets. The TCP protocol typically ensures that the transferred files are assembled back in the proper sequence and requires replacement for any packet lost or damaged during transfer. This process, known as *error correction* is a luxury, often sacrificed in streaming technology. When, during media streaming, the data are lost or destroyed, they are considered lost forever. This fact results in incomplete and, sometimes, even unintelligible, audio or video playback. Fortunately, human visual and auditory perception easily forgives a certain level of playback errors, since we can grossly perceive content, even when some video frame blocks or audio packets are lost. Thus, streaming technology is viable, even when lossless transmission is not feasible.

Streaming technology depends on the available bandwidth, because a steady data stream must be delivered on time to the media player, in order to achieve smooth media playback. That said, streaming requires low bit rate data transfer, so that it can be handled over a slow link. Typically, in Internet environments, such a data rate is much lower than the one used in digital TV broadcasting and clearly much lower than one provided by a DVD player. There are several ways to reduce the required bit rate:

- video frame spatial resolution (total count of frame pixels) can be reduced,

- video frame rate (number of frames per second) can be lowered, and

- video frame redundancy can be eliminated through video compression.

When one or more of these strategies are adopted, video playback quality is reduced. A user enjoying a high speed connection can play any media stream file, which is encoded for transmission at a lower connection speed, but probably poor video quality playback will result. A user with a slow connection, will face the problem of disrupted media reproduction or, at least, reproduction delays. The best solution offered by streaming media is to publish media content at multiple media streams, each encoded at different bit rates, so that their transmission adapts to a wide variety of end-user needs and connections. This approach is called *Multiple Bit Rate* (MBR) encoding.

### 9.2.3  Streaming categories

**Streaming on demand.** Once the files are encoded in a format suitable for streaming and are placed on a media server, they can be played back at any time by anyone on request. Users can choose to move backwards/forwards and either stop or resume playback of streaming media files. A major benefit of streaming on demand is that, since the files can be used at any time (and not at a given moment only), the provider is not required to posses excessive bandwidth to sustain a large number of connections. A prime application of streaming on demand could be distance learning.

**Live broadcasting.** Live Internet broadcasting (webcasting) involves real-time event encoding and uploading onto the media sever. Then, the server transmits the media stream straight to the intended audience. Live broadcasting requires much more bandwidth than that required by on-demand streaming, because all users are simultaneously connected to the server. Apart from the large bandwidth, live broadcasting also requires multiple media stream servers, for transmission load distribution. By distributing the load across multiple computers, the probability of a server shut-down is reduced. Thus, system fault tolerance increases and the probability of an unexpected transmission delay decreases.

### 9.2.4  Encoders, servers and media players

Encoders, servers and media player applications are the three basic building blocks of a media streaming system, as shown in Figure 9.2.1. Media (audio and video) files must be encoded by a *media encoder*, before being transmitted by streaming. After such files have been encoded, they should be uploaded on a media server. Servers respond to media playback requests coming from various clients and maintain a full-duplex link with the media player at user site during transmission. This bidirectional link is required, because the user can choose to stop playback or browse the content forwards/backwards. Such commands are then communicated by the media player to the media server for execution. Media players can offer, besides video playback, other functionalities, like full multimedia presentation with slides, music and narration. The most common media stream players are RealPlayer (produced by RealNetworks), Windows Media Player (Microsoft), QuickTime (Apple) and FlashPlayer (Adobe).

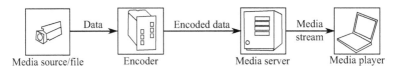

Figure 9.2.1: Structure of a media streaming system.

## 9.2.5    Protocols, file formats and codecs

The media streaming system components communicate with each other at various levels. Protocols, file formats and codecs provide the framework for this interaction. *Protocols* set the principles of information exchange between the system components. *File formats* describe how the data are stored to form a streaming file. *Codecs* encode and decode information contained in media files. Below, we explain these entities in detail.

At the lowest level, the *Hypertext Transfer Protocol* (HTTP) can be used for streaming media files across the Internet and for media player interaction with an HTTP server. This protocol is typically used to deliver web pages and is not particularly well suited for media streaming, for various reasons. Other protocols are also available, but there are no unified standards to this end. The interoperability and compatibility between the protocols used by the three above-mentioned main media streaming platforms is rather low. Apple and RealNetworks use the *Real Time Transport* (RTP) and *Real Time Streaming* (RTSP) protocols, while Adobe uses the *Real Time Messaging Protocol* (RTMP), Microsoft uses RTSP and a proprietary protocol, called *Microsoft Media Server* (MMS). However, MMS support diminishes.

Media streaming data must conform to a specific set of rules (file format), so that they are intelligible by both a media player and a media server. Unfortunately, each industrial media streaming platform uses primarily its own file format. MP3 audio format is widely used in streaming.

YouTube videos are encoded in a Flash Video format.

Once streaming media data are collected at the receiver, a media player decodes and prepares them for playback. This is performed using a video and/or audio decoder, e.g., the H.264 codec.

## 9.3   Media streaming process

The entire media streaming process is divided into four main stages:

1) *Media creation* refers to audiovisual content production for streaming.

2) *Media encoding* is the process of converting the audiovisual content in a format that can be streamed. This can be done in various ways, such as using special block-wise media encoding, or by running encoding scripts.

3) *Media authoring/publishing* is the media layout design and demonstration. The simplest way to demonstrate streaming media is to place them on-line as a hypertext link in a web page.

4) *Media hosting/delivery*, so that the users can access the streaming media. This stage includes hosting/delivery design, implementation, maintenance and analysis. These tasks interact with each other in a rather circular way.

Media encoding is the most complex stage in the media streaming process.

### 9.3.1   Streaming media encoding

Video codecs must adopt a bit rate distribution strategy over the various video frames, in order to improve transmission. Key frames have to be encoded first, followed by difference (P- or B-) frames. Consequently, video codecs generate a bit budget to be followed, when encoding individual video frames. The larger the video frame resolution is, the more bits are required for proper frame coding.

The strategy followed by video encoders for bit allocation to frames also considers the number of frames per second to be encoded. This number may change dynamically, depending on the video content. As encoding progresses over time, less frames can be encoded in low activity shots, so that more bits are allocated for high-activity shots. The choice of frame rate can be affected by the user, if he sets a maximum or minimum frame rate.

If a streaming media manager wants to address people having different connection bit rates, while providing the highest possible quality for everyone, he should encode different streaming media versions for each possible bit rate. This way, each file can be optimized for a specific connection speed, by determining the appropriate video frame size and frame rate, thus creating multiple streams. This process may produce additional files, depending on the platform used. QuickTime does not support multiple streams within a single file, while RealPlayer and Windows Media Player have the ability to integrate multiple streams at different transmission rates in a single file. These streams are automatically created during the encoding phase and offer important media delivery options.

Various streaming media encoding methods have been proposed that take into consideration all these factors and are suitable for different streaming media environments.

**Constant Bit Rate (CBR) encoding.** Usually, when we transmit video by streaming technology using hardware encoding, it is desirable to have a constant bandwidth codec. The encoder has a built-in data rate control unit, using a buffer to smooth out the peaks and valleys of the stream bit-load, in order to produce a constant data rate. The encoder controls the available buffer size and dynamically alters the compression rate to ensure that it achieves the target data rate. This method is referred as *Constant Bit Rate encoding* (CBR). The buffer size, which is used to create a constant transmission rate is determined by the encoder. Since a player can not begin playback before its buffer is full, video playback start is delayed. This is called *memory delay*. It usually causes a corresponding playback delay. It is easy to conclude that a large memory buffer ensures an encoded video of better quality because, in fast video shots, cache will be able to absorb the higher transmission rate peaks. Therefore, higher compression levels, which reduce compressed video quality, will be avoided.

The main tool for optimizing content quality in CBR encoding, is the use of a delay memory buffer, as mentioned previously. Increasing the buffer size, which is set by default to accommodate 5 sec of video, leads to a significant increase in quality. However, higher buffer size leads to bigger memory delays. An example, where memory increase is useful, is in movie encoding. It probably makes sense to have a greater start delay, e.g., 30 seconds, since it will not seem too long, in comparison to the duration of the movie. When the data rate is too low for a given (complex) scene, the video codec may miss frames to maintain the maximal data rate variations within the constraints imposed by the available CBR memory. When compromising memory delay and video quality, we must remember that a longer memory delay can bring higher video quality. We may want to choose first the buffer size and then the allowed video quality.

Another aspect that deserves attention is the distance of key frames (measured in terms of frame numbers). A greater distance usually leads to better video quality, because the codec smooths the transmission rate peaks caused by the key frame encoding. However, the key frames are synchronization references for the video stream, which are very important, if the player temporarily loses connection or receives damaged stream packets, because the media player seeks only key frames within a media stream. For this reason we should not allow a long distance between key frames.

**Two-pass CBR encoding.** In CBR video encoding, it would be very useful to know, in advance, what content will occur in future video frames. In this way, the encoder can make an optimal choice, as to how many bits should be allocated for each frame. For example, consider a newscast, containing an anchorperson (talking head) shot that changes to an advertisement scene. A talking head shot is easily coded, due to lack of a strong motion field. On the contrary, advertisements tend to have a high number of shot cuts to attract viewer attention. Thus, they require a higher bit rate for their encoding. If the encoder does not know that an advertisement will follow the newscast, it may allocate too many bits to the newscast shot, in an effort to improve its quality. Thus, few bits may be available for the advertisement, possibly leading to visible distortions.

*Two-pass CBR encoding* solves the problem of bit allocation, by scanning an entire video segment, before starting its encoding. During this first pass, an analysis is performed about the required theoretical bit rate for encoding the different frames of the video segment. This information is then used in the second pass, in order to determine how many bits should be allocated to each video frame. Since the encoder has complete knowledge of future coding needs, it can better accommodate sudden shot changes. This means that the overall video quality will vary much less, than in one-pass CBR coding. The main disadvantage of two pass encoding is that we need access to future information, which is not always available, e.g., in the case of live broadcasting. Another drawback is that the two-pass approach almost doubles encoding time.

**Variable Bit Rate encoding.** There are video streaming cases, where video content complexity varies: some video parts can be encoded with few bits, while other ones need many more bits. For such cases, *Variable Bit Rate encoding* (VBR) allows output data rate variations, according to the source content needs. Therefore, video quality can be better controlled, because there are no memory buffer restrictions. It should be noted that VBR pays more, when coding a combination of easy and difficult scenes. VBR encoding allocates less bits to easy scenes, thus leaving enough bits to produce good video quality in difficult scenes. VBR encoding offers best performance on long videos, e.g., movies. This is reasonable, because, in such films, there are many variations in scene complexity. In the past, VBR encoding was not supported well by hardware codecs. This is not the case any more, since many hardware codecs support VBR encoding, e.g., for audio streaming.

**Quality-based VBR encoding.** If our goal is to achieve a certain video quality and both our network and hardware can handle the data rate peaks generated by the encoder, *Quality-based VBR encoding* is the method of choice. In this case, the encoder uses a media quality scale, ranging from 1 (lowest quality) to 100 (best quality). When the encoder is requested to employ any of these quality levels, it attempts to reach the same quality level throughout the media file, so that there are few distortions, e.g., in fast scenes. Quality-based VBR encoding is rated using a combination of objective and subjective tests, so that it reaches approximately the required level of quality. Thus, when the encoder uses quality level 50, the achieved quality should be close to half the quality level 100. Of course, such a quality accuracy can never be achieved, because the objective quality measurements performed by the encoder do not necessarily agree with the viewers' subjective quality evaluation.

**Average bit rate (ABR) encoding.** This method allows us to maintain an average data rate, rather than a video quality level. It employs a two-pass procedure. In the first pass, the encoder analyzes the video frames, using a similar process to a two-pass CBR encoding. In the second pass, the encoder automatically determines the quality level that will allow achieving the average bit rate of choice. The main reason to use ABR coding is to reach the desired media file size, because fixed quality VBR encoding can lead to unpredictable file size, which highly depends on video content. We must be careful, since ABR encoding has the same restrictions, as fixed quality VBR encoding. Therefore, it is not particularly well-suited to streaming over unreliable communication channels having a fluctuating bandwidth. Furthermore, its advantages become evident, when used on media having significant duration and content variety.

It should already be clear that choosing the correct encoding method is crucial to obtain the best possible encoding quality. In many cases, the consequences of a wrong choice cannot be moderated by subsequent optimization. Decision-making should start by considering VBR first. Then, two-pass CBR and one-pass CBR encoding are examined. VBR encoding, when used on appropriate content, will produce much better video quality, compared to a same size video file that is CBR encoded. The difference in compression ratio may be approximately 2:1, meaning that we can get a VBR file that has the same quality, but half the size of the corresponding CBR one. Moreover, if the media source is a file rather than a live one, it is highly recommended to use two-pass CBR encoding. We get better quality than the one-pass CBR, without losing the advantages of CBR encoding.

Finally, in many cases of live broadcast stream encoding, one-pass CBR is the only available option.

## 9.3.2 Publishing and hosting streaming media

Publishing is the process of making streaming media files available to the public. In order to understand this process, we present some basic principles on how web browsers and network servers operate. When a user/client requests a page from a website, the following events take place:

- A web browser requests the website home page.

- The web server returns HTML code, which can contain references to images, text and other items that may come from different servers.

- The browser parses the received data and issues requests for files that are referred within the HTML code.

- Web servers receive these requests and send the appropriate files, together with the appropriate *Multipurpose Internet Mail Extensions* (MIME) files. HTTP/TCP/IP protocols are used for such communications, as shown in Figure 9.3.1.

- By using the MIME type information, the browser displays the received files or requests file visualization by other applications, resulting in the overall web page display.

The following different scenarios can be used for video file streaming:

- A streaming media file is transmitted via the HTTP protocol. The browser has built-in software, or a link to software, for stream decoding and playback.

- A media file is transmitted via the HTTP protocol and the browser leads the file to a separate media player.

- The file is transmitted via a different protocol and the browser leads the file to a separate media stream player.

- The file is transmitted via a different protocol and played by the browser, through a link to an appropriate software.

The original request must be communicated by means of the HTTP protocol, because this protocol is used by the web browsers and web servers alike, in order to transfer data. If the media file is then transmitted by streaming or via progressive transfer through HTTP, the web browser can

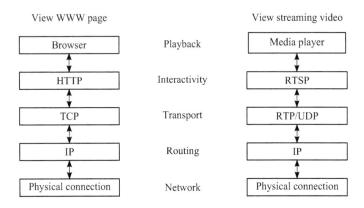

Figure 9.3.1: Browsing a web site and streaming media file playback.

reproduce it using a link to a media player or can send it to a separate media player for playback. To this end, control transfer control from the browser to the streaming media player is needed. This is done using *metafiles*. When the media player takes control, it may use a different protocol to receive the media file, as shown in Figure 9.3.2.

Metafiles are small files facilitating media play-back on streaming media players that use MIME types. These files are referred to as metafiles (RealSystem), Windows Media Files (Microsoft Media Player), or metadata (QuickTime). Metafiles contain the address of the true streaming media file and other information, such as a playlist or choices in the playback order.

When the web browser receives metafiles, it sends them to the appropriate streaming media player, according to the MIME file type. Streaming media player opens the metafile, finds the address of the media stream file and starts a separate communication with a streaming server on another port, using a different protocol. This control shift from the browser to the streaming media player, in conjunction with different port numbers and protocols used, explains the fact that we can listen to media stream radio stations and continue our normal Internet navigation.

Metafiles are a smart solution, but they can also cause problems. If someone has a few media stream files, the existence of the corresponding metafiles, one for each streaming file, is not a problem. However, for a big content provider that has thousands or even millions of streaming media files, the additional responsibility of managing an equal number of metafiles creates further problems. Metafiles can be easily copied or sent via email, because they are small in principle. Transmitted metafiles are beyond control and can create unforeseen multimedia content management problems.

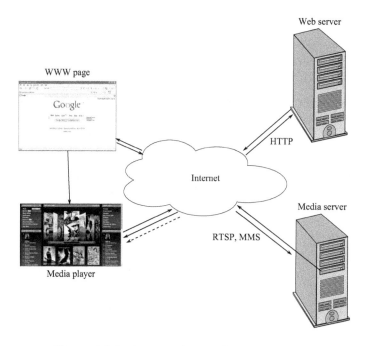

Figure 9.3.2: A streaming media environment.

### 9.3.3 Communication issues in media streaming

The bandwidth is a key issue in media streaming for two reasons. The most obvious reason is that digital audio and video files are much larger than that of most computer file types and their delivery requires high bandwidth. The second reason is sustaining consistent streaming media quality, which depends on the bandwidth available in every part of the network path used in a stream transmission. The network path can be divided into three parts:

- user-Internet connection,

- media server-Internet connection,

- internal Internet connections.

Unfortunately, no one can control user connectivity to Internet, which means that, if the user has bad connection, media server connectivity does not matter. We can simply limit this problem, by providing streams at different data rates to cater the widest possible audience needs.

Streaming media can be delivered to a user in three ways:

1) *Unicast.* A media server delivers a separate stream copy to each individual user, as shown in Figure 9.3.3. Multiple links denote multiple streams. On-demand media delivery always uses Unicast.

2) *Broadcast.* A single media stream is simultaneously delivered to multiple users. Each user has his own connection to the media server. Most live broadcasts use this model.

3) *MulticastMulticast.* A single media stream is transmitted over a network, using a special IP address. The streaming media packets are replicated in the network nodes to reach multiple viewers. When a viewer enters a multi-cast service, the media player is instructed to grab packet copies from a particular location in the network.

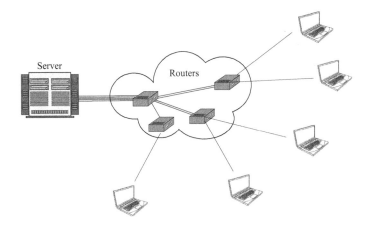

Figure 9.3.3: Unicasting.

Multi-cast protocols were developed to reduce data replication, when many recipients receive the same content. These protocols send a single stream from a media server to a target group, as shown in Figure 9.3.4. Depending on the network hardware infrastructure, the multi-cast transmission may or may not be possible. One disadvantage of multicasting is the loss of video control by the user. Radio or television content streaming usually hinders users' ability to control media playback. However, this problem can be mitigated by using media players with buffering. Multi-cast transmission is very important to *Local Area Networks* (LANs), where there is a single network router control. In such a setting, multiple media stream copies can be distributed on a LAN, with minimal impact on traffic congestion. However, multicasting across Internet, is still impractical. Combinations of multicasting and unicasting can be used to minimize bandwidth and maximize audience coverage.

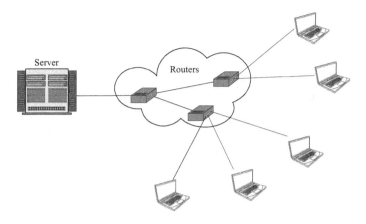

Figure 9.3.4: Multicasting.

## 9.4 Streaming audio and video file formats

*Waveform Audio File format* (WAV) is a container file format, developed by Microsoft to store uncompressed (usually) or compressed audio. Such audio content can be played, e.g., by the Windows Media Player, if the appropriate codecs are installed on the computer. The most common codecs used in WAV files are the uncompressed *Pulse Code Modulation* (PCM) and *Microsoft Adaptive Differential Pulse Code Modulation* (MS ADPCM). One minute of PCM audio can range from 644 KB up to 27 MB. The file size depends on the sampling frequency, the sound type (mono or stereo) and the bit number per audio sample.

*MPEG-1 Audio Layer 3*, known as *MP3*, is an audio compression format used in MPEG-1. MP3 was jointly designed by teams of engineers of Fraunhofer Institute (Germany), AT&T-Bell Labs (USA) and CCETT (France). It became an ISO format in 1991. It is a commonly used audio format for consumer audio storage and for music transfer and playback on media players. MP3 employs lossy audio compression. The compression method used is *perceptual coding*. It uses psychoacoustic models to suppress less perceived audio information, while compressing the rest of the audio information in an efficient manner. Thus, while it drastically reduces the audio file size, it provides almost comparable sound quality to that of the original uncompressed audio. An MP3 file can be created using low, medium or high bit rate. This results in low, medium or high audio quality, respectively.

*Audio Video Interleave* (AVI) format is a special case of the *Resource Interchange File Format* (RIFF). AVI is the most commonly used format for audiovisual content storage on computers. It is a container file format, used for storing compressed audio or video content that can be reproduced by media players, if the appropriate codecs are already available on the computer. The most common video codecs used in AVI files are:

1) *DivX* codec (brand name of DivX Inc.). It is used to heavily compress large video files, while retaining a relatively good visual quality. DivX codec employs MPEG-4 Part 2 compression.

2) *CinePak* codec. It was developed by SuperMatch and is designed to code video of resolution 320 × 240 pixels at a transfer rate of 150 KBps.

3) *MJPEG* codec. It compresses each video frame independently as a JPEG image.

The most commonly used audio codecs in AVI files are MP3 (for compressed audio) and PCM (for uncompressed audio).

## 9.5   Real Player

*RealPlayer* is a media player developed by Real Networks that allows users to listen to audio and watch video content. It allows RealAudio and RealVideo file playback, originating from the Internet or a local network in real time, without having to download and store the corresponding media files on PC hard disk. When selecting a RealAudio or RealVideo source, the application is linked to the web page and then automatically opens and plays the selected files. There are several functions that help in this direction: RealPlayer Control for ActiveX on Internet Explorer, RealAudio Xtra for Macromedia Shockwave Movie and RealPlayer Plug-In for the Netscape Browser.

The first RealPlayer version, called RealPlayer 4.0, appeared in 1995 as RealAudio Player and was one of the first streaming media players. Since then, RealNetworks offers a series of charge-free 'basic' versions as well as 'Plus' versions with additional features. RealPlayer version 11 was released in 2007. RealPlayer versions are available for MAC OS, UNIX, LINUX, Windows Mobile, PALM OS and SYMBIAN OS.

RealPlayer 11, supports new features, including Flash Video support and DVD/SVCD/VCD video recording capabilities. In addition, RealPlayer 11 Plus transfers easily online video to iPod and supports on-line radio for thousands of radio stations worldwide. It offers Digital Rights Management (DRM) support, so that publishers can restrict the use of digital content only to their clients. At this point, we shall analyze some of the additional functionalities provided by RealPlayer, apart from its main use as an audio and video player.

**Application profile.** RealPlayer supports the creation of playlists by providing drag and drop functionalities. It can also create a random playlist. It allows graphical displays, from light shows to graphics animations. This enhances user experience. RealPlayer supports sequential and random music playback, full screen video playback, equalizers and tools to improve audio and video quality and control.

**Media library and media browser.** This library allows content organization by track editing and titling. A media browser lets the user navigate in web pages, while playing digital media files.

**Audio recording and disc creation.** RealPlayer can create CD discs. The free version can create data and audio discs, the premium edition can also create MP3 CDs. Furthermore, RealPlayer Plus is able to record directly from a computer microphone.

**Format conversion.** The RealPlayer can convert files to supported formats, such as AAC (.M4A), RealAudio 10 (.RA), MP3, WAV and some WMA file types. RealPlayer cannot convert protected file formats, such as files downloaded using subscription services, for example protected WMA files, or RAX files.

**Additional functionalities.** RealPlayer music store offers song-on-demand. In addition, RealPlayer SuperPass allows users to have access to selected recording and live video broadcasts. Finally, RealPlayer 11 for Windows allows users to download videos from sites, like YouTube, and store them in MPEG-2 or MP4 format. Here we should mention that YouTube videos are encoded in a Flash format (SWF).

**File formats.** RealPlayer supports several digital media formats, such as MP3, MPEG-4, QuickTime, Windows Media files (AVI, WMA, WMV), RealAudio and RealVideo formats (RA, RV, RM) and Adobe Flash files (SWF). *RealAudio format* (RA, RAM) was developed by RealNetworks. Its first version was released in 1995. RealAudio 10 was released in 2006. It employs a wide range of codecs, offering low-rate to high-fidelity audio encoding. Low rate forms are used primarily on slow dial-up connections. The high rate quality forms are used primarily for high-fidelity music. The audio stream is played, while it is streamed from the media server. Many Internet radio stations use RealAudio to broadcast their programs on-line in real time. In 1997, RealNetworks began to support a video format called RealVideo. The combination of audio and video formats is called *RealMedia* (RM) format. However, the latest version of RealNetworks encoder uses suffix .RV for video files (with or without sound). Typically, these streams have constant bit rate (CBR). Recently, RealNetworks has developed a new container format for variable bit rate (VBR) streams, called *RealMedia Variable Bitrate* (RMVB) format. Suffixes *.RAM* (Real Audio

Metadata) and *.SMIL* (Synchronized Multimedia Integration Language) indicate file formats that sometimes appear as links on web pages.

RealAudio was developed as a media stream audio format. HTTP is the most common way to use RealAudio streaming, treating RealAudio files as normal web pages. Audio playback begins when the first audio segment has been delivered and continues, while the rest of the audio file is still downloading. This streaming mode operates better, when the audio content is pre-recorded. The first RealAudio version used a protocol called Progressive Network Audio (PNA) for audio streaming. Later, the *Internet Engineering Task Force* (IETF) accepted RTSP as a connection management format, while audio data are sent by the *Real Data Transport* (RDT) protocol.

In many cases, web pages are not directly linked to a RealAudio file. They, are connected to a .RAM (Real Audio Metadata), .SMIL or .SMI metafile. This is a small text file that contains a link for streaming media audio. When a user clicks on such a link, the browser downloads the .RAM, .SMIL or .SMI file and starts the media player at the user site. The player reads the PNM or RTSP URL from this file and starts stream payback. Downloaded .RAM files may ultimately be Real Audio (.RA) files and not just text files. RA files can be played by Windows Media Player and other media players based on DirectX (when the appropriate codec is available).

To download, record or store an RA file, we can use a media stream recorder that supports RealMedia, RealAudio or RealVideo formats and a relevant protocol (RTSP, PNA, or HTTP). WM Recorder is an easy to use and very powerful stream recorder, which can store Real Audio and Real Video streams. WM Recorder can record audio and video streams from RealPlayer. It can record media streams, even if we use Real Alternative, which is a codec capable of playing RealMedia files on Windows platforms, without installing RealPlayer.

## 9.6  Windows Media Player

*Windows Media Player* (WMP) is a media player and digital media library developed by Microsoft. It is used for audio, video and image playback. It works on PCs running Windows, Mac OS, Mac OS X, Solaris, and on mobile phones and PDAs running Windows Mobile.

The first release of the Microsoft Media Player was version 3. The big success came with version 6.1, which appeared in 1998. Since then, it is known as Windows Media Player. Over the years, new versions were released, providing new features and functionalities. Windows Media Player 11 was first designed for Windows XP (2006) and, then, it was included

Figure 9.6.1: Windows Media Player 12 screen.

on Windows Vista. Window Media Player 12 was released in 2009.

The main use of Windows Media Player is audio and video playback. Additionally, it can create audio or video CDs or rip music from CDs. Audio CDs can be ripped as WMA files at 48, 64, 96, 128, 160 and 192 Kbps, or as uncompressed WAV files. WMP can be synchronized with external devices, such as MP3 players or other audio or portable devices. It provides a digital media library for digital media content management based on ontologies, such as album, artist, genre, date. It also provides access to a number of on-line music stores, offering music rental or purchase.

WMP provides subtitling, if such information exists in the content. It can be connected to game consoles and other portable devices for data synchronization. Finally, it can cooperate with Internet Explorer, add tracks to the 'Now Playing' playlist and play music on web pages, by providing a built-in ActiveX control mode for Internet Explorer.

Windows Media Player supports various audio and video codecs and DirectShow filters. The supported file formats are the following ones: Windows Media Video (WMV), Windows Media Audio (WMA) and Advanced Systems Format (ASF). It also supports its own XML-based playlist, called *Windows Playlist* (WPL). Some Windows Media Player versions support Advanced Audio Coding (AAC) audio and MPEG-4 Part 10 (H.264) video. It can provide a digital rights management service for digital data, in the form of Windows Media DRM, to help protect copyright.

*Windows Media Audio* (WMA) is a format of compressed audio files, developed by Microsoft. Many consumer devices support WMA files, ranging from portable music players and mobile phones to DVD players. Originally developed to compete with the MP3 format, it never managed to dominate. WMA can support variable bit rate (VBR), constant bit rate (CBR) and lossless audio coding. Windows Media Audio can optionally support digital rights management, using a combination of cryptographic techniques, e.g., DES cryptography, RC4 stream cipher and the SHA-1 hash function. A WMA file is often encapsulated in an Advanced System Format (ASF) file, resulting in a WMA or .ASF file. WMA suffix is used only if the file contains strictly audio. ASF format explains how to encode file metadata (something like the ID3 tags of MP3 files).

The *Windows Media Video* (WMV) is a video file format, developed by Microsoft. WMV files are part of the ASF container format, which includes audio and video support. Using a different file suffix, one can install multiple media players on his computer and use them for playing audio and video streams. Various early versions of the WMV codecs were developed for low bit rate video streaming. There are many WMV codecs, but the most frequently used ones are WMV versions 7, 8 and 9. WMV versions 7 and 8 do not fulfill SMPTE requirements. In particular, the WMP version 7 (WMV1) codec seems to be based on the MPEG-4 Part 2 variant, developed by Microsoft. WMV version 9 follows a different direction than MPEG-4 and was promoted to become an independent SMPTE 421M standard, known as VC-1. It is an industrial video codec developed by Microsoft. It is contained in the specifications of Blu-ray, but there is a trend to be replaced by MPEG-4.

*Advanced Systems Format* (ASF) is a container file format that is used to store synchronized multimedia data, primarily based on the Windows Media format. It is suitable for local media playback and is specialized for media streaming. If appropriate codecs are installed on the computer, it is possible to play audio or video content, or both, using Windows Media Player files and ASF. It is possible to protect audio and video content, using the Windows Media Digital Rights Manager. ASF format does not describe how to encode video or audio, but rather describes the media video/audio stream structure. This means that ASF files can be encoded with any audio/video codec. One of the main advantages of ASF is its ability to efficiently deliver multimedia content to a variety of networks and protocols. ASF files are Multipurpose Internet Mail Extensions (MIME) files, which means that they provide e-mail support. Any media object can be placed in an ASF data stream, including audio, video, scripts, ActiveX controls and HTML files.

*Media Transfer Protocol* (MTP) is part of Windows Media toolset and is closely linked to the Windows Media Player. Windows Vista has integrated MTP support. MTP support on Windows XP requires the installation of Windows Media Player 10 or higher. Mac OS and Linux operating systems have software packages for its support. MTP is an innovative set of extensions of *Picture Transfer Protocol* (PTP) and supports transferring music/movie files to digital audio/media players, respectively.

## 9.7   QuickTime media player

The *QuickTime* media player was developed by Apple to handle various forms of digital video, audio, text, animations, music and various types of interactive panoramic images. It is available for Mac OS, Mac OS X and Microsoft Windows operating systems and provides the necessary support for software packages, like iTunes and Safari. It supports a large number of audio, image and video file types.

Particularly, QuickTime VR supports panoramic images, like the one shown in Figure 9.7.1. Such panoramic images can be formed easily by mosaicing successive, partially overlapping, images.

(a)

(b)

Figure 9.7.1: a) Original images, b) panoramic image.

QuickTime (MOV) file type is a container format, which can store audio, video and subtitles. It is very useful for media content editing that can be done on site, without copying the file. Since 1998 QuickTime format was the basis for developing the *MPEG-4 container format* (MP4), according to an ISO decision. However, MP4 files support more codecs, compared to MOV files, because MPEG-4 is an international standard.

The first version of QuickTime player was released in 1991. Since then, seven different versions were developed (QuickTime 1.x - QuickTime 7.x). In 2009, QuickTime Q was released, which is not compatible with previous versions. It supports recording and editing audio and video streams and their sharing in www environments, such as YouTube. Apple offers software development tools for QuickTime Q, such as the Movie Toolbox (for handling multimedia streams) and Image Compression Manager (for media compression).

## 9.8   FlashPlayer

Adobe Flash Player is a media player that supports audio and video streaming over Internet. Other media are supported as well, such as 3D graphics, still images and enhanced high-resolution bitmap support (larger than 16 Mpixel). Alpha channel transparency is offered as well.

Flash Player can open and play *ShockWave File* (SWF) media files (.SWF). Such files can contain animations and applets. YouTube videos are encoded in a Flash format (SWF). *LZMA* compression can compress SWF file sizes up to 40%, thus reducing download time. *Flash Video* (FLV) and audio may be contained in an SWF file. MPEG-4 Part 10 decoding is supported, allowing streaming of high-quality video for several real-time applications, such as video conferencing and webcasting. AAC or MP3 compressed audio can be decoded by the Flash Player. It supports the *JPEG-XR* still image compression format (ISO/IEC 29199-2 Standard) for very efficient lossless and lossy image compression.

Flash Player version 11 runs in various operating systems, such as Windows XP (and newer versions), Mac OS, Linux and Android (for mobile phones). It comes, as a plug in, in several WWW browsers, such as Internet Explorer, Mozilla Firefox and it is built in Google Chrome. SWF files ready for streaming can be embedded in a web page, using special HTML code. They can be streamed using the Flash Player that is embedded in the WWW browser. Flash Player provides webcam support. Finally, high-performance 2D/3D graphics are supported, by exploiting the GPU graphics rendering capabilities.

# 9.9 Videoconferencing over IP

*Videoconferencing* refers to two-way video and audio communication between two (point-to-point) or more (multipoint) sites/users. Although it has been around in analog form since at least 1930-1940 (e.g., in Germany), it has become practical in its digital form using digital transmission lines, such as the ISDN ones, and digital video/audio compression after 1980. Originally, digital videoconferencing was only moderately successful and was primarily used in business communications for reducing travel costs. The situation changed drastically with *Videoconferencing over IP* in 1990 and particularly, since the introduction of free Internet videotelephony services (e.g., Skype) in early 2000. Nowadays, desktop videoconferencing platforms use the computer microphone and a web cam as audio/video input, respectively and the computer loudspeakers and screen as audio/video output. Digital communication is performed over a LAN or WAN.

Powerful audio and video compression tools (e.g., the H.323 standard) can be used to reduce communication load and ensure reasonable quality of service over poor or unreliable communication networks. The videoconferencing systems consist of several layers (planes). In the *Signal Plane* of a videoconferencing system, the signals follow certain standards, e.g., the H.323 or *Session Initiation Protocol* (SIP) protocols to control IO connections. The *Media Plane* of a videoconferencing system describes audio/video multiplexing and streaming. It can use various protocols, e.g., the Real-time Transport Protocol (RTP) and Real-time Transport Control Protocols (RTCP). RTP can describe the codec used and technical parameters, e.g., video frame resolution and rate. RTCP can handle streaming errors.

*Skype* is a very popular videoconferencing application firstly used for desktop communication. Nowadays, it offers calls anywhere in the world over Internet, mobile and fixed telephone networks. It is also a videoconference and instant messenger platform with the ability of sending SMS or other files among users. Audio and video streaming is used for real-time videoconferencing. Skype runs on Windows, Mac and Linux operating systems and on mobile phone platforms, such as Android OS and Symbian. It allows communication with peers among users, by voice using a microphone, video using a webcam or by instant messaging over the Internet. Registered Skype users are identified by a unique Skype name that may be listed in the Skype directory. Voice chat allows telephone calls between pairs of users and conference calls. Skype audioconferencing currently supports up to 25 users simultaneously. Text chat allows group chats, emoticons, storing chat history and editing of previous messages. User profiles and online status indicators are also included. Calls to other users within the Skype service are free of charge, while calls to *Public Switched*

*Telephone Network* (PSTN) telephones and mobile phones are charged via a debit-based user account system. Skype competitors include SIP and H.323-based services, such as Linphone, as well as the Google Talk service, Mumble and Hall.com.

Skype videoconferencing between two users was introduced in for the Windows and Mac OS X platforms in 2006, while Skype 2.0 videoconferencing for Linux was released in 2008. Currently, Skype videoconferencing between up to five people is available. Skype for Windows supports high quality video offering full-screen and screen-in-screen modes, similar to those of mid-range videoconferencing systems.

Skype uses the G.729, SVOPC or SILK audio codecs for audio streaming. ITU-T G.729 is an audio compression standard that compresses the digital voice in packets of 10 msec duration. It codes speech at 8 kbps using the *Conjugate Structure Algebraic Code-Excited Linear Prediction* (CS-ACELP) codec. Because of its low bandwidth requirements, G.729 is mostly used in *Voice over IP* (VoIP) applications, where bandwidth must be conserved, such as conference calls. G.729 extensions provide rates of 6.4 kbps and 11.8 kbps for worse or better speech quality, respectively. G.729 has been extended with various features, commonly designated as G.729a and G.729b. The *Sinusoidal Voice Over Packet Coder* (SVOPC) is an audio codec, which is used in VoIP applications. It is a lossy speech compression codec designed specifically for operating over communication channels suffering from packet losses. It uses more bandwidth than other bandwidth-optimized codecs, but it is packet-loss resistant. Finally, Skype uses the proprietary SILK audio codec that is intended to be lightweight and embeddable.

Skype uses the VP7, VP8 or H.264 video codecs for video streaming. VP8 is an open and royalty free video compression format created by On2 Technologies, later acquired by Google. The H.264 codec can be used for 720p and 1080p high definition point-to-point and multipoint video conferencing.

# 10

# DIGITAL VIDEO

# INTERFACE

# STANDARDS

For digital video playback on screen, we need to achieve a connection (*video interface*) between a digital video source (e.g., a computer, digital camera, DVD player) and the display device. The two prevailing digital video interface standards, namely HDMI and DVI, are presented in this Chapter.

# 10.1 Introduction to HDMI

*High-Definition Multimedia Interface* (HDMI) is a connection format for transmitting digital audio and video. It is primarily used for local cable transmission of uncompressed digital audio/video streams. It provides an interface between any compatible digital audio and video source and playback device. HDMI connections are used in digital television sets, DVD and Blu-ray disc players, HDTV cable and satellite set-top boxes, providing consumers with high sound and picture quality. HDMI technology seems to be the best solution for transporting digital audio and video, probably replacing Firewire and DVI. It is supported by a group of companies, including Sony, Hitachi, Silicon Image, Philips and Toshiba. They worked together to create the first HDMI working group. HDMI was also supported by many movie production companies, such as Fox, Universal, Warner Bros and Disney and by service providers, such as DirecTV, EchoStar (Dish Network) and Cable Labs. HDMI is a common digital interface standard for computers, high definition video and commercial electronics. It has been adopted by more than 700 companies and is installed in hundreds of HDMI compliant devices. It allows computers to deliver high quality digital audiovisual content, including high definition movies and multi-channel audio. HDMI is continuously evolving to abreast with market needs. New products implement new versions of the HDMI standard and still have backwards compatibility with older HDMI versions.

HDMI is the best digital audio and video interface standard, because it merges all audio and video cables in one. Thus, the wired jungle behind the home entertainment systems disappears. This is very good news for consumers, but bad news for cable manufacturers. However, it seems that cable manufacturers have found an answer to this problem, since HDMI cables are still very expensive.

## 10.1.1 HDMI features

In this section, we discuss the main HDMI features.

**Audio and video in one cable.** HDMI has the advantage of carrying both digital audio and video over a single cable. Computer hardware must be designed in such a way, that the audio signal is routed from the sound card to the graphics card, where it is appropriately multiplexed with the digital video signal for HDMI transmission.

**Increased color depth.** Until now, analog and digital color computers were limited to 24-bit color depth, producing 16.7 million colors. This color palette used to be called *true color*, because the human eye cannot easily distinguish small color differences in this palette. By increasing the image resolution in HDTV, the human eye can spot overall color quality differences in 24-bit color images, though it can not easily distinguish each color separately. The first HDMI versions were limited to 24-bit color, but HDMI version 1.3 allows 30, 36 and even 48-bit color depth. This significantly increases the perceived color quality. The only restriction is that both the graphics card and the monitor must support HDMI version 1.3.

**HDCP.** HDMI includes *High-definition Digital Content Protection* (HDCP) specifications. This ensures that digital content can not be eavesdropped, as it is transmitted to the screen for rendering. Each HDMI-compatible graphics card and monitor must support this feature.

**Backward compatibility.** HDMI is backward compatible to single-link Digital Visual Interface (DVI) digital video (DVI-D or DVI-I, but not to DVI-A) that is used in computer monitors and graphics cards, as described subsequently in this Chapter. By using an adapter cable, the HDMI connector can be plugged into a DVI digital video port. This is very useful for consumers who want to buy a system supporting HDMI output, when their TV or computer screen only has a DVI input. It should be noted that this applies only to digital video and not to audio. Therefore, the HDMI audio and remote control features will not be active. Furthermore, the device with DVI input must support HDCP, otherwise the signal transfer will not be achieved. Finally, it is worth mentioning that, while a display monitor with DVI input can be connected to an HDMI computer port, an HDMI display screen cannot connect to a DVI computer port.

HDMI supports already existing high-definition video formats, such as 720p, 1080i and 1080p/60. It also has the flexibility to support enhanced definition standards such as 480p or 576p, and standard definition digital TV formats, such as 480i (NTSC) or 576i (PAL). Additionally, the HDMI version 1.3 has the ability to offer even higher resolutions (up to 1440p), because of the increased transfer bandwidth.

Initially, HDMI started by transporting eight uncompressed 192 kHz 24-bit audio channels, surpassing all existing audio standards. In addition to that, HDMI can carry any type of compressed audio, such as Dolby (including Dolby Digital EX 7.1, Dolby Digital Plus 7.1 and Dolby TrueHD) and DTS, such as DTS-ES 6.1 and DTS-HD Master Audio sound. Newer HDMI sources can deliver 6-channel 96 kHz uncompressed audio from a DVD-Audio disc.

HDMI, as well as DVI technology, use the *Transition Minimized Differential Signalling* (TMDS) digital data transmission standard for video (and audio) transmission. TMDS encoding offers serious advantages, such as interference reduction in copper wires. It is based on the 8-bit to 10-bit word conversion. These words are selected to have interesting properties, e.g., proper 0 and 1 distribution to support a low DC level. The 10-bit TMDS offers 1024-word combinations: 44 combinations are used for control, e.g., for horizontal and vertical synchronization and 460 combinations are used to represent 8 bit words (instead of the typical $2^8 = 256$ combinations). Most of the 8 bit words have two different TMDS codes, while some have only one TMDS code. The TMDS codes are chosen, so as to reduce the DC signal level. Finally, 560 combinations are not used. In order to transmit video, audio and data, TMDS uses three types of transmission periods:

1) *Video data period* used for video transmission.

2) *Data island period*. It is used to transmit audio and various data types. Such a transmission occurs during the video horizontal and vertical blanking intervals.

3) *Control period*. It occurs between video and data island periods.

## 10.1.2   HDMI versions

There are many different HDMI versions providing full backwards compatibility with earlier versions. Although each new version uses the same HDMI cables, they can increase transmission bandwidth. The supported audio formats may vary in each version. All versions must be capable of transmitting high-definition 1080p video.

**HDMI 1.0 (2002).** It decodes most audio formats contained in DVD and digital television signals, including Dolby Digital and DTS. It uses a single cable for both digital audio and video connection at a maximum rate of 4.9 Gbps. It supports up to 165 Mpixel/sec video (1080p 60 Hz or UXGA) formats and eight-channel 192 kHz/24-bit sound.

**HDMI 1.1 (2004).** It is improved over the previous version, since it supports DVD audio, which means that users with compatible disks and players can listen to 5.1 channel surround sound, without the use of six separate RCA audio cables.

**HDMI 1.2/1.2a (2005).** HDMI 1.2 technology adds features and capabilities that make HDMI more accessible, both in the consumer electronics and in the computer industry markets. The main improvement in version 1.2 is the addition of *Super Audio CD* (SACD) and *Direct Stream Digital* (DSD) support, which means that users do not need to rely on iLink or analog cables to listen SACDs. This version also supports, a so far unused, Type A connector. It also supports both RGB and $YC_bC_r$ color formats. HDMI 1.2a introduced the HDMI Compliance Test Specification

(CTS) for use by the HDMI Authorized Testing Centre (ATC). Each cable manufacturer must submit to ATC any new HDMI cable, whose length exceeds that of already tested cables, for review. One device passes the CTS 1.2a test, if all its connections are included in a links list approved by ATC.

**HDMI 1.3/1.3a/1.3b (2006).** It supports Dolby TrueHD audio and DTS-HD Master Audio, used in Blu-ray players. Furthermore, HDMI 1.3 supports Dolby Digital Plus (DD+) or DD- or Enhanced AC-3 (E-AC-3) audio, which uses lossy compression at 6.1 Mbps. This is a massive improvement compared to conventional Dolby Digital 5.1, which runs only at 0.64 Mbps. Dolby Digital can carry up to 13 audio channels, compared to the 5.1 channels of Dolby Digital 5.1 surround sound. Its data rate is equal to that of the Dolby True HD and DTS-HD Master Audio. HDMI 1.3 has the following characteristics:

1) Greater bit rate. HDMI 1.3 increases its range up to 340 MHz (10.2 Gbps) to support future HD display characteristics, such as higher spatial resolution, bigger color depth and higher refresh rate.

2) Higher color depth. HDMI 1.3 supports 10-bit, 12-bit and 16-bit (RGB or $YC_bC_r$) color depths, which is higher than the 8-bit color depth of the previous HDMI versions.

3) Color range. HDMI 1.3 supports the xvColor color standard (IEC 61966-2-4 xvYCC), reaching almost perfect color.

4) Smaller connector size. HDMI 1.3 offers a new smaller connector for portable devices, such as HD camcorders, which must be connected to HDTV TVs.

5) Synchronization. HDMI 1.3 includes automatic audio synchronization, enabling devices to automatically synchronize with precision. Audio and video synchronizing in user devices is a big challenge, because of the complex digital signal processing operations used to enhance content quality.

**HDMI 1.4/1.4a (2009).** It supports high $4K \times 2K$ resolutions, e.g., $3840 \times 2160p$ and $4096 \times 2160p$ for digital cinema, 3DTV (stereoscopic TV) distribution and a new micro HDMI connector. HDMI 1.4a extends 3DTV broadcast content support at 720p, 1080i and 1080p resolutions and 24/50 Hz frame rates.

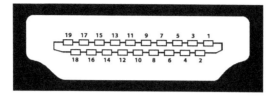

Figure 10.1.1: Type A HDMI female plug.

Figure 10.1.2: Type A HDMI male plug.

### 10.1.3    HDMI connectors and cables

HDMI has expanded to include three connector types, each targeting a different market. A type A HDMI connector has 19 pins as shown in Figures 10.1.1 and 10.1.2, dimensions 13.9 mm × 4.5 mm and can support SDTV, EDTV (Enhanced Definition Television) and HDTV. It is the most frequently used plug. Type A connector is compatible with any DVI-D single link. HDMI connector Type B is a higher resolution version defined in HDMI 1.0 and is not used in general. It has 29 pins (21.2 mm width), allowing it to carry the HD video channel for high-definition screens at a WQSXGA resolution (3200 × 2048 pixels). It is compatible with the dual-link DVI-D. The HDMI Type C mini-plug, is used in portable devices, such as HD video recorders. It is smaller than Type A (10.42 mm × 2.42 mm), but has also 19 pins.

When buying a HDMI compliant device, the consumer must consider the HDMI inputs and outputs needed. Lately, we observe an increase in HDMI inputs and outputs in consumer devices. For example, HDTV sets frequently have 3 or 4 HDMI inputs, due to the massive use of HDMI. They often have an additional input for connecting game consoles or cameras. It is very important to decide the number of devices that will become part of a home entertainment system, in order to make sure that it has the required number of HDMI inputs and outputs.

The cable length is a very important criterion for selecting an HDMI cable, especially with respect to its audiovisual format support. One issue that should be mentioned is the internal wire thickness, or *gauge* (unit for measuring a wire diameter). For example, if the internal wire diameter of a HDMI cable is 28 gauge, it can carry the audiovisual signal at a distance of up to 15 meters, under ideal conditions. For very long connections, alternative solutions can be used, such as the CAT-5 cable that can extend the transmission even over 90 meters.

## 10.1.4 HDMI advantages

HDMI technology offers a plethora of advantages, in comparison to analog video standards, such as composite video, S-video or component video. First of all, HDMI is a digital standard, which means that it provides the best audiovisual quality in inherently digital connections, because there is no need to perform A/D and D/A conversions, neither to audio nor to video signals. The quality difference over analog interfaces is remarkable, especially at higher resolutions, such as 1080p. Furthermore, HDMI addresses quite well the problem of video transmission noise and manages to provide smooth and bright images. Another HDMI benefit is its ease of use, because it combines video and multichannel audio in one cable.

Moreover, the digital nature of HDMI allows very good support to digital displays, such as LCD monitors and Plasma or DLP projectors. A HDMI cable can precisely match the screen resolution to video input resolution. HDMI allows image conversion to the desired aspect ratio (specifically, 16:9 or 4:3). Furthermore, it provides device control with a single cable, enabling remote control capabilities. Also, HDMI versions support Blu-ray content playback in high definition of up to 1080p. HDMI 1.3 supports lossless Dolby True HD audio and DTS-HD Master Audio audio, specifically developed for Blu-ray disc soundtracks. The increased color depth (30, 36 or 48 bits) is another HDMI advantage, since it allows to generate billions of colors and great visual detail. Finally, HDMI supports the TOSLINK optical audio transmission, which is a fiber optic connection, usually made of 1 mm optical fibers or of several quartz glass fibers. TOSLINK technology can offer very high audio transfer rates to a home entertainment system.

The only HDMI constraint is its digital content protection mechanisms, based on the HDCP support. Thus, consumers should check, when they purchase HDMI-compliant devices, that they are compatible with HDCP.

## 10.2    Introduction to DVI

*Digital Visual Interface* (DVI) is a digital video transfer standard for computers, designed and developed in 1999 by the *Digital Display Working Group* (DDWG). It was originally designed for transferring uncompressed digital video from a computer to a VGA screen. Later implementations maximized the visual quality on LCD and Plasma screens.

The main advantage of DVI is that it uses only one cable to transmit an RGB video signal. The video transfer speed is significantly greater than that of analog interfaces. DVI combined with HDCP was the preferred video transfer format, before HDMI. There is a trend in TV and DVD systems manufacturers to include HDCP on DVI connections. This means that consumers using DVI technology should check whether their hardware is compatible to HDCP. Finally, digital DVI (DVI-D) is partially compatible to HDMI.

### 10.2.1    DVI technology

Today almost all computer monitors are digital (usually LCD) ones. If an LCD monitor does not have a digital input, an analog connection must be used: the graphics card must convert the digital signal to analog and the LCD monitor should do the reverse conversion from analog to digital signal, as shown in Figure 10.2.1. This solution causes significant image quality loss. If a digital DVI connection is available, there is no need for such lossy signal conversions, resulting in high image quality that is more evident at higher image resolutions.

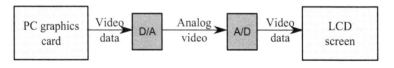

Figure 10.2.1: D/A and A/D signal transformations in an analog computer-monitor connection.

DVI is based on the TMDS transmission standard that is also used in HDMI connections. This explains the compatibility between the HDMI and DVI interfaces. This fact requires at least one TMDS link, although sometimes two TMDS channels are used. A single TMDS link consists of three channels for RGB data and one channel for clock, as shown in Figure 10.2.2. In TMDS transmission, 8 bit video data are converted into 10 bit words. The produced signal has undergone DC term suppression. This enables a very good transmission, while minimizing electromagnetic

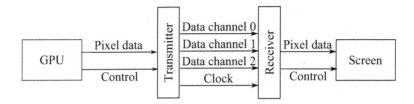

Figure 10.2.2: Single TMDS link in a DVI connection.

interference. Hence, reliable data transfer over long DVI cables is allowed.

All DVI equipment should transmit a video signal over a 5 m long cable. Almost 8 m long DVI cables can be used, possibly together with a DVI signal amplifier. Tests on various DVI-compatible home devices produced good connections over cables that were up to 10 m long. Unfortunately, data loss may occur even over a DVI link. In such a case, the consumers may perceive static pixels on screen. Further signal deterioration results in picture flickering. Tests on 12 m cables generally resulted in signal loss and severe image quality deterioration. The use of cable lengths larger than 12 m resulted in complete transmission failure. When long DVI-I cables are used, complete image loss may occur. In such cases, analog VGA or digital HDMI connections are a good alternative solution. If we have to use DVI connections anyway, the DVI-D cables are the best option.

## 10.2.2 DVI types and functionalities

DVI cables are available in three different formats: DVI-A, DVI-D and DVI-I. A flat blade pin at the left plug side indicates whether the cable is digital or analog. If it is stand alone, this indicates a digital DVI-D cable as shown in Figure 10.2.3. If it is surrounded by four other pins, then the cable is DVI-A or DVI-I. The pin number varies, depending on whether the cable is single link, dual link or analog. Two groups of 9 pins indicate a single link cable; one group of 24 pins indicates a dual link cable, as shown in Figure 10.2.3. Two separate groups of 8 and 4 pins indicate a DVI-A cable.

DVI-A (DVI-Analog) is an analog standard used for connecting analog video sources (e.g., VGA computer graphics cards) with analog displays, such as a CRT screen. In DVI-A plugs, the flat pin is surrounded by four pins. There are adapters for SVGA to DVI-A conversion and vice versa.

DVI-D is a digital connection standard used to connect digital video sources, e.g., graphics cards to digital (LCD, Plasma) monitors. There are two types of DVI-D cables: single-link and dual-link DVI-D, as shown in Figure 10.2.3. Both single-link and dual-link DVI-D connections use

Figure 10.2.3: Single-link DVI-D (left) and dual-link DVI-D connector (right).

TMDS transmission. The cable choice (single-link or dual-link) depends on the desired application. Single-link DVI-D offers a transfer rate of 1.65 Gbps, supports video resolutions up to 1920 × 1200 pixels and pixel clock frequency in the range from 25 to 165 MHz. Dual link DVI-D can achieve better performance and can virtually double the transmission rate. It supports pixel clock frequencies up to 330 MHz and video resolutions up to 2560 × 1600 pixels. It provides 2 Gbps transfer rate and it is backward compatible to single-link DVI-D.

DVI-I is a multiple type cable, capable of transmitting both digital-to-digital and analog-to-analog signal. It should be mentioned that the DVI-I cable is not able to connect a digital output to an analog input or vice versa. A DVI-I plug can be connected to any type of DVI cable. However, we have to make sure that both the signal source and receiver support the same signal type (digital or analog). DVI-I supports either single or dual TMDS links, as shown in Figures 10.2.4, 10.2.5.

At this point, we should mention that digital and analog DVI cables cannot be interchanged. This means that neither DVI-D can work on an analog system, nor a DVI-A can work on a digital system. For connecting an analog source and a digital screen, an electronic VGA to DVI-D converter is needed. Similarly, a DVI-D to VGA converter is needed for

Figure 10.2.4: Single-link (left), dual-link (right) DVI-I connectors.

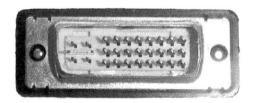

Figure 10.2.5: DVI-I connector.

connecting a digital output to an analog monitor.

## 10.3   HDMI and DVI comparisons

DVI is a video interface standard designed to maximize the visual quality of digital display devices, like LCD displays and digital projectors. HDMI is an interface standard for both audio and video connections and provides more features in a single technology. Thus, audio and video can be transferred via a single cable, achieving better quality and reducing the cable number in consumer systems. In addition, HDMI is compatible with DVI. HDMI offers *Consumer Electronics Control* (CEC) functionalities, which permit users to control devices remotely.

Another great advantage of the HDMI standard, as opposed to DVI, is plug size. The DVI plug standard is similar in size with the VGA plug. The HDMI connector size is about one third the size of a DVI connector. Furthermore, HDMI versions 1.3 and 1.4 include mini and micro HDMI connectors for portable computers and devices, such as digital cameras and camcorders. Finally, we should mention that HDMI is a newer technology with much room for further development, as opposed to DVI, which is an older technology.

# 11

# DIGITAL VIDEO

# PERIPHERAL

# DEVICES

The peripheral devices for digital video display and storage have undergone dramatic changes in the last decade. New optical mass storage devices (e.g., Blu-ray discs) have been developed that are capable of storing HD resolution movies in one optical disc. New TV and computer monitor technologies (e.g., Plasma and LCD) enable high-quality HD video display. New digital video projectors enable a true cinema experience at home. Auto-stereoscopic TV displays emerge. The technologies of peripheral devices are detailed in the subsequent sections.

# 11.1   Introduction to DVD

When Sony and Philips introduced the first digital *Compact Disc* (CD) in the market in the late '70s, they provided the first taste of the digital age in music. CD has experienced great success and universal acceptance, by virtually all consumer electronics manufacturers. Despite the great success of CD technology, the advances in media compression and laser technology were relentless and, shortly after its appearance on the market, a debate started on its successor. The target was to increase the optical disc capacity, while increasing the playback speed, in order to enable the storage of an entire high definition movie on one side of a single disk. In 1994, seven film industries, namely Columbia (Sony), Disney, MCA/Universal (Matsushita), MGM/UA, Paramount, Viacom and Warner Bros (Time Warner) decided to create a new optical disc standard, called *Digital Video Disk* (DVD) or *Digital Versatile Disk*, which would have the following characteristics:

- storage capacity that allows to store 135 minutes of a feature movie on one disk side,

- superior image quality to existing optical disks,

- support of 3 to 5 different languages on a single disk,

- protection from piracy,

- support for widescreen viewing,

- parental control.

In 1993, two dominant manufacturing alliances were created: a) Sony and Philips, which announced independently their joint MMCD standard: a compact disk, whose readout was based on a red laser beam and had a capacity of 3.7 Gbytes on one side and b) a group of seven companies, namely: Hitachi, Matsushita (Panasonic), Mitsubishi, Victor (JVC), Pioneer Thomson (RCA/GE) and Toshiba that supported the SD (Super Disc). The dispute continued until 1995, focusing on storage size, aiming to meet the film company requirements. This delay, however, worried computer manufacturers. So, in April 1995, five computer companies (Apple, Compaq, HP, IBM and Microsoft), formed a technical advisory board, which pushed the opponents to converge on a standard that would incorporate the following features:

- common storage and file format standard that could be used both by computers and movie players,

- compatibility with existing CDs and CD-ROMs and future recordable and rewritable discs,

- same cost with existing CD and CD-ROM disks,

- disk independence from its package,

- information reliability similar or better than that of CD-ROM,

- increased and expandable storage capacity,

- high performance, both in video playback and data transfer.

To fully meet these requirements, the advisory board proposed the adoption of the Universal Disk Format (UDF) file system, which supports disk recording and readout and was developed by the *Optical Storage Technology Association* (OSTA). OSTA had already agreed to further develop UDF, so that it would be compatible both for computers and video playback systems.

Finally, at the end of 1995, the final DVD standard specifications were announced by the two manufacturer alliances. The new standard covered the basic DVD-ROM format and incorporated most recommendations made by Hollywood studios and computer manufacturers. Subsequently, a new manufacturer alliance was formed, called *DVD Consortium*, consisting of Philips, Sony, the seven major players of the SD alliance and Time Warner. DVD patent rights were shared between these players: Matsushita was awarded 25%, Pioneer and Sony 20% each, Philips, Hitachi and Toshiba another 10% each, and Mitsubishi, JVC and Time Warner shared the remaining percentage of a total of 4000 patents, as shown in Figure 11.1.1.

The first DVD came out in 1999 and, over the next years, it was established as a home entertainment and computer industry standard. DVD has completely replaced the conventional analog VHS video cassettes for movie storage in the consumer market. Almost all films were digitized on DVD disks. Sophisticated computer games with increased capabilities were made to fit on a single DVD disk.

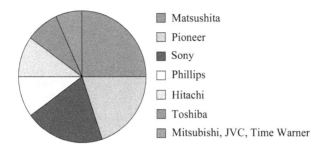

■ Matsushita

□ Pioneer

■ Sony

□ Phillips

□ Hitachi

■ Toshiba

▨ Mitsubishi, JVC, Time Warner

Figure 11.1.1: Patent pie in DVD-Consortium.

## 11.1.1   DVD technology

A DVD is usually made of polycarbonate compounds, but can also be made of acrylic, or a similar transparent material. Digital information is stored in spiral *tracks*, consisting of a series of *pits* (no reflection) or *lands* (reflection) on a laser-reflective surface. A laser beam is used to read the pits/lands and, hence, the stored information. A DVD cross section is shown in Figure 11.1.2. DVD does not differ externally from a CD. It has a thickness of 1.2 mm and 12 cm diameter. The *track pit* (or *groove spacing*), i.e., the distance between the tracks, is 1.6 $\mu$m on CD, 0.74 $\mu$m on DVD and 0.32 $\mu$m in Blu-ray. The minimum pit length is 0.834 $\mu$m in CD, 0.4 $\mu$m in DVD and 0.14 $\mu$m in Blu-ray. The red laser wavelength used in DVD is 640 nm, while the Blu-ray and CD wavelengths are 405 nm and 780 nm, respectively. The length of the spiral track, where data are recorded, is 12.5 km for DVD-5 (capacity 4.7 GByte) and 25 km for DVD-9 (capacity 8.5 GByte). Similarly, the CD spiral track is 6 to 7.5 km long. Finally the Blu-ray spiral track length is 27 km and 54 km, for 25 GByte and 50 GByte capacities, respectively.

On the first DVD layer, the data is written from the center to the perimeter, while on the second layer (if it exists), they are written in reverse mode (*Opposite track path* mastering, OTP), as shown in Figure 11.1.3a, to avoid delays in data transfer, recording and read-out speeds. The data can be written on two layers and in a parallel mode, called *Paral-*

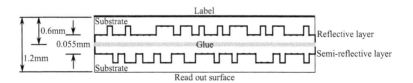

Figure 11.1.2: DVD disk cross-section.

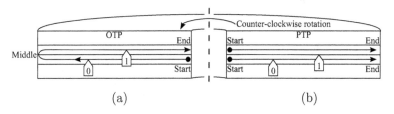

Figure 11.1.3: Write/read operations in double layer DVD.

*lel track path mastering* (PTP), as shown in Figure 11.1.3b. The employed *Error Correction Code* (ECC) is better than in CDs, rendering DVD more resistant to mishandling (e.g., scratches, dirt).

DVDs are divided in three areas, the Lead-in area, the main intermediate data recording area and the Lead-out area. Lead-in and Lead-out areas set the beginning and end of a data storage session. They are very important in multisession DVD recording, or in case we want to append data. As multisession DVDs are not fully compatible, the Lead-in and Lead-out area specifications are important.

The main DVD types are defined according to their storage capacities (in GByte). Furthermore, DVDs are divided into those having a diameter of 12 cm and those having a diameter of 8 cm (mini-DVD). Secondly, DVDs can be classified according to their features and use types (recordable, rewritable, video, audio, etc.). The categories of 12 cm DVDs are the following ones:

### Single-layer (SL) DVDs:

- DVD-5 4.7 GB SL. It is the most prevalent DVD format. Its consumer acceptance and mass production has dropped prices to those of recordable CDs.

- DVD-R SL, DVD-R/RW (rewritable), DVD+R SL, DVD+R/RW.

- DVD-RAM SL (Random Access Memory) version 2.1. Its structure is similar to that of a hard disk. It is much more robust, than the common recordable DVDs. They are ideal for camcorders and desktop video recorders/players. Unfortunately, they are relatively expensive and not necessarily recognizable by all DVD devices. Its specifications do not allow low-cost manufacturing. The use of hard drives in camcorders makes their future use uncertain.

- DVD-10 9.4 GB Single Layer Double Sided (SLDS).

### Dual layer (DL) DVDs:

- DVD-9 8.5 GB DL,

- DVD-R DL, DVD+R DL, DVD-RAM DL version 2.1,

- DVD-18 17 GB dual-layer double-sided (DL DS).

Mini-DVDs are primarily used in digital camcorders. They are divided in single and double-sided media, with capacities of 1.4 GBytes and 2.8 GBytes, respectively. The DVD capacities are shown in Table 11.1.1.

Table 11.1.1: DVD disk characteristics.

| Type | | Sides | Layers (total) | Diameter (cm) | Capacity (GBytes) (GB) |
|------|------|-------|---------|----------|-------------------|
| DVD-1 | SS SL | 1 | 1 | 8 | 1.46 |
| DVD-2 | SS DL | 1 | 2 | 8 | 2.66 |
| DVD-3 | DS SL | 2 | 2 | 8 | 2.92 |
| DVD-4 | DS DL | 2 | 4 | 8 | 5.32 |
| DVD-5 | SS SL | 1 | 1 | 12 | 4.7 |
| DVD-9 | SS DL | 1 | 2 | 12 | 8.54 |
| DVD-10 | DS SL | 2 | 2 | 12 | 9.4 |
| DVD-14 | DS DL/SL | 2 | 3 | 12 | 13.24 |
| DVD-18 | DS DL | 2 | 4 | 12 | 17.08 |

## 11.1.2    Digital audio and video storage in DVDs

DVD-Video discs store digital video. Video playback requires either a standalone DVD-player or a PC with DVD drive and a software video reader/decoder. Typically, movies are compressed using the DVD-Video format, which is MPEG-2-based, so that one movie can fit in a single DVD, without significantly losing image quality. The DVD-Video and DVD-Audio specifications were defined in the DVD format. The feasible data transfer rates on DVD media range from 2 to 10 Mbps. The highest achieved image quality corresponds to a 10 Mbps transfer rate. However, video compression produces acceptable video quality even at a transmission rate in the range of 2 Mbps. *DVD-Video* supports:

- MPEG-1 or MPEG-2 video compression up to 1.8 Mbps or 9.8 Mbps, respectively.

- PAL (576i) or NTSC (480i) interlaced video resolution at 720 × 576 or 640 × 480 pixels, respectively. Video resolution of 352 × 288 pixels at 25 frames/sec.

- Audio coding: PCM up to 6 Mbps, DTS up to 1.5 Mbps, MPEG-1 Audio Layer II up to 912 kbps and multichannel AC-3 surround sound up to 448 kbps. Dolby AC-3, despite its low bitrate, is the most commonly used audio format and provides excellent audio quality.

- Up to 32 different subtitles.

*DVD-Audio* offers multi-channel sound with a sampling rate of up to 192 kHz, 24 bits per audio channel and a data transfer rate of nearly 9.6 Mbps. Audio is not always compressed, because one DVD has up to 12 times more capacity than one CD. DVD-Audio players are still not that frequently used compared to CD audio players. A convenient solution is to play DVD-audio on a computer.

DVDs that are recorded following the ISO9660 standard file system, also called *Compact Disc File System* (CDFS), have filename length and file size restrictions. File size must be up to 2 GBytes. Eight subdirectories are allowed. File names must be up to 8 characters (ISO9660 Level 1) or up to 180 characters (ISO9660 Level 2) long. The total number of directories and subdirectories must not exceed 65535. A DVD recorded in DVD-ISO meets the ISO9660 standard and is compatible with all operating systems and devices. On a *Universal Disk Format* (UDF) filesystem, files can reach 2 TByte in size and there are no restrictions on file name length. Although there are many versions of UDF, version 1.02 is the most popular one. Blu-ray disks follow the UDF 2.60 file standard.

For worldwide DVD-video distribution, the earth is divided into six regions, due to different movie pricing and release policies. In the past, multi-region DVD players could be found. However, even now, this restriction can be bypassed by an (illegal) DVD player firmware change.

# 11.2 Introduction to Blu-ray

*Blu-ray Disc* (BD) is the brand name of a new generation of optical storage disks. Their main uses are high-definition video recording and playback and the storage of huge amounts of data. The Blu-ray disc has the same dimensions as a standard CD or DVD, but its capacity is up to 25 GB on one layer, or up to 50 GB on a dual layer format.

Blu-ray disc specifications were produced by the *Blu-ray Disc Association* (BDA), a group of more than 180 companies worldwide, representing consumer electronics, computers and movie production. Currently, it is headed by representatives of the following companies: Apple Computer, Dell, Hewlett Packard, Hitachi, LG Electronics, Matsushita, Mitsubishi,

Pioneer, Philips, Samsung, Sharp, Sony, Sun Microsystems, TDK, Thomson Multimedia, Twentieth Century Fox, Walt Disney Pictures and Warner Bros Entertainment.

The high-definition video optical disc concept arose as a consequence of the emergence of HDTV. In 1998, commercial HDTVs began to appear on the market. However, there was no commonly accepted and inexpensive way to record and playback high-definition content. Apart from the Digital VHS (JVC) and HDCAM (Sony) industrial standards, there was no device with the required storage capacity to accommodate HD video content. Also, it was already known that using lasers with shorter wavelengths would enable optical storage at a higher spatial density. This became possible when blue lasers diodes were invented. However, a lengthy lawsuit, involving patent rights, delayed their commercial appearance.

The first consumer BD device was a BD-RE recorder that came out in April 2003 and was only available in Japan. However, there was no standard for already recorded video and no movies were released for this player. The Blu-ray disc standard wouldn't be established until years later, since Hollywood studios required a new and safe system of copyright protection or Digital Rights Management (DRM), before they would accept it.

During the "first war" of high-definition optical disc standard, which lasted till 2008, the Blu-ray Disc format was competing with the HD DVD format. In 2008, Toshiba – the main supporter firm of HD DVD – announced that it will no longer support this format, hence essentially proclaiming Blu-ray as the winner in this war. There were two major reasons leading to this decision:

- alliance changes between major film producers and retail distributors and

- Sony's decision to include a Blu-ray player in the PlayStation 3 video game console.

The first BD-ROM players appeared in June 2006, along with several movie titles released in the new format. The first releases used MPEG-2 video compression, as in DVD. In September 2006, the first releases, using the newer video codecs VC-1 and MPEG-4 AVC, were presented. The first movies that used a dual-layer Blu-ray disc (of a 50 GB storage capacity) came out in October 2006. In July 2006, Sony released the first mass consumption Blu-ray disc device that supported rewritable discs for computers. It could record on single and dual-layer BD-R and BD-RE discs.

The Blu-ray standard is covered by several patents belonging to various companies. In 2010, the BD4C licensing group formed by Mitsubishi, Thomson, Toshiba and Warner Bros started licensing their patents describing procedures that are essential for the production and distribution of Blu-ray discs.

The name Blu-ray resulted from the use of a blue-violet laser to record and read data. The letter "e" in blu was deliberately omitted, so that the Blu-ray term could be registered as a trademark. Because of the use of blue laser, which has a shorter wave-length (405 nm), substantially more data can be stored in a Blu-ray disc compared to a DVD, which uses a red laser (of 650 nm). A dual layer Blu-ray disc can store 50 GB, almost six times the capacity of a dual-layer DVD.

Blu-ray can store video encoded in MPEG-2, MPEG-4 and VC1. The supported video resolutions are up to 1080p. Many such movies in Blu-ray format are already available in the market. It takes about 14 GB to store one hour of HD video, which amounts to thirteen hours of standard video. Blu-ray discs support the multichannel 5.1 or 7.1 surround audio standards.

Most Blu-ray disc players use 24p (24 frames per second) True Cinema technology. In video technology, 24p refers to a video format that really operates at 24 fps (or formally at 23.976 fps, when using NTS video equipment) with progressive scanning. Initially, 24p technology was used in non-linear digital film editing. Either NTSC or PAL video processing workflows can be used for 24p material production. The PAL solution is simpler to handle.

## 11.2.1 Blu-ray technology

Blu-ray discs have a higher storage capacity than traditional DVDs, as shown in Figure 11.2.1. They also offer new levels of interactivity. Users can connect to the Internet and directly download subtitles and other interactive movie features. With Blu-ray, the user can:

- record high definition television (HDTV) broadcasts, without any loss of quality,

- randomly access any spot in a movie,

- record a TV program, while watching another disk,

- create playlists,

- process or restructure TV programs already recorded on disk,

- automatically search for empty disc space.

Blu-ray disc was originally designed in several different formats, while DVD and CD started with read-only formats and were only later supported

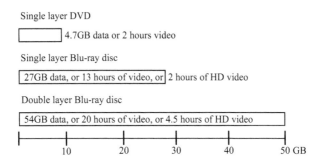

Figure 11.2.1: Optical disc capacity.

by recordable and rewritable formats. Blu-ray supports the following formats:

1) BD-ROM (read only) for pre-recorded content,

2) BD-R (recordable) for PC storage,

3) BD-RW (rewritable) for PC storage,

4) BD-RE (rewritable) for HDTV recording.

Blu-ray disks store digitally encoded video and audio information in spiral tracks defined by grooves, as shown in Figure 11.2.2, that start from the disc center and spiral towards its perimeter. The reflected laser beam is read, in order to play the movie or program that is stored on the DVD. The optical disc capacity increases when grooves become narrower and the pits smaller. The smaller the pits are, the greater the precision of the read-out laser beam should be. The blue laser ray focuses with greater precision than the red laser used in DVD and can read information recorded in pits that have a length of just 0.149 $\mu$. Such pits are more than two times shorter than the pits in a DVD, as shown in Figure 11.2.2. Also, the Blu-ray reduced track pitch from 0.74 $\mu$m to 0.32 $\mu$m. Smaller grooves and smaller pit length enable a Blu-ray disc to store 25 GB of information on a single layer, which is about five times the amount of information that can be stored on a DVD.

Dual-layer discs simply add another recordable layer stacked behind the first one. In this case, the metal surface behind the recordable layer that is closest to the laser source is semi-transparent, allowing the laser beam to pass, when it focuses at a deeper layer.

A Blu-ray disc has about the same thickness (1.1 mm) with that of a DVD (1.2 mm). However, the two disc types store data differently. In a DVD, the data lie between two 0.6 mm polycarbonate layers, as shown in

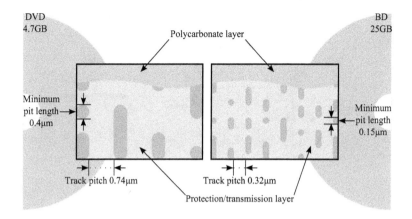

Figure 11.2.2: DVD and BD disc structure.

Figure 11.1.2. The existence of the polycarbonate layer above the data layer may cause *birefringence* (or *double refraction*), due to the fact that the layer beneath may refract the laser into two separate rays. If the angle between the two rays is too large, the data can not be read. Also, if the DVD surface is not exactly flat (and for that reason it is not exactly perpendicular to the beam), the laser beam may be distorted (*disc tilt* problem). All these issues lead to a complicated DVD manufacturing process.

Compared to standard DVD, a Blu-ray disc was initially more vulnerable to scratches, because the data layer in the Blu-ray disc is closer to the disc surface, as shown in Figure 11.2.3. Therefore, the first discs were enclosed in a protective case. However, advances in polymer technology eventually made these cases unnecessary.

Blu-ray Disc overcomes the previously mentioned DVD read-out problems, by placing the data on the top of a 1.1 mm polycarbonate layer, as shown in Figure 11.2.3. Having the data on top, double refraction is avoided and, therefore, readability problems are reduced. Furthermore, since the recording layer is closer to the objective lens of the reading mechanism, the disc tilt problem is virtually eliminated. Because the data are closer to the disc surface, a hard exterior disk layer is placed on top to protect it from scratches, dirt and fingerprints.

The Blu-ray disc design reduces its manufacturing costs. Traditional DVDs are manufactured by bonding the two discs. The recording layer is placed between them. The process must be done very carefully in three steps to avoid double refraction:

1) two polycarbonate substrate discs are fabricated using injection molding,

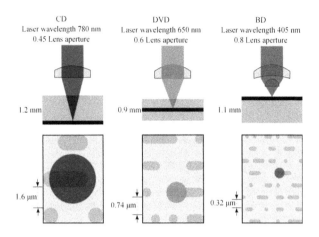

Figure 11.2.3: CD, DVD BD read-out by a laser beam

2) the recording layer is added to one of the disks,

3) the two discs glued together.

In a Blu-ray disc, only a single 1.1 mm thick polycarbonate disc is formed, which reduces costs. This reduction balances the cost of applying the hard protective layer on top of the recording surface, so that the final price is not greater than the price of a regular DVD.

The Blu-ray disc provides higher data transmission rates (36 Mbps), compared to DVD (10 Mbps). A Blu-ray drive can write 25 GB of data in just one and a half hour. Finally, the Blu-ray discs are better equipped, in terms of security, than DVDs. They have a unique ID (based on a secure encryption system) that protects digital content from piracy and copyright infringements.

## 11.3    Video projectors

A *video projector* receives an input video signal and displays the corresponding image on a reflective ("silver") screen, using a light source and a lens system. An example of a digital video projector can be seen in Figure 11.3.1. All video projectors use bright light to project the image on screen. Current projector technology allows various image projection adjustments, e.g., aspect ratio, luminance/contrast change and projection geometry correction. Video projectors are widely used for presentations in conference rooms, classrooms, or in home theaters. Common image resolutions that are supported by various projectors are: SVGA (800 × 600),

Figure 11.3.1: Digital video projector.

XGA ($1024 \times 768$), 720p ($1280 \times 720$) and 1080p ($1920 \times 1080$ pixels). Often a 720p resolution projector is compatible with the 1080p technology (for displaying, e.g., Blu-ray HD-video content) and reproduces such content at reduced resolution.

The projector cost is determined by its image resolution, brightness and noise/contrast characteristics. Most modern projectors provide sufficient illumination for a small screen in a dark room or under controlled illumination conditions (primarily for indoor projections). For larger screens or for indoor daylight projections, the projector requires a brighter light source. Source brightness is measured in *lumens*, which is the unit of measuring luminous flux, i.e., the light power that is emitted by a light source, as perceived by the human eye. One lumen is the amount of light emitted from a source that uniformly radiates luminous intensity of one *candela* (cd) within a solid angle of one *steradian* (sr): $1\ lm = 1\ cd \times 1\ sr$. A common 100 Watt incandescent light bulb emits about 1700 lumens, while an 100 Watt sodium vapor lamp emits approximately 15,000 lumens (i.e., it is about nine times brighter). The *American National Standards Institute* (ANSI) has established a standardized procedure for testing projectors. The luminous flux of projectors that have been tested according to this process is measured in *ANSI lumens*. This allows a precise comparison of the technical specifications of various projectors. The testing specifications are defined in the standard document IT7.215 (1992). Peak lumens is a measure of luminous flux commonly used in CRT video projectors. In this framework, a white area of a size equal to 10 % or 20 % of the total screen area is used, while the rest of the screen remains black. The light power is measured only in nine such areas and, then, the results are averaged and rescaled to provide the peak lumens over the entire projection screen. Projector brightness of 1500 to 2500 ANSI lm or lower is suitable for smaller screens with controlled lighting or low ambient illumination. A brightness between 2500 and 4000 ANSI lm is needed for medium sized screens with a little ambient or dim illumination. A brightness of more than 4000 ANSI lm is suitable for very large screens in large rooms, with no control over illumination conditions (for example, in an auditorium).

*Projector contrast* is expressed as the ratio of the brightness of the darkest (black) and brightest (white) image regions. When the contrast ratio is high, video images and graphics look clear and vivid. Contrast ratios between 1500:1 and 2000:1 are considered good, whereas contrast ratios above 2000:1 are excellent. ANSI contrast measurements are very reliable.

*Color reproduction* during projection is very important as well. It is typically related to the color depth (24/36 bits per pixel) and other technical projector characteristics. Good projectors provide natural color tones, good color reproduction in very bright/dark image regions and color stability over time.

3DTV content projection is a plus offered by good video projectors. 3DTV content viewing is more comfortable using video projectors/screens, rather than monitors, since the display screen is much larger. This results in better quality of experience.

Finally, projector weight and portability are very important factors in certain market sectors, e.g., in trade shows. In such cases, screen portability can help as well.

The size of the display screen is important: because the luminous flux does not change, as the screen size increases, the perceived image brightness decreases. The typical screen sizes are measured in inches along the screen diagonal, ignoring the fact that larger screens require more light (proportional to the screen surface and not to the length of its diagonal). An increase of the screen diagonal length by 25 % will reduce the mean image brightness by 35 %. A diagonal length increase by 41 % would reduce the image brightness by half the original brightness.

## 11.3.1   Video projection technologies

CRT projectors use *Cathode Ray Tubes* (CRT), one for each red, blue and green channel. They require little maintenance, unlike projectors using expensive lamps that must be replaced periodically, because they burn out. CRT projectors are based on a rather old technology and cease to be popular, because of their big size that renders them rather inappropriate for home theater use. However, they can support the largest screen size for a given projector price.

LCD projectors use LCD light valve polysilicon panels for projection. A prism splits the light source illumination and directs it to these three panels, one for each RGB channel. The gated panels are controlled electronically, so that certain RGB channel pixels are open or blocked. The red, green and blue beams are recombined by a lens to reproduce the color video on screen. It is a simple, inexpensive projection technology, which is common for home theater and business use. The most common problem in LCD projectors is the *Screen Door Effect* (SDE): since the fine lines separating the panel light valves (pixels) are also projected on screen, we perceive the video as being viewed through a mosquito screen or mesh. Therefore, fine details, e.g., the optical texture of grass on a soccer field seems blurred. Recent progress has minimized this problem. Other projectors (e.g., CRT ones) do not suffer from this problem.

*Digital Light Processing* (DLP) projectors employ tiny electronic mirrors laid out in a grid on a semiconductor chip to perform image projection. This technology is commonly known as *Digital Micro-mirror Device* (DMD) and was developed by Texas Instruments. The micro-mirror chip has the same resolution as the displayed image. The micro-mirrors can be controlled to reflect to the lens or not. The speed of this on/off operation can produce gray scale tones. There are single and triple DMD projector versions. In the case of a three DMD chip projector, a prism directs the light of a metal-halide lamp to three DMD chips. The light is then recombined using a lens. In the case of an one DMD chip projector, color image projection is performed by using a color spinning wheel, placed between the light source and the DMD chip. Most color wheels consist of red, green, blue and, sometimes, blank regions. Some others have also yellow regions, or regions that correspond to all six primary positive and negative colors (red, green, blue, cyan, yellow and magenta).

The most common problem with one DMD projection is a visible "rainbow" (visible color separation), perceived by some people when moving their eyes. The so-called *Rainbow Effect* (RBE) is a stroboscopic phenomenon that forces some people to see red, green and blue flashes. It is due to the way the human eye and brain perceive moving objects displayed using a wheel of colored filters spinning at high speed. This effect is mainly a problem in video, rather than in static slide projection. It is more visible, when white areas are moving quickly over a very dark background or vice versa. The presence of white or gray tones are necessary to have a full perception of this effect. It affects only a small percentage of viewers. However, some people (about 5 % of the general population) are very sensitive to this phenomenon. The three DMD system does not suffer from this effect. Modern DLP projectors with higher wheel spinning speed (2× or 4×) and optimized color wheels have minimized this phenomenon. DLP projectors are also used in rear projection TV screens.

Finally, there is another projection technology called *Liquid Crystal on Silicon* (LCOS), which is a hybrid technology between LCD (transmissive) and DLP (reflective) projector technologies. It uses a reflective CMOS liquid crystal technology chip for light modulation. The liquid crystal cells are overlaid on a reflective substrate and can modulate light reflection. Color video projectors use three LCOS chips. LCOS projectors may use *Light Emitting Diodes* (LEDs) as light source, thus, eliminating the need for replacement bulbs. The *Direct-drive Image Light Amplifier* (D-ILA) projector by JVC is based on LCOS technology.

The typical lifetime of projector lamps, used in both home theater and business projectors, is 2000 or 3000 hours, for full or low power use, respectively. This is the case for traditional high pressure mercury-vapor lamps used in many projectors. Rather expensive xenon lamps are used in some expensive projectors. They usually have a shorter life. Most manufacturers state that the life of a lamp only extends to the point when its brightness is reduced by half and not till they stop functioning altogether.

## 11.3.2   Projection screens

Various types of projection screens exist. *Silver screens* are largely a matter of the past that nowadays only retains its metaphorical meaning. However, silver lenticular screens enjoy a certain popularity in 3D movie projection using polarized light. Metallic screen (e.g., silver or aluminum ones) do not interfere with light polarization and, therefore, are suitable for 3D (stereo TV) content visualization. White matte screens are easy to manufacture and provide very wide viewing angles. Currently, they are very popular.

Pearlescent and glass-beaded screens provide narrower viewing angles and more reflected light. High contrast (gray) screens absorb the ambient illumination and are ideal for high contrast projection in rooms with uncontrollable ambient illumination.

# 11.4   Display monitors/screens

## 11.4.1   LCD displays

*Liquid Crystal Display* (LCD) displays are based on a thin layer of liquid crystals placed between two transparent electrodes and two perpendicularly polarized filters. A backlight source is used to create the image. The light passes through the first polarized filter and becomes polarized by itself. An electrical stimulus changes the orientation of the liquid crystal molecules and, hence, the light polarization passing through the liquid crystal layer. Depending on the controlled light polarization angle, the polarized light may or may not pass through the second filter. Thus, we can control the output image luminance at pixel level, by using a pixel-level LCD activation in a multiplexed way. *Thin Film Transistor* (TFT) uses an active matrix of transistors (one transistor per pixel) to control better pixel brightness. Color LCD display can be obtained by using a set of additional RGB filters. Thus, each pixel can be split in 3 RGB subpixels that can be controlled independently producing a very large color palette. TFT technology reduces screen panel thickness. Other benefits are weight and energy consumption reduction, compared to other display types. LCD displays are used either as computer or TV monitor or both.

LCD technology is very old. In 1888, botanist Freidrich Reinitzer discovered the liquid crystals and, in 1890, he began to produce the first synthetic liquid crystals. In the 1950s, new materials were developed that made LCD manufacturing possible. In 1967, the wet *Twisted Nematic* (TN) crystals were discovered and the first functional LCD screen was manufactured. In 1979, the first color LCD screen was produced that used TFT technology. The first commercial LCD color TV screen appeared in 1985. Its display size was 2 inches. Now they are LCD screens with a size of well over 40 inches. Currently, seventh-generation LCD displays were announced by major manufacturers, like Samsung, Sony, LG, Philips and Sharp, having a large LCD panel size, ranging from 40 to 108 inches. Improvements in LCD technology have reduced the technological gap with Plasma displays, allowing producers to offer lighter screens, higher resolution and lower power consumption. LCD TVs are now more competitive against Plasma TVs on the market. The LCD displays now outnumber Plasma ones, particularly in the important display sector of 40 inches and above, which, until recently, was dominated by Plasma screens.

## 11.4.2   Plasma displays

*Plasma Display Panels* (PDP) are flat displays commonly used in large TV sets (over 37 inches or 940 mm). In such displays, many tiny cells, located between two glass panels hold a mixture of noble gases (neon and xenon) and a very small amount of mercury. The gas is electrically excited into plasma, which then excites mercury and, finally, the phosphorus atoms, which are painted at the interior of cell surface, to emit light. Plasma displays are often confused with LCD ones, which use a very different technology.

Plasma video screen is an invention of the University of Illinois at Urbana-Champaign (1964). The original monochrome (orange, green, yellow) screens were very popular in the early seventies, because they required neither memory nor circuitry to update the images. They were abandoned in the late seventies, as semiconductor memory made CRT displays cheaper than Plasma. But the relatively large size and thin body of Plasma screens, made them suitable to be used in reception halls and meeting rooms. Plasma screens were first used as computer terminals in 1981.

Screen sizes have increased with the advent of Plasma screens. Until recently, their much better brightness, faster response time, larger color spectrum and wider viewing angle, in comparison with the competing LCD technology, rendered them as one of the most popular technologies for high definition flat screens. For a long time, LCD technology was considered only to suit to small TV sets and could not compete with Plasma technology in larger screen sizes, especially from 40 inches (100 cm) upwards. Since then, improvements in LCD technology have rather bridged the technology gap. The lower weight, decreasing prices, higher resolution (crucial for HDTV) and, often, lower power consumption of LCD displays made them more competitive with Plasma displays, even for displays larger than 40 inches, where Plasma technology largely dominated.

Plasma displays are bright (1000 lux or more), have a wide color palette and can be manufactured in large panels, up to 380 cm (150 inches) diagonally. They have a very low brightness black level, compared with the rather high brightness black level of an LCD display. The panel thickness is only about 6 cm (2.5 inches), while the total thickness, including electronics, is less than 10 cm (4 inches). Plasma displays use as much power consumption per square meter as CRT screens. The power consumption varies considerably, depending on image content. The luminous scenes consume significantly more energy than the darker ones. The nominal power is typically 400 Watts for a 50 inches (127 cm) screen. Newer models use 250 to 350 Watts for a 50-inch screen, when set to cinema mode. Most Plasma monitors are preset to modes which consume twice this power (approximately 500 - 700 Watts), for household use. The lifetime of the latest generation Plasma displays is estimated at 60,000 hours of actual operation, or 27 years, when operating 6 hours per day. In this time span, the maximum brightness will deteriorate to half of the original one.

## 11.4.3 Rear-projection TVs

DLP *rear-projection* TVs are just a DLP video projector in a box. They are low-cost solutions but, generally speaking, they have high operational costs. Although cheaper than either Plasma or LCD screens in very large sizes (42-50 inches), they are not much cheaper than Plasma screens and definitely not cheaper in the long run. DLP rear-projection TVs use an electric lamp that should be frequently replaced and can cost from 200 to 400 USD. Their life varies, in the range of 6,000-8,000 hours, although it may be considerably less. Eventually, one should buy a lamp every two years or earlier, if they watch TV regularly. In total, a DLP rear-projection

TV may cost twice as much as a Plasma TV, in a time span of five to six years of normal use. Such a TV set can cost three or four times more than a Plasma screen over its life expectancy. Finally, they are bulky and can not be hung on the wall.

As far as the field of view is concerned, DLP rear-projection TVs improve but still do not offer comparable field-of-view to that of Plasma TVs. Although their image quality improves, they lag in image quality against their competitors. Many people complain of visual illusions and image blockiness. Because of all these disadvantages, several TV manufacturers stopped, or plan to stop, the production of DLP rear-projection TV sets.

## 11.4.4 Display monitor technology comparison

A key advantage of Plasma screens is their durability, since the average lifespan of a Plasma TV is 50,000 to 60,000 hours, practically without maintenance. When its brightness will reduce to 50 % of the original one, it is still 2 or 3 times brighter than a normal TV. Another advantage is its wide view field, since a Plasma display can offer a 180 degrees field of view without any image quality loss. Plasma displays are 4 to 5 times brighter than an average TV. Additionally, Plasma screens have great contrast ratio (1000:1 or higher).

Plasma screens have competitive prices: a 42 inch TV Plasma monitors costs about half that of a 40 inches LCD display, although market prices change. They have virtually no time delay in image displays, in contrast to LCD displays. Plasma displays offer very natural colors in image display. Finally, one should mention the following advantages of Plasma screens:

1) They are very thin. A Plasma screen can be hung on a wall and takes up as much space as a picture frame.

2) Almost all Plasma screens have a 16:9 aspect ratio.

3) Many Plasma screens have upgradeable video cards, in order to be compatible with future video standards.

Plasma screens have some disadvantages. They can suffer from the *burn in* phenomenon (image retention), if a static image remains on screen for a long time. For this reason, it is inappropriate to use Plasma displays as computer monitors. If the burn-in phenomenon accidentally occurs, some Plasma screens have a *white flash* function, which reduces the problem (and screen life). Plasma screens are not available in sizes below 37 inches. Most Plasma screens do not have television receivers (tuners), but the expensive models. Some Plasma TVs have cheaper optional low-quality TV receivers. Another disadvantage are *defective pixels*. All major Plasma screen brands have pixel quality policies that can allow one or two dead pixels per screen. These are not observable in a 50-inch display, having more than 983,000 pixels, unless one is in close range in front of the screen. If Plasma screen supports the so-called orbiter operation, it will significantly reduce the likelihood of pixel failure.

The advantages of LCD screens can be summarized as follows:

- They are good for still images and can be used as computer monitors.

- They have quite reasonable prices, especially for smaller models (less than 30 inches).

- Quality monitors have good brightness levels.

- An LCD screen can be hung on a wall and takes about the same space as a picture frame.

- They have a low operating cost per hour.

- They have a long life (30 to 50,000 hours).

- They are called "Green TV", because they are friendly to the eyes, have low power consumption and have a significantly long life.

LCD screens have an inherent time delay when displaying images. This problem can not be surpassed. When an object moves rapidly in a scene to be displayed on an LCD screen, this delay causes an optical illusion. Basically, there is a tendency that similar pixels in the image form uniform pixel groups (blobs), since screen displays can not keep pace with object motion. The new LCD screens have smaller time delays, with fewer optical illusions that, in fact, are not observable, especially on screens smaller than 30 or 35 inches. For larger screens, time delays can sometimes be quite annoying. Another drawback is the poor black level, since the back-light illumination cannot be completely blocked. Therefore, the black areas are rather very dark gray. Even the best LCD monitors have rather narrow viewing angle. When one looks at the screen perpendicularly, the picture looks great. As one moves sideways, the image quality decreases and, eventually, the image disappears. Realistically, in a good LCD TV, the picture must be visible for a viewing angle range of 90 degrees (45 degrees on each side).

There are many LCD screens on the market, but very few have good video processing capabilities. If an LCD screen is manufactured as a computer monitor, it usually has rather poor video display quality. If we want to use an LCD screen as a TV monitor, we should buy a monitor designed for video, rather than an LCD computer screen and a TV tuner. For dual use, it is best to buy an LCD TV with PC input, rather than a LCD computer monitor with a tuner. LCD screens are rather expensive for sizes above 35 inches. An important drawback of the LCD screens is that they may have defective pixels. All major brands have pixel quality policies, which may allow only a few defective pixels. A 20 inch LCD screen has more than 300,000 pixels. Thus, one or two non-functioning pixels are not observable, unless someone is very close to the screen. However, we should note that the computer users are much closer to their LCD computer monitors than to their Plasma (or LCD) TV monitors. Finally, it has been observed that many LCD displays tend to offer a "digital display" look and feel of the image. In such cases, they do not seem to reproduce colors naturally.

# DIGITAL CINEMA

## 12.1 Introduction

Cinema was the last entertainment industry to be embraced by the digital revolution. Until recently, movies were only filmed and reproduced on celluloid film, in more or less the same way movies have been filmed after the introduction of cinematography in the late 19th century. Even today, in several movie theaters, huge machines rotate reels of 35 mm film, projecting the image on the silver screen, in almost the same way, as in the last 50 years.

The digital revolution, which has already transformed the music and home video industries, has already a huge effect in the motion pictures industry. Episode II of Star Wars: "Attack of the Clones" (2002), directed by George Lucas, was the first movie, whose production was exclusively based on digital technology. Thus, a new era has emerged for cinema. The transition to digital cinema already changed cinema industry and will, undoubtedly, continue to do so, since its impact has just started being sensed.

## 12.2    Definition and advantages of digital cinema

*Digital Cinema*, or *D-cinema*, refers to digital technology used in the production, post-production, distribution and projection of motion pictures on screen. However, this definition does not include all aspects of digital cinema. Cinema can be defined as the art of presenting pictures on "the big screen" at a visual and audio quality not usually found in other media, e.g., in television. Cinema is all about visual and audio quality. By designating cinema as "digital", it is implied that its quality is at least that of a 35 mm celluloid film.

In digital cinema, motion pictures and sound are recorded digitally. Computers are used to process movies or even construct entire scenes from scratch, to enhance color and create Visual Effects (VFX), subtitles and titles, as shown in Figure 12.2.1.

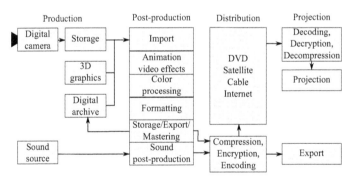

Figure 12.2.1: Workflow in digital cinema.

The final movie version is compressed, encrypted and distributed on hard/optical discs, or via Internet or satellite to movie theaters. For movie projection, instead of using a conventional movie film projector, digital projectors with high luminosity, transfer rate, resolution and color quality can be used.

Digital Cinema is a relatively new term. In the last twenty years other terms have been used as well, such as Digital Film, Digital Cinematography, Electronic Cinema. However, only recently there were new serious attempts under way to substitute movie distribution on celluloid. *Digital Film* (D-Film) mostly refers to the final digital form of the movie. *Digital Cinematography* mostly refers to the use of electronic cameras for filming. *Electronic Cinema* (e-cinema) is a term closely related to Digital Cinema. The main difference between Digital Cinema and Electronic Cinema is that the first one supports only pictures of 2048 × 1080 (2K) pixel resolution or greater. Smaller resolutions fall in the class of Electronic Cinema. Electronic Cinema can develop independently of digital cinema and has proven to be viable in certain applications, e.g., in the production of low cost advertisements. Digital Cinema specifications, in addition to supporting full-length movies, refer to any audiovisual content that may have similar quality requirements.

Digital Cinema confers many advantages in processing, transmitting and projecting cinematographic material. Digital information is much more amenable to processing than analog information. A computer can handle digital image very easily, but can not easily process an analog audiovisual stream. Presentation quality is one of the main characteristics of Digital Cinema, which offers high image resolution and sharpness, excellent audio quality and visual effects that render spectators' experience unique and exciting. Digital data files allow for new faster, easier and more economic digital movie distribution methods, such as Internet, cable or satellite distribution. Digital technology makes motion picture distribution safer against piracy, by allowing digital file encryption and subsequent decryption in the movie theater only by legitimate users, who posses the appropriate decoding keys. Digital cinema also allows for the presentation of new forms of content at movie theaters. Sporting events, education, live or recorded music concerts or cultural events, such as opera or theatrical plays create new audiences.

## 12.3   Digital cinema standardization efforts

The *Society of Motion Picture and Television Engineers* (SMPTE) convened the DC28 Technology Committee in early 2000, in order to discuss the many issues introduced by the full adoption of digital cinema and to produce its application guidelines and recommended practices. At more or less the same time, the *Digital Cinema Initiatives* (DCI) consortium was formed by the most important Hollywood studios. DCI operates together with the National Association of Theater Owners (NATO) and the DC28

Committee, to establish an open set of digital cinematographic standards, which ensure a uniformly high level of technical performance, reliability and quality control in digital cinema. The *European Digital Cinema Forum* (EDCF) was formed in 2001 in Stockholm, in order to encourage the development and application of Digital Cinema in Europe. EDCF communicates with other related organizations to help adopting appropriate global standards for Electronic and Digital Cinema, but does not produce any specifications by itself. EDCF is interested in mastering, image compression, transport delivery, security, theater systems, audio, acoustics, projection and server systems for Digital Cinema.

In Germany, four Fraunhofer research institutes have joined forces to form the Fraunhofer Digital Cinema Alliance, aimed at developing future digital cinema technologies. In France, the French National Organization for Standardization (AFNOR) has published quality requirements on image file resolution, which are fully compatible with DCI standards. In Japan, the Digital Cinema Consortium of Japan (DCCJ) is a non-profit organization, which contributes to the development, testing and evaluation of high quality digital cinema standards and their infrastructure. DCCJ aims are:

- to collect information and studies on digital cinema technology status and future trends, in order to encourage the use of digital cinema,

- to communicate with other relevant organizations, in order to aid the establishment of global digital cinema standards,

- to provide technical support to users, so that they can set up a digital cinema system,

- to support producers in the creation, distribution and presentation of digital movies.

## 12.4   DCI technical standards

DCI has defined very detailed and comprehensive digital cinema specifications as early as of 2005 and has updated them since then (version 1.2). DCI specifications are internationally used as digital cinema standards. Basic DCI specifications cover picture compression, audio/acoustics, text, transmission and encryption.

Digital image size must be either 2K or 4K, corresponding to 2048 × 1556 pixel (actually 3 Mpixel) and 4096 × 3112 pixel (actually 12 Mpixel) image resolutions, respectively. Such resolutions correspond to a 35 mm celluloid film frame scan and to an aspect ratio of 4:3. However, film scanning is not necessary in digital cinema. Therefore, 2K and 4K are defined as 2048 × 1080 pixel (actually 2.2 Mpixel) and 4096 × 2160 pixel (actually 8.8 Mpixel) resolutions, respectively, and correspond to a 16:9 aspect ratio, as shown in Figure 12.4.1. For comparison with digital television, SD TV resolution is 720 × 576 pixels (actually 0.4 Mpixels), at an aspect ratio of 4:3, while HD TV resolution is 1920 × 1080 pixels (actually 2 Mpixels), at an aspect ratio of 16:9.

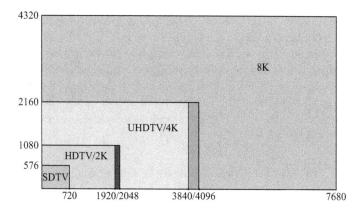

Figure 12.4.1: SDTV, HDTV, 2K, 4K, UHDTV and 8K image resolutions.

"Spiderman 3" and "Ocean's 13" were the first movies produced in 4K definition. For 2K pictures, the frame rate should be 24 or 48 fps (frames per second), while for 4K pictures the frame rate should be 24 fps. Each pixel has 36 bits color depth, allowing 12 bits for each color coordinate and a palette of $2^{36}$ (68,719,476,736) colors.

The recommended image compression standard is JPEG 2000 (.JP2) and the maximal data rate is 250 Mbps. JPEG 2000 has been standardized by the *Joint Photographic Experts Group* (JPEG) of the International Organization for Standardization (ISO) and has been published as ISO 15444-1 standard. JPEG 2000 uses a wavelet-based image compression technique, which does not require image division in blocks, as the popular JPEG does. Therefore, it yields fewer blocking artifacts. Additionally, it conveys 20% better image compression, at significantly higher image quality. The main benefits of JPEG 2000 are:

- support of lossless and lossy compression in a single coder-decoder,

- multiple aspect ratios and resolutions,

- intra-frame coding, which does not require motion estimation and compensation,

- scalable image reproduction. A low resolution image version can be shown after the reception of a small part of the image file and can be enhanced progressively, after receiving more data. The first layer which can be transmitted and displayed, corresponds to the image background, which is, usually, its least important part.

Concerning audio, its bit depth is 24 bits/sample and its sampling frequency is either 48 kHz or 96 kHz. In audio reproduction at 24 fps, there are 2000 audio samples per frame for 48 kHz and 4000 audio samples per frame for 96 kHz. In audio reproduction at 48 fps, there are 1000 audio samples per frame for 48 kHz and 2000 audio samples per frame for 96 kHz. An audio system for theaters must have the capability to alter the sampling rate, when needed. The produced digital audio should support 16 full bandwidth channels. The general description of the first 8 channels is given in Table 12.4.1.

Table 12.4.1: Audio channel use in digital cinema.

| Pair/Channel | Channel No | Name | Description |
|---|---|---|---|
| 1/1 | 1 | L/Left | Front left loudspeaker |
| 1/2 | 2 | R/Right | Front right loudspeaker |
| 2/1 | 3 | C/Center | Center loudspeaker |
| 2/2 | 4 | LFE/Screen | Subwoofer |
| 3/1 | 5 | Ls/Left Surround | Surround left loudspeaker |
| 3/2 | 6 | Rs/Right Surround | Surround right loudspeaker |
| 4/1 | 7 | Lc/Left Center | Back left loudspeaker |
| 4/2 | 8 | Rc/Right Center | Back right loudspeaker |
| 5/1, 5/2, 6/1, 6/2, 7/1 | 9-16 | | Unused |

The user-defined channels can contain an alternative language, commentary, etc. Audio files should follow the *Broadcast Wave Format* (BWF). BWF is an audio standard developed as a successor to WAV by the *European Broadcasting Union* (EBU). It supports file metadata to facilitate the exchange of audio data among various computer platforms and applications. These metadata are stored as extended parts of the standard WAV digital audio file header.

Concerning text, subtitles and commentaries, when available, they can be of the following forms:

- Text burned in the digital cinema image files.

- Subpictures. They are intended for the complementary transmission of visual data (usually of subtitles) in a motion picture and have been designed for a graphical overlay on the main image of a motion picture. The subpicture standard is a binary image file (bitmap) having *Portable Network Graphics* (PNG), ISO/IEC 15948:2004 format. Its resolution is the same with the resolution of the digital motion picture.

- Text (usually subtitles) and a presentation way, so that it can:

  1) be shown in a certain font (time-stamped text, textual information which can be shown at predefined times) and be overlaid to the main image by the central theater server, or the inline processor or the digital cinema projector;

  2) be displayed in LED subtitling screens, driven by a subtitle processor receiving data from the digital cinema central server;

  3) be shown in separate projection systems, driven by a subtitle processor.

Concerning transmission, the final composition shall be compressed, encrypted and packaged to form the *Digital Cinema Package* (DCP), using *Material Exchange Format* (MXF) and the *Extensible Markup Language*

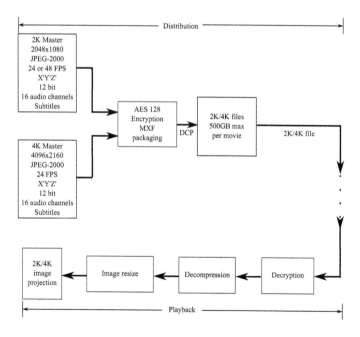

Figure 12.4.2: Digital cinema system based on DCI specifications.

(XML). MXF is a container format, which supports a number of separate information streams, encoded by a variety of codes. Encryption uses *Advanced Encryption Standard* (AES) 128 standard, which receives an 128 bit text fragment for encoding and produces a corresponding 128 bit encrypted text (ciphertext). AES 128 encoding uses a secret key. Generated keys are distributed using the so-called *Key Delivery Message* (KDM). Decoding is similar to encoding.

The Digital cinema system structure following the DCI standards is shown in Figure 12.4.2. This system uses a hierarchical image structure with 2K and 4K image resolutions.

## 12.5  Audio and picture production

Movie production includes audio and picture recording. An example of digital audio recording equipment is shown in Figure 12.5.1. They produce BWF audio files and are widely used for motion picture and television productions. They use surround microphones to record 3D audio. A significant advantage of nonlinear digital recording instruments is their ability to transfer recordings much faster than real time, by means of Firewire or *Universal Serial Bus* (USB) connections.

Either 35 mm (24 mm × 18 mm) celluloid cameras or HD digital cameras can be used for picture recording. Digital Cinema cameras (*DC-cameras*) have been already developed supporting 2K or 4K image resolution. They were designed to give the same style and feel, compared to traditional film cameras. These cameras have high-quality cinematographic lenses and sensors. An image sensor chip with a mosaic filter has replaced film. They have the same optical characteristics with analog cameras and use an optical viewfinder, as shown in Figure 12.5.2.

DC cameras use portable high-capacity and high-transmission rate storage devices, in order to store the huge volume of digital picture data. About

Figure 12.5.1: Nonlinear digital audio recorder (*courtesy of Zaxcom*).

Figure 12.5.2: 2K digital cinema camera (*courtesy of ARRI, Germany*).

20 to 50 GBytes are required for recording individual scenes. A complete uncompressed 2K movie requires up to 20 TByte. Much more TByte are required for a 4K movie, where each second of picture recording produces about 1 GB of data.

## 12.6 Digital cinema post-production

If a 35 mm celluloid film camera has been used, the original camera negative has to be scanned using a film scanner, such as Imager HSX by Imagica and Arriscan by ARRI, or higher resolution Telecine equipment, such as URSA by Cintel International and Spirit by Thompson. Movies are usually scanned in *Digital Picture Exchange* (DPX) files, which is an SMTPE standard, in 2K or 4K resolution, possibly with simultaneous color adjustment. A (constantly reducing) number of current cinematographic productions are still performed this way. Generally speaking, the artistic world has been reluctant to fully migrate to direct digital recording. Data files are adjusted appropriately and an output file is produced, called *Digital Source Master* (DSM) of the movie.

DSM files can be converted to a *Digital Cinema Distribution Master* (DCDM) file or a film duplication master or a home video masters or an archive master file. The DCDM workflow is shown in Figure 12.6.1. DCDM contains all digital material required for playback and includes image/audio information, subtitles, comments, animations, optical and sound effects, etc. Audio, image and text conform to the DCI standards. DCDM files can be directly played by the media playback equipment (e.g., projector and sound system) for projection quality control, or for synchronization and composition integration. *Composition* refers to all content and metadata required for a movie, trailer or advertisement projection. The mastering procedure includes image compression, encryption and packaging.

DCDM files are compressed using the JPEG 2000 standard for picture

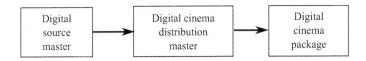

Figure 12.6.1: DCDM workflow.

coding. Compressed movies are encrypted using the AES 128 encryption standard and packaged using the MXF and XML standards to form the *Digital Cinema Package* (DCP), as shown in Figure 12.6.1. DCP is simply a set of MXF files comprising of the audiovisual content and a set of XML files, containing metadata for each single file and dictating the playback sequence. Each distribution reel contains the track files, which may be images, audio, subtitles or any other multimedia data and/or metadata tracks. For reproduction, a *Composition PlayList* (CPL) is created, which prescribes the sequence of the DCP reels and contains all data and metadata required for a unified presentation of a movie, a trailer or an advertisement. It consists of one or more reels. The encrypted content can be digitally signed, so that any composition playlist modification can be detected. There is a separate composition playlist for every movie version or language version. A DCP for a full length movie with English sound and Greek/French subtitles shall contain two separate composition playlists, as shown in Figure 12.6.2.

Conversion to DCDM, mastering and packaging are complex procedures and they are performed in a Digital Cinema Lab (DCL). DCL equipment may include:

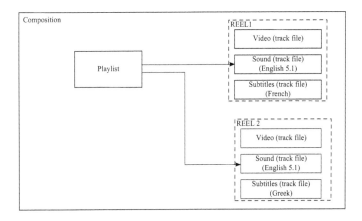

Figure 12.6.2: Composition playlist structure

- mastering workstations used for JPEG 2000 compression, encoding, packaging and encryption,

- computer infrastructure, such as file servers, high capacity storage devices, fast video and sound processors, networked computer systems,

- audiovisual content control and projection tools, such as computer monitors, digital projectors and audio control instruments,

- software for color correction, image processing, visual effects and image restoration, such as Film Master by Digital Vision, Photoshop and Premiere by Adobe, 3D Studio Max, Smoke, Flame and Maya by Autodesk, Final Cut by Apple, Boujou by 2d3 and MatchMover by Realviz and Avid tools.

- production and post-production tools (digital cinema cameras, film scanners, video devices, DVD authoring tools, film copy devices, media filing systems).

## 12.7 Digital cinema distribution

DCP files are conveyed to theaters using either physical media, such as optical disks (DVD, Blu-Ray), hard disks, or electronically, via satellite or a terrestrial broadband network. Decryption keys are provided separately, as a part of a *Key Delivery Message* (KDM), which is separately sent to each theater. Technicolor, Deluxe, XDC, Access Integrated Technologies, Microspace, Communications Corporation, Kodak, DTS, Ascent Media, Dolby and Arts Alliance Media are involved in digital cinema distribution.

The use of physical media to transfer DCP files, efficiently replaces one physical medium (film) with another one (disk). DCP file delivery from studio to theater may last several days. Furthermore, there may be theaters that will try to cut their costs by pirating used physical media. Electronic distribution greatly reduces transmission cost and time. Satellite distribution requires an antenna, which is typically larger than the antenna of a regular home receiver. DCP files can be transmitted directly by satellite to many theaters anywhere in the world. The recommended terrestrial broadband network can be the optical fiber one, because it delivers the required speed. Regular PSTN lines (e.g., ADSL) do not, currently, provide a satisfactory transmission rate. In contrast to satellite, terrestrial networks allow point to point transmission, which means that only the intended recipients receive the DCP files. In electronic distribution, data files can be stored and forwarded, whenever it is required.

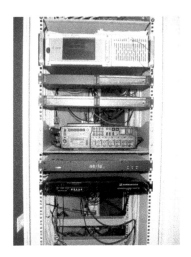

Figure 12.8.1: Projector and audio computers inside a digital cinema projection room (*courtesy of the Science Center and Technology Museum "NOESIS"*).

## 12.8    Digital movie playback in theaters

Theaters receive the DCP files and the decryption key and use them to reconstruct the DCDM files, which include all image, audio and text files of a cinematographic composition. The theater system for digital cinema presentation is divided into the *Playback System*, the *Projection System*, the *Audio System* and the *Theater Management System* (TMS), also called *Screen Management System* (SMS). The playback system includes the storage unit and the Media Block, which can be physically together, or separated. The projection system includes image projectors. The audio system includes an audio processor and a sound box. Some of these playback devices, such as the projector and the sound devices, may be in the same safety box. In multiplex theaters, theater systems must provide multiscreen functionalities.

A *playback file server* stores DCP files for eventual playback. The file servers can be near each screen or centrally located. In the second case, all content is centrally stored and feeds a multiscreen system. A combination of central and local storage may be the best solution for multiscreen systems. The storage system must be fault-tolerant. If a hard disk fails, the system must keep on with the playback, without interruptions. The cinema playback file server must not be confused with simple video servers. According to DCI standards, playback file servers must support a flow of

307 Mbps or higher for compressed image, uncompressed audio and text data and must have high enough capacity to allow for continuous digital cinema playback. Playback file servers use the composition playlist for data synchronization. The stored content is AES encrypted. Decrypted data are never stored in the storage system. Therefore, there is no danger of illegal copying.

Figure 12.8.2: Audio rack inside a digital cinema projection room (*courtesy of the Science Center and Technology Museum "NOESIS"*).

The *Media Block* is a device or a group of devices, which convert the packed, compressed and encrypted cinema data to synchronized raw image, audio and text in real time. The movie content can reach the Media Block completely unpacked or partially packed, depending on the employed storage method. Media Block uses the decryption key to perform content decryption and JPEG 2000 decoders for image decompression. If the Media Block and the projection system are not physically in the same safety box, then the Media Block must convey data via a *Link Decryptor Block* to the projection system. Text information can be displayed using either an alpha channel (a mask that controls image transparency), or an overlaid subpicture. In case of time-stamped text, a corresponding text renderer can be used. Alternatively, these tools can be integrated in the image projector. A Media Block should sustain a data rate of 10 Gbps. It should also be interconnected with the rest of the theater system at three levels. The first level is needed for accessing the packed digital cinema content. The second level is the raw output to the projector subsystem, the audio processor or any extra devices. The third level is the Media Block playback

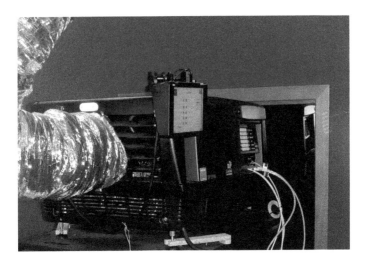

Figure 12.8.3: Digital cinema projector (*courtesy of the Science Center and Technology Museum "NOESIS"*).

subsystem control.

The *Projection System* converts the digital picture information to light, which is projected on screen. A projection system can support many interfaces and various digital cinema architectures. In case the Media Block is installed on the projector, then all of the content is forwarded through a single data interface. When the Media Block is external to the projector, then the appropriate Link Decryption Block is needed for the projector interface. Alternative content may originate from an external interface, even if the Media Block is installed in the projector. In addition to the main image, a projection system may also project text and still images on screen. This requires additional interfaces from the Media Block, in case it is not installed in the projector. Two major technologies are used in digital cinema projectors, namely *Digital Light Processing* (DLP) and *Digital-Image Light Amplifier* (D-ILA). An example is shown in Figure 12.8.3.

DLP has three basic benefits, compared to alternative existing projection technologies:

- it allows high quality color or monochrome image projection without noise,

- it is more efficient than other alternatives (e.g., LCD technology) because the Digital Micromirror Device (DMD) used in DLP does not require polarized light,

- the dense location of micromirrors produces images at the highest perceivable image resolution.

D-ILA has other benefits:

- it allows maximal pixel density and supports high image resolutions,

- it allows powerful light emission, even at high resolutions,

- it provides high image contrast.

The audio system receives uncompressed digital sound from the Media Block, converts it to analog and directs it to the appropriate sound box, which consists of loudspeakers and a subwoofer. Sixteen channels are provided for audio playback and 5.1 and 7.1 surround audio formats are supported. An audio processor provides the digital audio to analog conversion. In addition, it may provide an intermediate program or music. The main interface of an audio system receives the digital sound delivered by the Media Block to the cinematographic audio processor. Other interfaces refer to status and control information.

In a digital cinema system, each theater must have a single *Screen* (or theater) *Management System* (SMS). It creates a show playlist from individual playlists and can exchange it as a file with other screen management systems. Multiple show playlists are allowed. An example is shown in Figure 12.8.4. The screen management system provides an interface to the user for local theater control, such as starting, ending and editing a show playlist. It may control and run diagnostic tests for theater equipment and convey appropriate information to the theater technical manager. An example of events in such a system is shown in Table 12.8.1. The screen management system may be local or remote and it may use one computer or a computer network.

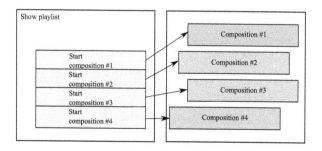

Figure 12.8.4: Digital cinema show playlist.

Table 12.8.1: Events in a theater management system.

| SMS Events | SMS Action |
|---|---|
| Corrupted Composition Playlist Received | Validate received DCP |
| Movie prepped for playback is modified | Check prepped movie against CPL |
| Movie playback queries | Show playlists and execution statistics |

## 12.9   The future of digital cinema

Digital cinema is based on a modular architecture, which allows component replacement or upgrade in the future, without a complete system replacement. Its hardware and software is designed to be easily upgraded, as progress is made in relevant digital cinema technologies.

Concerning the production procedure, digital cinema camera technology is geared to high-resolution, high-speed and multicamera (three-dimensional image) recording. Scientists work on new omnidirectional camera systems, which will be able to record live panoramic images with an angle of almost 150° degrees and a resolution of up to 8K. This system will have a structured format, which will allow for the installation of up to 12 cameras. This means that even 360° images could be produced. Researchers work on hybrid high-resolution high-speed and low-cost cameras, which will convey information for the entire three-dimensional space. The prospect is three-dimensional vision and real three-dimensional digital cinema (holographic) projections, to be discussed in Chapter 13. Other significant research fields are real three-dimensional sound recording and high speed/capacity storage.

In post-production, research is performed to produce more efficient and low cost picture and audio processing tools. This means workflow and management improvement and huge data file handling. The existing production meta-tools are not well adapted to large data quantities that follow, e.g., the 4K standard. In addition to this, there is need for higher capacity and faster data storage.

Additionally, new standardized physical media are needed for data transfer to theaters. Digital technology creates new business models for cinemas, such as *Cinema on Demand* (CoD), where the cinema operator may search and acquire movies on a 24 hour basis, without having to wait for regular movie distributions. Consequently, cinema operators can gain flexibility in programming their shows, something they had never had before.

As far as playback is concerned, there is a need to reduce the projector cost and also to improve flat screen, as well as three-dimensional display technologies. Scientists work on high-resolution multiprojection systems, where movies can even be projected on convex surfaces and can be used for special events, e.g., in theme parks and conferences. New forms of image and audio playback technologies are invented, e.g., three-dimensional holography or real three-dimensional sound with *wave field synthesis*, which create an optimal audiovisual ambience for each member in a cinema audience. Such systems give a natural spatial audio impression to the audience in virtually the entire auditorium, since the audio playback system produces natural sound for each seat in the theater.

# 13

# THREE-DIMENSIONAL

# DIGITAL TELEVISION

## 13.1 Introduction

*3D television* (3DTV) provides both visual and depth perception to the viewers, enabling them to have a feeling of the 3D structure of the displayed scene. Typically, stereo imaging can be used to this end (stereo TV), displaying a left and right video channel. An example of such an image pair can be shown in Figure 13.1.1. *Three-dimensional* (3D) *imaging* and display techniques first appeared almost simultaneously with classical photography (*two-dimensional imaging*). TV was almost immediately fol-

Figure 13.1.1: Stereo frame pair (*courtesy of the 3DTVS FP7 project*).

lowed by experimental stereoscopic three-dimensional television (3DTV).
The idea of three-dimensional display has a long and interesting history,
going back to the three-dimensional stereoscopic photographs of the '50s,
to the 3D movies and holography of the '60s and '70s and extends to
current technologies, notably computer graphics and virtual reality. The
demand for three-dimensional display is steadily growing and becoming
more important, as its applications grow, e.g., in scientific and medical
imaging, games and commercial (e.g., sports) television. Various three-
dimensional display methods were presented in the last decades, but none
was capable enough to create a massive market. All developed technologies
have their individual characteristics, their advantages and disadvantages.
Generally speaking, the interest in all forms of three-dimensional television has recently grown, both in the research community, as well as in the
entertainment business. This is already manifested through commercially
successful 3D movies, like Avatar and Up, the release of new movie titles in
3D DVD and Blu-ray and the start of 3DTV broadcasting. An impressive
increase of 3D audiovisual content is expected in the near future, either
produced professionally or user-provided in social media platforms. 3DTV
delivers stereoscopic video at home, while 3D cinema is typically seen in
theaters. 3DTV broadcasting of sports events using satellite/terrestrial
HDTV networks started in 2002 in Japan and Korea. As early as 2004,
real-time capturing and broadcasting of multi-view video started being
implemented. So far a multitude of international TV channels, including
major broadcasters, like Sky 3D, ESPN 3D, Canal+ 3D and 3net provide 3DTV services. Many more broadcasters are expected to offer 3DTV
broadcasting soon. The 2012 Olympics were also broadcasted in 3DTV.

A complete 3DTV system normally has the following building blocks:
*3DTV image capture*, *post-production*, *representation*, *compression*, *transmission* and *rendering* (visualization), as shown in Figure 13.1.2. Currently,
3DTV systems capture, broadcast and display stereo video, consisting of
a left and a right video channel. However, three-dimensional scenes can
be captured in many ways, e.g., by using several cameras simultaneously

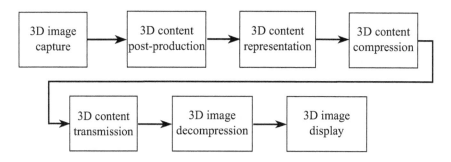

Figure 13.1.2: 3DTV chain.

(*multiview imaging*). Such multiview images are shown in Figure 13.1.3. Furthermore, it is desirable to allow various ways of rendering the three-dimensional content, depending on the maturity of the three-dimensional screen technology. For this reason, scene capture and rendering should be independent in future 3DTV: scene information, after being acquired, should be converted to appropriate scene representations, by means of computer vision techniques. Visual rendering shall be performed using computer graphics methods. The viewer shall interact with the intermediate scene representations, e.g., by changing the view angle. Concerning compression, it is reasonable to extend the established single-view video compression techniques to *multiview video compression*, exploiting the intrinsic spatial redundancy of the content produced by several cameras for the same scene. Three-dimensional video encoding attracts great research interest and leads to standardization activities in the context of ISO-MPEG. Digital transmission of three-dimensional content using streaming techniques is another active research field. As far as visualization is concerned, various methods have been developed and used, such as autostereoscopy, holography and volumetric display.

Figure 13.1.3: Three views of a scene (*courtesy of the i3DPost FP7 project and CVSSP, University of Surrey, UK*).

# 13.2    Three-dimensional image capture

Three-dimensional television starts with the digital capture (recording) of a dynamic real world scene, which contains several moving actors/objects and continues with the conversion of the recorded data to an appropriate representation format. In contrast to conventional television, where only the visual representation (image) of the scene must be recorded, true three-dimensional television usually demands the acquisition of the complete geometrical information about objects in the scene, so that one can view the scene from different view points. The scientific challenges are two-fold: both the three-dimensional scene geometry and the relevant visual information (texture) have to be recorded.

Various technologies have the ability to satisfy the two previously mentioned requirements. It is possible to perform 3D scene recording, using several conventional cameras recording simultaneously (*multi-view imaging*). The simplest way to record a scene is the stereoscopic one, using only two cameras, which capture the same scene from slightly different positions. The two views are stored, transmitted and eventually delivered to the viewer. Typically a set of 2 up to 20 cameras are used in a multi-view capture system. Such camera systems are usually calibrated. The key point in the subsequent 3D scene representation is finding common points of interest (feature points, landmarks) on the various video frames and their transcription to a three-dimensional virtual scene model. Furthermore, it is possible to record a 3D scene with a single video camera. Here, the multi-view system is replaced by one video camera, which records the scene from different view-angles. The basic current limitations of this method is that the recorded scene must be still, or that the objects must be modeled in such a way, so that their three-dimensional geometry can be reconstructed from a single image.

Beyond the use of video cameras, there are other methods for recording three-dimensional information, such as 3D scanning, using structured light. This technique is based on a laser source and an optical detector (camera). The laser source emits a light beam (stripe) on the object surface to be captured and the camera detects the reflected light stripe. The stripe displacements allow the extraction of the 3D object geometry. The main advantage of this technique is the high accuracy of the 3D geometrical information.

## 13.3    3D scene and 3D video representations

The problem of 3D scene representation (or modeling) arises immediately after 3D image capture. The simplest method for 3D scene representation is to use the data we obtain directly from 3D image capture, without extra processing. If two cameras are used, we have the conventional stereo video pair corresponding to the left/right eye, respectively. In this case, the 3D content can be delivered to broadcasters either as a) two separate time-code synchronized files, for the left and the right video sequence, respectively or b) in the side-by-side format, where the right and left channel are downsampled horizontally and are stored in one video frame, thus producing only one stereo video file. However, these two methods provide only implicit 3D scene representations. Their advantage is that they consist of two or more video sequences that can be easily compressed and transmitted using standard video compression methods. They can also be fairly easily displayed in classical 2D and in 3D video displays. If more than two video cameras are used, we obtain multiview video and we use it for 3D scene representation and transmission.

In order to successfully represent the 3D scene geometry from multiview or stereo video in a more advanced way, a camera calibration must be performed, resulting in the estimation of internal and external camera parameters. For camera calibration, a light point source can be used, which moves all over the camera capture volume. Calibration information, like internal and external parameters (position, rotation, lens focal length, etc.) of the cameras are calculated using the recorded video. Automatic camera calibration, performed during the scene capture, is an active research field.

Based on the camera calibration parameters, the position of a three-dimensional point of the scene is associated to its projections in all camera views. Using the image coordinates $p_l, p_r$ of a three dimensional point $P$ in at least two views (two cameras), the inverse problem can easily be solved,

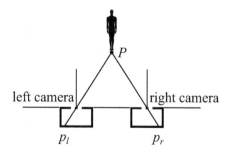

Figure 13.3.1: Determination of the 3D coordinates of point $P$ from its projections $p_l$, $p_r$ on the left and right camera image planes.

(a) (b) (c)

Figure 13.3.2: a) Left channel video frame, b) right channel video frame, c) disparity map (*courtesy of the 3D4YOU FP7 project and the Hertz Heinrich Institute*).

thus determining the three-dimensional coordinates of this point in space, as seen in Figure 13.3.1.

In the first step, *feature points* (landmarks), such as corners, are located in one stereo view, as shown in Figure 13.1.1. In a second step, the position of each fiducial point of the first view is found in the other stereo view, by using *correspondence search* (*feature point matching*) techniques and the local image texture. This correspondence search procedure is quite simplified, because the stereo camera calibration parameters define *epipolar lines* on both views. Landmark correspondence search must be performed only on the epipolar lines. This search provides the so-called *disparity map*, as shown in Figure 13.3.2. Usually, the object surface points that are nearest to the two cameras appear brighter, compared to points that are further away. In a third step, the three-dimensional coordinates of a point in space are determined from its disparity, if image calibration parameters are known. These 3D points can also be tracked and their position can be corrected, resulting in extra reliability in the 3D coordinate calculations. The resulting 3D *point cloud* is the simplest way to represent a 3D scene.

As soon as the three-dimensional coordinates of the scene points have been determined, a three-dimensional model of the object surface can be created, usually by 3D point triangulation. The surface model can be described using a triangular grid, whose vertices are the 3D landmark coordinates. A triangular mesh is shown in Figure 13.3.3.

Alternative representation methods are the polygonal grids, the *B-spline* (NURBS) surfaces and surface models derived by recursive surface subdivision approaches. The latter one, provides a good compromise between non-smooth polygonal grids and NURBS surfaces. Subdivision surfaces allow the representation of arbitrary object topologies and fine surface structures with controllable smoothness.

In the last modeling step, the camera views are reprojected on the three-dimensional model, thus defining its 3D visual appearance, also referred to as *3D model texture*, as shown in Figure 13.3.3b. In advanced systems, the texture of a given 3D surface patch can be derived from multiple views.

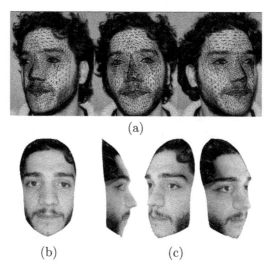

(a)

(b)                    (c)

Figure 13.3.3: a) 3D triangular face grid, b) its texture, c) three different side viewss.

Thus, each object surface patch may have various texture maps, allowing for a more realistic object visualization from different view-angles. Such object models containing both 3D shape and texture information can be stored, e.g., in *Virtual Reality Modeling Language* (VRML) files. A three-dimensional object model can be represented and visualized from any arbitrary viewpoint, using OpenGL or any other 3D graphics visualization software/library.

As the number of available views grows, the explicit three-dimensional information used in modeling geometry can decrease. There are several approaches for 3D object representation, starting from the previously mentioned accurate three-dimensional 3D geometry representation with a single texture, to the multiview object imaging from many view-angles. Depending on the requirements, there is a wide spectrum of three-dimensional scene and object representation techniques, as shown in Figure 13.3.4. They vary in the type and amount of the geometric information used for scene and object modeling. At one end of this spectrum, there are very accurate geometric scene and object models at any time instance, which are produced using computer vision methods. The conventional three-dimensional models that can be visualized by 3D in computer graphics belong to this category. In this case, relatively few views are needed for the representation of the object geometry and texture. At the other end of the spectrum, a very dense visual sampling of the scene view in space and time (and no use of explicit geometrical models) is employed for three-dimensional object representation. The most significant benefit of this approach is the resulting high image quality for real world scene visualization, compared to the quality produced by explicit geometric modeling techniques. Another significant benefit is that it requires a much smaller computation cost for scene visualization, that is independent of scene complexity. In the following, the various 3D object representation methods, shown in Figure 13.3.4, will be concisely presented.

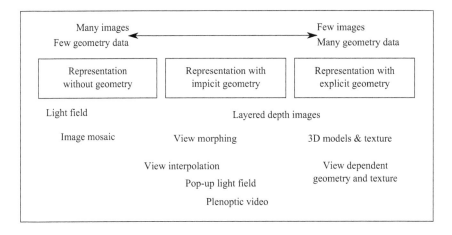

Figure 13.3.4: 3D scene representation taxonomy.

**Light fields.** Proposed in 1996 by Levoy and Hanrahan, they allow free three-dimensional virtual viewpoint motion in a bounded volume. They are based on the assumption that light rays are reflected from the surface of an object, which is enclosed in a bounding box. The system records all light rays leaving one side of the bounding box, by placing a very dense two-dimensional image sampling grid, which is oriented towards the bounding box. The orientation of this grid and its placement are done based on the recording geometry of the capturing cameras. Usually there are two cameras, placed with their axes parallel to each other and positioned very close to each other, to visualize an object from one side. For the visualization of all object sides, six such representations are needed.

**Image mosaicing.** When image mosaicing of an outdoor scene is desired, an outward oriented camera is placed on a horizontal arm, which rotates on a circular trajectory. A series of images is taken along this trajectory, thus creating a panorama of the scene. For this reason, this visualization is also called *panoramic*. Then, using few geometrical information regarding camera position/orientation, it is possible to represent the three-dimensional scene. This approach works well, since there is a redundancy of the recorded images, which overlap spatially on purpose, as shown in Figure 9.7.1.

**View morphing and view interpolation.** In this case, the scene geometry can be assumed to be decomposed in fitting planes and local parallax information. We usually start viewing the scene from specific locations/view angles. If we wish to create a scene view from other locations/view angles, the virtual views are interpolated based on the available true views, used as reference planes, in order to preserve visualization quality. Depth deviations from those of the true scene and from the fitting planes may cause visual distortions. Alternatively, view morphing may be used instead of view interpolation.

**Layered depth maps.** Depth maps confer information on object geometry, as seen from a particular view point. Such a depth image is shown in Figure 13.3.2c. In depth maps, only object points that are visible from the specific view point are visualized. Layered depth images combine depth information from many view points. This is accomplished by appending to each depth image pixel several layers, each containing depth information for surface points, which are located on different planes on the scene along a view line. This way, objects in the front and in the back of the scene are accumulated in the same representation. Thus, the use of additional computer vision methods for the representation of the three-dimensional geometry is avoided.

**View-dependent geometry and texture.** The calculation of three-dimensional object models from real views is not always feasible. For this reason, methods have been suggested, which create intermediate object representations or models, for describing the geometry from each new virtual view. These models can avoid some of the shortcomings of depth map representation. Depth maps can not be used for backward mapping, while the forward visualization of discrete depth values may lead to visual holes. In order to circumvent this problem, the creation of a model, which uses a local grid approximating the scene surface for each view, has been suggested. Using this grid, the color of each pixel is determined based on backward mapping.

## 13.3.1   3DTV video representations

Various approaches can be used to represent and transmit 3D video information. They can be split in two major representation approaches: the ones that use explicitly depth information and the ones that do not. *Conventional Stereo Video* (CSV) is currently the standard way to represent 3D video by two (left/right) video sequences. *Multi View Video* (MVV) contains two or more scene views taken from different viewpoints. If the viewpoints are arranged in a sequential order and were taken at slightly different view positions, then any two consecutive views could form a CSV pair. MVV can feed auto-stereoscopic 3D displays that require more than two stereo views.

More advanced 3DTV formats contain explicit scene depth information, using the previously described depth maps. The *Video-plus-Depth* (V+D) format contains a single video channel and its depth map. Currently, there are cameras that can support V+D format. Other 3D scene views can be derived from V+D information, by using *Depth Image Based Rendering* (DIBR). V+D format allows backwards compatibility to existing 2D receivers and offers easy brightness, contrast and color adjustment by the user. It supports autostereoscopic multi-view displays, from limited viewpoints around the original camera position, by employing DIBR. Instead of using simple depth maps, we can use layered depth maps in the *Layered Depth Video* (LDV) format, where an additional depth layer, containing occluded background information, can handle occlusions during rendering. *Depth Enhanced Stereo* (DES) combines the left/right-eye sequences of classical stereo with additional dense depth maps and achieves better 3D scene rendering results using DIBR. *Multi-View Video-plus-Depth* (MVD) is multiview video with additional dense depth maps for each view. The CSV, V+D, MVV and MVD 3D video formats are illustrated in Figure 13.3.5.

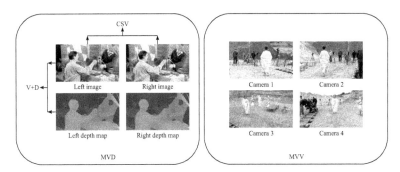

Figure 13.3.5: 3DTV video formats.

# 13.4    3D video content compression

As mentioned in the previous section, there are several 3D scene and video representations. Having specified the 3D representation format, the next step is its efficient compression. There are many different data compression techniques, which correspond to different 3D video content representations. For example, there are various techniques for the compression of three-dimensional grids, depth maps, or for multi-view video compression. The level of maturity for each technique varies and is highly correlated to its age and commercial use.

A basic compression scheme concerns pixel-based visual information, such as stereoscopic and multi-camera video. This compression approach is the oldest one, it is very well developed and has brought up significant innovations. Classical single-view video compression has been intensely studied for many decades. As a result, the latest generation video encoders, such as the H.264/MPEG-4 AVC standard, offer excellent compression performance. Such compression methods have been extended to stereoscopic video. Their commercial use is not as widespread as single-view video compression, but the relevant technology is mature enough.

A significant stereo video compression can be achieved by considering the *binocular suppression theory* for stereo video coding. The perceived binocular quality of a stereo sequence, having different sharpness at the left and right eye views, is rated close to that of the sharper view. Therefore, a stereoscopic video sequence, whose one view has a reduced resolution, could be transmitted at a lower bitrate compared to the full resolution video, while maintaining the same binocular quality. One of the two views can be transmitted at reduced spatio-temporal resolution, resulting in the *Mixed Resolution Format* (MRF).

For stereoscopic video compression, we can use the high spatiotemporal correlation of the visual information provided by the right and left cameras and achieve a satisfactory compression. Its extension to multicamera video compression is relatively new and deserves particular attention. The compression of such data has been intensively studied and, as in the case of stereoscopic video, it employs the high spatiotemporal correlation in the visual information provided by several cameras viewing the same scene. Video compression standards, such as H.264/MPEG-4 AVC, already allow the compression of such data.

Depth map information can be compressed as well. The nature of the dense depth maps is the same with that of two-dimensional images, as seen in Figure 13.3.2c. Therefore, classical image/video compression techniques can be used to this end. However, in this case, there is a margin for further improvement, by using algorithms which exploit the depth data statistics and their (normally) low-frequency spectral characteristics. The scene depth information provided by depth maps can be combined with multiview imaging in order to perform better data compression. The principles of depth data encoding can be extended to cover layered depth maps as well.

Light field encoding is also an interesting research field. Up to now, static light fields have been studied, as has been previously mentioned.

Compression algorithms proposed for such data are of great interest and have similarities to multiview video compression methods.

Three-dimensional mesh data are widely used in computer graphics. For this reason, their compression has been extensively studied in the last decades. However, further improvements are possible, especially for multiresolution and animated polygonal/triangular grids.

# 13.5    3DTV broadcasting

## 13.5.1    3DTV broadcast formats

In the early phase of 3DTV deployment, 3D broadcast pioneers utilized existing HDTV infrastructure as much as possible, in order to deliver stereoscopic 3D content within a conventional HDTV video frame. Thus, they decided to use the so-called *frame-compatible* approach, also called 3DTV *Phase 1* in DVB. This approach has several variations. In the *side-by-side mode*, the left and right frame of the 3D video are downsampled by a factor of two horizontally and are delivered side by side, within the same HDTV video frame. The HDTV receiver at home can relay the 3DTV video unaltered to a 3D display for rendering. The side-by-side mode has the advantages that a) there is no need for a specialized 3D receiver and b) the 3D video compression and broadcasting technology is not specific to the 3D content particularities. Hence, broadcasters can utilize the existing HDTV broadcast infrastructure. With little extra effort, the HDTV receiver could even relay one channel to a classical 2D TV display. The disadvantages of the side-by-side mode is that a) it cannot directly feed a 2D video display and b) it reduces horizontal video resolution by half.

One disadvantage of frame-compatible solutions is the lack of backwards compatibility with 2D displays, which is essential for the business model of many broadcasting channels. Another problem is the reduced 3D video compression performance, since this approach is agnostic to the 3DTV content being broadcasted. This problem is more severe when limited bandwidth channels are used, e.g., DVB-T ones. The newer *service-compatible* approach, called *Phase 2* in DVB, ensures technology compatibility between 2D and 3DTV platforms. Video plus depth data approaches can be used to this end, by transmitting a 2D full resolution HDTV video channel plus additional multiplexed depth information. Such an explicit depth information can consume an additional $10 - 30\%$ transmission bandwidth. In principal, other depth data formats can be used as well. Conventional 2D HDTV receivers discard the depth information and relay the 2D full resolution HDTV channel to a 2D display. A Phase 2 3DTV receiver can relay the entire 3DTV stream (HDTV signal plus additional depth data) to a 3D display.

## 13.5.2  3DTV format standardization

3DTV format standardization started in mid-nineties, when the MPEG committee standardized stereoscopic video compression using the V+D format. MPEG-4 *Animation Framework eXtension* (AFX) framework uses the V+D format and Depth Image Based Rendering (DIBR) for 3D scene visualization, using slight virtual viewpoint variations from the original camera viewpoint. Furthermore, MPEG-C Part 3 container format specifies V+D 3D video content transmission, as shown in Figure 13.5.1. Point cloud and multi texture 3D scene reconstructions are also supported in the MPEG-4 AFX tools.

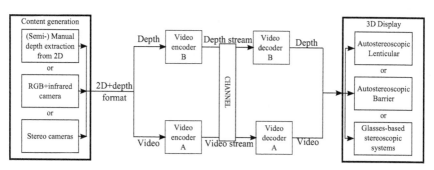

Figure 13.5.1: Video plus depth transmission.

The *Multi-View Coding* (MVC) standard is an extension of MPEG-4 Part 10 (Advanced Video Coding, AVC), towards free viewpoint television and 3D television. MVC enables the construction of bitstreams that represent more than one view of a video scene, by taking into consideration the fact that multiple view redundancies of the same scene improve multiview video compression. The encoder receives several temporally synchronized video streams and generates one bit stream. The decoder receives the bit stream, decodes it and outputs the various video streams. The *Joint Multiview Video Model* (JMVM) was issued in 2008 for testing and evaluating this technology. Two MPEG-4 MVC profiles were developed (2009): *Multiview High Profile* that supports an arbitrary number of views and *Stereo High Profile*, supporting only stereoscopic video. The Multiview Video Coding extensions were completed in 2009.

The previously described Multiview video-plus-depth (MVD) video format is another standardization approach that was developed as a successor to MVC and V+D formats, because advanced 3D video applications, e.g., auto-stereoscopic multiview displays, as well as free viewpoint video were not well supported by existing standards, since they require at the decoder either 3D scene visualization continuity over various viewpoints or a very large number of different output views. MVC does not support visualization continuity and becomes inefficient for large view numbers. The V+D representation only supports a very limited viewpoint continuity around the available original view, since, e.g., occlusion problems increase dramatically in a virtual view, as the virtual viewpoint distances itself from the original camera position. The MVD standard is designed to support these new requirements. MVD encodes multiview video and depth in separate coding streams. It includes metadata for image-based rendering of virtual views from V+D video. The video and the depth sequences are encoded independently, resulting in two bit-streams. A special case of MVD, *Multiple Video-Plus-Depth with 4 Views* (MVD4) format consisting of the four post-produced video streams and the four generated depth streams has been proposed for 3DTV coding. The combined use of MVC coding and MVD4 is an efficient way to implement scalable 3DTV transmission.

*3D Video Coding (3DVC)* is an ongoing MPEG 3D video compression standardization activity that targets a variety of 3D displays, e.g., multiview ones, presenting simultaneously $N$ views (e.g., $N=9$) to the user. For efficiency reasons, only few views (e.g., $K=1,..,3$) are transmitted. For those $K$ views, additional depth data must be provided. At the receiver side, the $N$ views to be displayed are generated from the $K$ transmitted views with depth, by depth-image based rendering.

Finally, *MPEG 3D AudioVisual* (3DAV) format provides another advance in 3DTV compression. It supports user interactivity, e.g., by allowing viewpoint changes, omnidirectional video, interactive stereo video and free viewpoint video.

## 13.5.3   3D video transmission

The determination of the optimal technologies for 3DTV data transmission in real time via communication networks requires thorough investigation of various transmission techniques and their adaptation to the special requirements of this new service. In many cases, it is expected that the three-dimensional video transmission infrastructure will be based on Internet technology and, more specifically, on the Internet Protocol (IP). TCP/IP architecture has proven to be adaptable and succeeded in accommodating the requirements of multimedia communications, as we can conclude from the introduction of IP-based services, which offer audio and/or video communication (voice-over-IP). The transmission of three-dimensional television signal over the TCP/IP protocol appears to be the natural extension of such services. In this setting, the use of proper error detection and correction techniques are very important. If, during transmission, there is loss of three-dimensional geometry information, it can not be readily replaced in a straightforward manner, as is the case with the visual signal errors occurring in single-view television. Another aspect of three-dimensional television, which has no parallel in single view television, is the dependency of the displayed video on the view-angle of the viewer. The displayed video must adapt, when the viewer moves, hence changing his/her view angle. Otherwise, the visualization of the presented scene will look unrealistic. This fact may enforce the transmission of multiple views, thus greatly augmenting the bandwidth requirements. Currently, network-based transmission and delivery methods for multiview video are still under development.

## 13.6   3DTV display techniques

3D display is the last, but most important, element in 3DTV production and delivery chain, because it visually presents the final result of the entire 3DTV chain to the viewer. Therefore, the 3D display quality will be judged directly by the consumers and will determine the overall acceptance of the 3DTV technology. 3D display has a long history, starting in the 20th century with the discovery of stereoscopy and, later on, of holography. Such discoveries, especially stereo vision, were the catalyst, which led to significant developments in stereoscopic and volumetric display methods. Furthermore, developments in virtual reality technologies led the computer and optical industries to the production of novel, better and portable 3D display devices.

The main requirement of a 3D display is depth perception by the viewer, using view disparity. Normally, two slightly different views of the same scene are projected on each eye to create the sense of depth. Wrong view disparity is a frequent reason that creates uncomfortable viewing experience to the viewer and alienates him/her from the scene action. The solution of such *Quality of Experience* (QoE) problems will boost the acceptance of the three-dimensional television in the consumer market. To this end, various questions arise, e.g., whether the viewer wants to watch a show on a table-top 3DTV display device or if he/she prefers to immerse in the 3DTV content. Other important display quality parameters are image resolution, field-of-view width, screen luminance, viewing distance, service to one or more viewers and, of course, device cost. 3DTV display technolo-

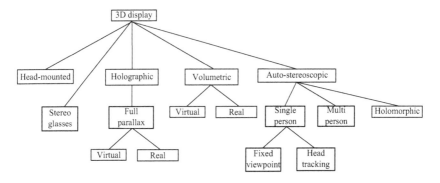

Figure 13.6.1: 3DTV display taxonomies.

gies can be classified in the following categories, as illustrated in Figure 13.6.1: stereoscopic vision glasses, head-mounted displays, holographic displays, volumetric displays and autostereoscopic displays. In the following sections, the pros and cons of each three-dimensional display method are presented in detail.

## 13.6.1   Stereoscopic vision glasses

Stereoscopic vision employing a computer screen displaying both the left and right view and using suitable glasses is the oldest 3D display technology. It is a very popular low cost solution, due to the use of conventional computer screens, with some appropriate display adaptation. Several glass types are used for stereoscopic vision. The central idea of this technology is to use such glasses that allow the left/right eye to see only the left/right view, respectively, when both views are projected on the same screen in a multiplexed way.

**Blue/red glasses.** When wearing a pair of glasses with a red and a blue lens (for the left and right eye, respectively), as seen in Figure 13.6.2 and, simultaneously, presenting the view intended for the left/right eye colored in red/blue color, respectively, on any color display device, each one of the two views is invisible to the other eye. Thus, the desired result of stereoscopic visualization is achieved. However, the visualization colors are quite distorted. Furthermore, when the user removes the glasses from his/her eyes, his/her color perception will be fully restored only after some seconds. Alternatively, other complementary color pairs (e.g., red/green) can be used, leading to similar problems.

**Glasses with oppositely polarized lenses.** The light emitted by a light source, such as the sun or a light bulb, oscillates along all directions

Figure 13.6.2: Blue/red glasses.

perpendicular to its propagation direction. When the light propagates through a polarized lens (or filter), it oscillates only along a direction parallel to the orientation of the lens polarization. This light is called polarized. When it hits a polarized lens, whose polarization axis is perpendicular to incident light polarization, then the light is blocked. Based on this polarization property, when the light being emitted from two projection devices is polarized horizontally and vertically and is presented to the viewer wearing a pair of glasses with horizontal and vertical polarization lenses (Figure 13.6.3), then each eye sees only the view having the respective polarization. Therefore, by projecting appropriate images on two screens emitting horizontal/vertical polarized light and merging the two images in one, with the use of a suitable mirror, it is feasible to achieve stereoscopic vision using glasses with oppositely polarized lenses. The disadvantage of this solution is that the viewer should not rotate his/her head, since the alignment of the polarized lenses to the horizontal/vertical directions is of vital importance for achieving stereoscopic view.

**Liquid crystal display (LCD) shutter glasses.** They are special glasses, whose "lenses" are a pair of electronically controlled LCD light shutters (Figure 13.6.4). These shutters are synchronized with each other, in such a way that, when one is open and allows incident light propagation, the other one is closed and blocks light. When these glasses are synchronized with a screen displaying alternating views for the right and left eye

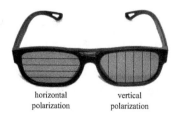

horizontal          vertical
polarization        polarization

Figure 13.6.3: Glasses with opposite polarized lenses.

Figure 13.6.4: LCD shutter glasses.

at a rate of at least 120 Hz, it is possible to achieve color stereoscopic display. When the view alternation is very slow, an intense image flickering is observed, since each eye sees video at half the display refresh rate, hence rendering stereoscopic vision difficult or even impossible. For this reason, the most suitable choice is a screen frame refresh rate that is equal to or higher than 120 Hz (typically 200 Hz). However, few screens can achieve such a refresh rate at high image resolutions.

## 13.6.2   Head-mounted displays

Head-mounted devices, such as binoculars and helmets, put a small screen in front of each eye. Each one of these screens may be fed with the corresponding left/right image and, thus, cause the required sense of depth. Displays with head-mounted devices, such as the ones using Liquid Crystal on Silicon or Retinal Scanner Devices are difficult to penetrate in the mass media market, because they limit user mobility and comfort. It is also universally acceptable that average users do not like to wear such devices, especially when socializing, e.g., in their living room or in a club. Head-mounted display devices are typically used for virtual reality applications, when *user immersion* is desired.

## 13.6.3   Autostereoscopic displays

*Autostereoscopic visualization* refers to any 3D display method that generates stereoscopic images, without the use of special glasses or other head-mounted devices. In the case of autostereoscopic vision, we attempt to achieve binocular vision with the use of screens, which, by construction, can direct the left/right view to the left/right eye, respectively. For this purpose, we use various optics methods, such as light reflection, diffraction or refraction. As the correct view should reach each eye of a single viewer, head-tracking or eye-tracking devices may be used. For exactly same reason, autostereoscopic systems have limitations on the viewer number they can support for simultaneous viewing of high quality stereoscopic images.

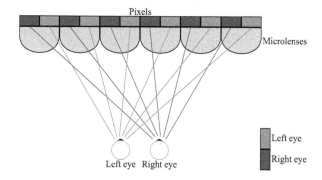

Figure 13.6.5: Autostereoscopic display with lenticular lenses.

The particular characteristics of flat LCD or Plasma screens, such as the fixed and factory-predefined pixel position and the excellent visualization geometry, made them suitable for autostereoscopic displays. Thus, the user can perceive depth without the use of additional equipment like glasses, giving the sense of "looking at the scene through a window". The enabling optics technology is similar to that encountered in various flat surface objects, like rulers etc., which can display different printed images, depending on the view-angle. This can be achieved, e.g., with the use of transparent lenticular lenses, which appropriately refract the image which is displayed beneath, as shown in Figure 13.6.5. The stereoscopic view is formed by two or more images, depending on scene motion, which are multiplexed, next to each other in very thin strips, having a width equal to that of the streaks of the lenticular lenses. Thus, depending on the view-angle, only one of the two multiplexed images is rendered visible by each eye. When observing such a multiplexed image with both eyes from a distance, it is very probable that each eye sees a different image of the stereoscopic image pair. Thus, three-dimensional visualization is possible, by using LCD or Plasma screens fitted with special lenticular lenses. They convey the depth sense in a satisfactory way. Nowadays, this is one of the most promising three-dimensional display technologies.

## 13.6.4 Holographic displays

In holographic displays, images are formed with an appropriate light wave capture and reproduction, including luminosity (oscillation amplitude), wavelength (color) and phase difference information. For 3D scene capture, *coherent light* is used, which produces the holographic video (*interference pattern*). During display, this video must be lit with coherent light and projected on a special screen, via a system of lenses and mirrors. Thus, the exact wavefield of the captured light is reproduced. The produced image is impressive. It changes with view angle, as if the portrayed object was present in front of the viewer, as seen in Figure 13.6.6.

Figure 13.6.6: Holographic display (*courtesy of MediaScreen GmbH*).

The use of holography is limited by the physical problems of light wave capture and display, particularly when using coherent light. The great volume of information, which must be recorded, stored, transmitted and displayed, sets severe limitations to existing computer technology. Holography can be developed in limited parallax systems (e.g., stereoscopic holography), which mitigate some of the aforementioned limitations. Generally speaking, although holography is a rather old technology (invented in 1947 by Gabor), holographic visualization is still in its infancy, due to existing technical difficulties.

## 13.6.5   Volumetric displays

Volumetric displays produce an image by projecting light inside a physical volume, which is permanently or periodically filled with a photoreflective or self-luminous material, as shown in Figure 13.6.7. They are generally based on light diffusion for generating three-dimensional displays. Either flat semicircular or helical revolving screens are used for image visualization. Generally, the generated images have rather limited spatial resolution.

Presently, most commercially available solutions for volumetric display are based on the multiple and rapid projection of two-dimensional images

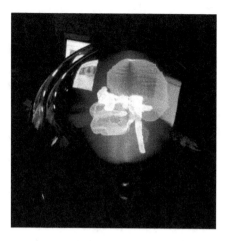

Figure 13.6.7: Volumetric display (*courtesy of Optics for Hire*).

on semitransparent rapidly revolving surfaces. This technique creates the illusion of a semitransparent three-dimensional image, which the user may examine from various view angles, exactly as he/she would do with a real three-dimensional object.

Another solution is the rapid alternating projection of two-dimensional images on a stack of rectangular electronic liquid crystal shutters the size of a monitor. A video projector, which is synchronized with the electronic shutters, projects rapidly on each of them a sequence of images, each corresponding to a slice of the three-dimensional scene. Thus, it is feasible to render the third dimension in a satisfactory way, despite the limited number of depth layers defined by the electronic shutters.

## 13.7   3DTV market

Actual market studies from various research institutes indicate a bright future for the 3DTV markets. Some key figures are the following ones:

- 35 3D movies released in 2010,

- 50 new 3D movies confirmed,

- growing demand for 2D to 3D film conversions,

- 25 3D TV channels in operation (end of 2010),

- 3D TV market penetration in 2014 for Western Europe 20% (forecast),

- 400 3D computer games available (end of 2010).

The 3D market is considered to be one of the main media market drivers for this decade. It has been greatly boosted by the 3D movie success (e.g., Avatar) and the ensuing availability of stereoscopic displays intended for the living room.

**3D Television channels.** A number of TV channels are currently broadcasting or plan to soon start broadcasting in 3D. Although 3DTV channels are still a small minority, compared to the number of cable and satellite TV channels, their number is rapidly growing, despite the international financial crisis that creates investment problems. Many of the above channels only broadcast 3D content some of the time, while the rest is filled up by regular HDTV programs. Some of them, such as 3net, broadcast 3D 24/7. There is a strong preference for sports content in the current 3DTV channels. However, sports are far from forming the majority of the 3DTV content, as most channels also show 3D films, concerts, documentaries and other content. Finally, it should be stressed that almost all of the channels have appeared rather recently, with the pace of appearance accelerating rapidly.

**3DTV content.** Although there have been periods of intense 3D motion picture production in the past 40 years, the last few years have shown a great increase in the production of 3D films, as shown in Figure 13.7.1. This increase has been accompanied by the unprecedented popularity and profitability of 3D films. The number of theaters that showed 3D films increased greatly from few tens to thousands in less than 5 years. Now more than 70% of the theaters can project 3D films. The proportion of viewers that chose to view the films in 3D increased significantly. Furthermore, in sports, most recent major sporting events have been broadcasted in 3D, such as the 2010 Football World Cup and the 2012 Olympics in London. This trend is bound to boom in the coming years.

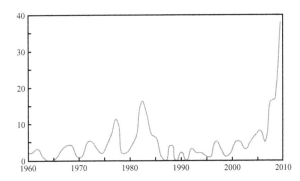

Figure 13.7.1: Number of 3D films produced per year in the last 40 years.

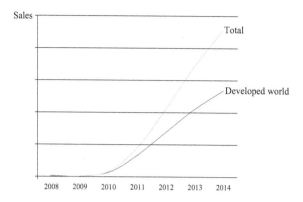

Figure 13.7.2: Trends in the 3DTV market growth.

**3D Television hardware.** Driven by the increase in 3DTV content and promoted by electronics manufacturers, sales of 3D television sets are expected to soar in the following years, as shown in Figure 13.7.2. The discrepancy in the predictions is great, but the overall trend is the same: the growth is expected to be explosive. Essentially, from the next 1-2 years onwards, all high-end TV monitors will be 3DTV compatible.

The increase in the value of the 3DTV hardware market will probably be fuelled by the fall in the prices of individual sets, from around 1000-1500 USD today to about half of this in about 4 years, when the technology will mature. Thus, the 3D TV set market in 4 years can be expected to range from 40 to 80 billion USD.

This analysis shows that the 3DTV market will thrive in the coming years. It is foreseeable that this will lead to an explosive growth of the 3DTV content market. However, the size of the 3DTV content sector cannot be directly estimated right now, due to the lack of appropriate statistics. But keeping the number of 3DTV channels in mind and taking the 3DTV hardware sales estimations into account, the availability of 3DTV content will grow significantly, despite the fact that currently 3DTV content is more difficult and expensive to shoot and produce.

**Online user-fed 3DTV content.** In addition to traditional forms of 3D video (movies, television), an increasing amount of video content appears on the Internet. The definitive website for Internet video is, of course, YouTube, which supports 3D video with a number of visualization options (e.g., for red/blue glasses or autostereoscopic display). The number of 3D video clips that have been stored in the site has increased by 10-fold in a period of 1.5 years, as shown in Figure 13.7.3 for the period 7/2009-12/2010.

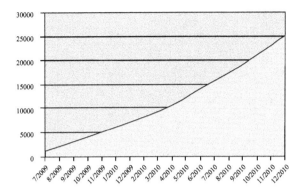

Figure 13.7.3: Number of 3D video clips on YouTube.

At the end of 2010, over 1% of the videos uploaded to YouTube were in 3D, despite the fact that 3D video acquisition was still very difficult for non-professionals, since, e.g., 3D cameras are very scarce. Furthermore, special 3D video www sites exist, e.g., www.3dvideoclips.net. Such 3D content over open platforms is expected to soar soon, with the advent of 3D mobile telephony and of cheap 3D cameras. Currently, consumers can buy mobile phones that display small 3D images on autostereoscopic displays. Many such devices appeared in the market in 2010-2012. 3D mobile conversations are expected to rise sharply, despite the fact that certain criticisms regarding usability persist.

**Other 3D content sectors.** 3D media production and distribution is currently pushed by most of the significant players in the media value chain. The most obvious support stems from the movie production business, recognizing that 3D movies earn extra money for them. The consumer electronics industry is a strong supporter as well, looking for the next innovation wave, following the already widely introduced HDTV services. However, digital convergence adds an extra momentum to the 3D market development. *Connected TV* and *Hybrid Broadcast Broadband TV* (HBBTV) will facilitate 3D-capable content portals. Another part of this extra momentum is provided by computer games, where all major game platforms are already 3D-capable. The 3D game platforms for handheld game consoles (e.g., Nintendo 3DS) are currently the main driver for the development of autostereoscopic displays.

Another huge area for 3D video content is the Digital Signage market. Especially autostereoscopic content and autostereoscopic displays are intensively developed for this application area, in order to build large distribution networks and content management systems for 3D video content.

# 13.8   3DTV prospects

The concept of three-dimensional television existed for many years. However, only recently its technology has been developed to such a degree that its wide deployment is possible. A big push to three-dimensional television was given by the great commercial success of three-dimensional motion pictures, such as movie "Avatar" (2009). The problems of capture, representation, compression and transmission of three-dimensional content have already some mostly satisfactory solutions, although they are still active research topics. The greatest problem awaiting solution is that of stereoscopic display without glasses. It is not possible to accept 3DTV technology in a living room, if it will require the use of glasses or other viewing accessories. Furthermore, stereoscopic vision creates vision adaptation problems and, more importantly, eye weariness. Many viewers of three-dimensional motion pictures admit taking off their glasses regularly. Furthermore, it is very important to allow simultaneous stereoscopic vision to many viewers, without reduction in viewing quality. Manufacturing of autostereoscopic big screen television, with wide view angle, very large color palette, correct support of parallax and convenient viewing would set the standard in 3D television market. There are already some autostereoscopic Plasma or TFT screens in the market, which support some of the aforementioned characteristics. Most TV set manufacturers already deliver autostereoscopic high-end TV screens. However, a satisfactory solution of the stereoscopic view problem is still an open issue.

Although most ingredients for 3DTV success are here, its explosive growth is yet to be confirmed. Several 3D quality criticisms persist and a trend to move media progress to other directions, e.g., in Ultra HDTV, may put this success at risk.

# 14

# VIDEO STORAGE, SEARCH AND RETRIEVAL

## 14.1 Introduction

Video databases are widely available either in broadcasters or in production/post-production houses or, increasingly so, in social media sites, like YouTube. The video information stored in such databases is immense in size. It is typically (manually) annotated by text and tags/keywords. Nowadays, video search is performed mainly using such keywords.

Decades ago, the search for just a few words in a large number of text files posed significant difficulties. Similarly, today, the search for specific content in digital video files is difficult. While text search engines are widely available today, content-based video retrieval is still an open issue. Many techniques have been proposed to lead the way to the new and exciting world of content-based video retrieval. These studies concentrate mainly in video analysis and (hopefully automatic) description and also on video indexing, search and retrieval from video databases. In this Chapter, low-level and semantic video analysis and description techniques are presented. Furthermore, the MPEG-7 standard on audiovisual data description is overviewed. MPEG-7 profiles that are suitable for audiovisual content description in XML files (e.g., AVDP) are detailed. Finally, the current form and functionalities of the audiovisual archives are described. New topics, like label propagation for video annotation, relevance feedback and user profiling are presented as well.

## 14.2    Hierarchical video structure

The hierarchical video decomposition presented in Figure 14.2.1 is a common practice serving two purposes. It exposes the semantic video characteristics and can provide a framework for the spatiotemporal analysis and description of the video content.

First a *temporal video decomposition* can be performed. A video (e.g., a movie) consists of a sequence of scenes. A *scene* is a sequence of shots. A *shot* is a sequence of consecutive video frames, which are captured without interruption by a stationary or a continuously moving camera. Thus, a movie scene, which contains alternating views of two persons consists of multiple shots. A scene is defined as a collection of one or more continuous shots, focusing on an object or objects of interest, or on physical scene, or on a semantically meaningful part of the story (narrative). For example, shots showing a person walking in a corridor and entering a room could constitute a scene, if the person has been captured by different cameras. Three camera shots, showing three different persons walking down a corridor may constitute a scene, if the object of interest is the corridor and not the persons. Video scene must not be confused with physical scene (also called *set*), where action takes place, thought they sometimes coincide semantically. In the following sections, we shall present methods for segmenting a video stream into shots and scenes.

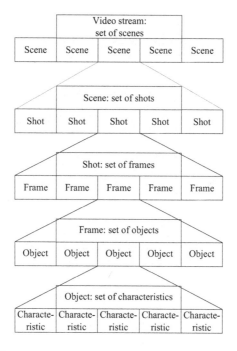

Figure 14.2.1: Hierarchical video structure.

## 14.2.1 Shot/scene cut and transition detection

There are various types of shot transitions. A *shot cut* is an abrupt shot change. A *fade-in/fade-out* is a slow change in shot luminance which usually leads to, or starts with, a black frame. A *dissolve* takes place when there is a spatial blend of the frames of two successive shots for the duration of the transition, so that the luminance of the images of the first shot decreases and that of the second shot increases. A *wipe* occurs when the pixels of the second shot gradually replace those of the first shot with a local motion, e.g., from left to right. Of course, many other gradual shot transition types are possible. All these shot transitions are very popular tools for movie editing. The extent of their use though depends on the editor's style. For example, once popular fancy shot transitions go out of style and the classical simple transitions (e.g., the abrupt cuts) reemerge.

Abrupt changes are easier to detect, compared to gradual ones. The techniques for abrupt cut detection can form the basis for more recent techniques for the detection of gradual shot transitions. Most abrupt shot cut detection methods examine two video frames $f$ and $f'$ and define a *dissimilarity* metric $D(f, f')$. If its value exceeds a threshold, a transition between two shots is detected. Various similarity/dissimilarity measures can be used to this end, meaning, e.g., color/texture/motion/object shape similarity within a shot (and dissimilarity between two successive shots). The simplest such metric between two consecutive video frames is the *Mean Square Difference* (MSD) of their pixel luminances. Also, the simple color, or luminance, or motion *histogram difference* between the frames $f$ and $f'$ can also be used to this end. More complicated methods based on the same principles can be used for gradual shot transition detection.

Shot detection can also be considered as a video frame clustering problem over time. The video frames within each shot should be similar. They should be dissimilar across consecutive shots. Once video frames are clustered into consecutive shots, shot transitions are easy to detect at or close to the shot start/end frames. The same color/texture/motion/object shape similarity measures can be used for video frame clustering, as the ones used for shot transition detection.

Another approach to shot cut detection utilizes human interaction to improve performance, while, at the same time, preserving content integrity. A human annotator selects a few key frames in various representative shots. Then, a label propagation method can propagate the shot labels to other frames automatically, to finally compile a list of video shots. Content (e.g., color/texture/motion) similarity between successive labeled and unlabeled video frames can be used for label propagation. This procedure requires limited time and effort, in comparison to manual shot annotation.

Shots can be classified into several classes, most notably in long shots, medium shots and close-ups, as already described in Chapter 6. This can be typically done by finding the region of the main actor body and comparing its size with the video frame size. Long shots contain a lot of background (and the actor body). Medium shots contain part of the human body. Close-ups contain the actor face. Therefore, human body and face localization is performed first, in order to decide on the shot type.

Video scenes have a highly semantic nature. Therefore, scene detection is much more abstract and difficult than shot detection. As audio (music) is used by movie directors to underlie scene continuity across shots, audio analysis (e.g., detection of same musical motif or background noise) can be used to group shots into scenes or to detect scene transitions. Alternatively, shots can be detected by clustering consecutive shots, e.g., based on their background similarity denoting action in the same physical scene.

## 14.2.2    Key frame selection and video summarization

Given a long video sequence, a user may want to extract a number of *key frames* for video description and fast browsing. Their number may vary from 5% to 10% of the total frame number in the original video. Sometimes they are also called *representative frames*. The key frames should be able to summarize well the video content. Therefore, this task is called *video summarization*. Unfortunately, video content description is highly subjective and application-dependent. Therefore, there is no mathematical model, which defines the exact requirements for key frame selection. Many techniques for key frame extraction are based on shot cut detection, while other approaches employ the visual content and motion analysis. An easy way to perform video summarization is to select few representative video frames per shot, e.g., the first ones or the central ones (in terms of shot duration) or the central ones, in terms of video frame similarity. In the last choice, few video frames are selected per shot, which are the most similar to the rest of the shot video frames. Frequently, shot key frames are considered to be the ones which correspond to local minima of motion velocity, i.e., the key frames are recognized by the stillness of their visual content. In other cases, outlying video frames are selected to complement the central ones for shot summarization. This philosophy is based on the mathematical (and journalistic) notion of information: rare events carry more information than frequent events, e.g., when a person bites a dog, this event is interesting, the opposite event is not.

When video snippets, rather than video frames, are used for video description, then we have *video skimming*. It is performed along the same principles with video summarization, the difference being that we use short video snippets, rather than individual video frames.

Video summarization can be used to create an image gallery to describe a video visually. Video skimming is closer to trailer production. However, trailer production is a more sophisticated task, typically created by experts, since it is designed to capture audience attention (and interest to watch the full movie). Video skimming is more difficult in 3DTV, since the human eye can get very tired by fast depth transitions between the various 3DTV video snippets. Therefore, skimming must be performed with great care in 3DTV, in order to produce gradual depth changes and an acceptable overall result.

## 14.3 Spatiotemporal video description

In many cases, video metadata are created (usually manually) up to shot or scene level. This is understandable, since manual video annotation is a time consuming and unmerciful task. However, the current (semi)-automatic video analysis tools can provide detailed annotation granularity at frame or object level, as already described in Chapter 5. Therefore, we can perform *spatial decomposition* of a video frame into objects and

Figure 14.3.2: Face detection results (*courtesy of the 3D4YOU and MUS-CADE FP7 projects and the Hertz Heinrich Institute*).

background. Objects, including persons and faces, can be detected by object/person/face detection algorithms. They are typically described by object *Regions Of Interest* (ROI), as shown in Figure 14.3.2. Objects can be tracked over time within a video shot, thus creating moving ROIs (called VideoObjects in video coding). This results in a spatiotemporal video decomposition into moving object ROIs that have a certain motion trajectory, as shown in Figure 14.3.3.

Shot background can be found as well, typically by moving object detection and subtraction. It can be described by a full frame image, or by a panoramic image, or by a 3D graphics model.

Humans are, very frequently, the primary actors in a movie. Therefore, the description of their presence, identity, status and activities is a very important task in video analysis leading to *human-centered* (also called *anthropocentric*) video descriptions. For example, facial image clustering allows us to automatically cluster facial images of the same actor into one cluster. Face recognition allows to tag facial image clusters with the corresponding actor names. Facial expression recognition allows to recognize

Figure 14.3.3: A moving person and its ROIs (*courtesy of the i3DPost FP7 project and CVSSP, University of Surrey, UK*).

and tag various expressions in facial images, e.g., smile, anger. Human activity recognition allows to recognize human actions, e.g., walk, run, bend. Such anthropocentric video analysis tools are at various degrees of maturity and adoption. For example, face and even smile detection are currently used in various cameras to aid inexperienced users. Although they are error-prone, they provide rich metadata at object, shot and scene level that are very useful for a variety of applications, e.g., in video surveillance, human-centered computer interfaces and in semantic video search. When such video descriptions are stored in an XML file, fast searches can be performed of the form 'find a video shot where actor X smiles', 'find a video scene where actors X and Y converse'.

# 14.4    Semiautomatic approaches for video description and search

Semiautomatic approaches have also been proposed for content-based video retrieval. Most videos are annotated manually. Different people may have different semantic interpretations for the same video scene. Thus, to eliminate this confusion, adaptive and flexible approaches can be used. One approach is to use automatic tools for video analysis and description, as presented in the previous section. Then the human annotator can edit and amend the automatically extracted video descriptions. Another approach is to let an annotator annotate one video or some of it scenes/shots/frames/objects and then use label propagation tools to propagate annotations from one video to another one or from one shot to another one and so on, at varying granularity levels.

Another approach is to continue annotating the video during video search. Each time a user searches for a video with text-based query, text annotation tables are searched. When the query is satisfied, the query terms are added to the annotation text. Using such relevance feedback mechanisms that combine retrieval and annotation, the system can include different descriptions for the same video clip, while preserving, at the same time, semantic soundness.

# 14.5    Multimodal description of audiovisual

## content

Both audio and video features can be employed for audiovisual content description and retrieval. The general structure of audio and image feature fusion is shown in Figure 14.5.1. The mean audio intensity is used as a measure of shot significance. It has been shown that shots, which have a higher audio intensity, are more significant than those that have a lower than average audio intensity. For audio streams, the audio features are extracted from low-level audio characteristics. For video streams, the visual features are extracted using motion estimation with luminance histograms and pixel differences. Then, each feature sequence extracted from either audio or video channels is used for the identification of audiovisual content semantics. This way, e.g., in case of scenes containing humans, four different shot types can be identified: dialogue, monologue, action and generic video.

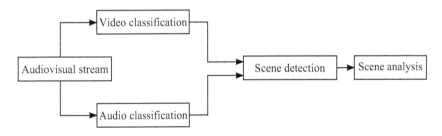

Figure 14.5.1: Audio and video features for audiovisual content description.

Video description techniques, using both the audio and video channels, have been proposed and have been further improved with the addition of text (subtitle) processing. Figure 14.5.2 shows the block diagram of such a method. Initially, the input audiovisual stream is split in an audio and a video stream. Subsequently, the audio stream can be classified in at least four classes: speech, music, environment noise and silence. Different music genres, environmental noise types or audio events (e.g., explosions) can be detected/recognized. In case of speech, the audio stream is further segmented in different temporal segments, depending on the current speaker. Therefore, speaker turns should be detected. Speaker turn detection can be assisted by subtitle information, in case it is available. Simultaneously, video shot detection and key-frame extraction are performed in the video stream. Following this, color/motion correlation between shots is calculated and an extended shot clustering is performed, so that shots, whose

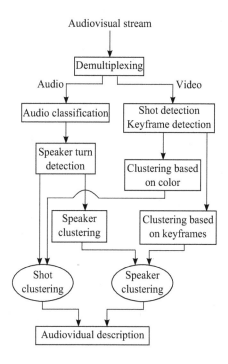

Figure 14.5.2: Multimodal audiovisual content analysis.

objects or the background color are closely correlated (for example shots which were acquired in the same 3D physical scene), are grouped together. In the next step, the results of audio and video analysis are merged to improve shot clustering into video scenes. At this point, the results of speaker change detection can be combined with the results of color-based shot grouping, to find the scene transitions. The fusion rule is that shots within audio segments corresponding to one speaker, which are chromatically correlated, are grouped and marked as correlated. In other words, a shot sequence will be grouped in a scene, only when the correlation analysis of the visual content and the audio segmentation detect a common scene transition. In order to detect key persons, as far as audio is concerned, the audio segments, marked by the speaker change points, are further grouped. In video, the shots can be grouped based on key-frame or facial region clusters. Then, the following heuristic rules are used for the detection of potential key persons in audio and video data:

1) The speech/image duration ratio of human actors is usually higher than the corresponding speech/image duration ratio of other persons. This is the case, e.g., for anchorpersons in news broadcasts.

2) The main actor ROIs are more centrally located in the video frame.

3) The shot type is defined according to the main actor ROI in relation to the video frame size.

Semantic particularities can be observed in some video genres. E.g., in news broadcasts, the temporal dispersion of the speech/image duration of the anchorpersons is higher than the corresponding speech/image duration ratio of other persons. That is, the anchorperson will appear from the start until the end of a news broadcast. In the news video case, the visual and audio analysis results can be recombined, resulting to a valid anchorperson shot detection. The fusion rule used here is the logical conjunction between the anchorperson video shots and their speech segments.

Another method involving both visual and audio content for video indexing is shown in Figure 14.5.3. Audio processing starts with speech-silence detection, which is performed using the mean volume of the audio signal and the zero crossings rate, leading to signs of potential scene changes. The audio features are extracted only from voiced frames. For this reason, the video frames must be divided in voiced and unvoiced ones. This division is based on the low- to high-frequency power spectrum ratio of the audio channel, which is calculated using the *Short Term Fourier Transform* (STFT). In the voice segments, voice analysis can lead to speaker recognition. The extracted audio features can model well the speaker. Training audio data from various speakers can be used to this end. Furthermore, *Text To Speech* (TTS), also called *speech recognition*, methods can be used to transcribe the speech signal into text. Subtitle information can assist voice detection, when available. In this case, TTS may be optional. Video processing starts with the detection of shot transitions, using color differences. Subsequently, face detection is performed, assuming that faces can be characterized by skin-like color and have elliptical shape. Facial analysis follows, to estimate first the eyes and subsequently the mouth position. Mouth tracking is used to determine if a person speaks or not *(visual speech)*. Cross-modal audio and video analysis facilitates the detection of shot transitions, using the detection of speech-silence periods. Additionally, face analysis facilitates speaker identification, especially in case when strong background noise corrupts the audio channel, e.g., in street scenes.

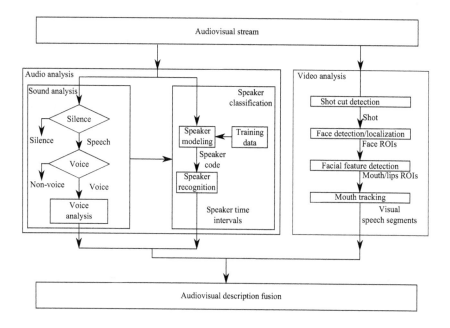

Figure 14.5.3: Audiovisual content analysis.

## 14.6   The MPEG-7 content description standard

In October 1996, the MPEG standardization committee, initiated an effort to create a digital media content description standard, for various media data types. The audiovisual data which can be described in MPEG-7 may include static images, 2D graphics, three-dimensional object models, audio, speech, video and composition information on how all these elements are combined in a multimedia scenario. The MPEG-7 standard does not aim at a specific application. The MPEG-7 representation tools do not depend on digital media content encoding and storage modes. However, the MPEG-7 standard can exploit the advantages existing in the encoded digital content (e.g., in MPEG-4 format). MPEG-7 aims to standardize:

a) A basic core of *Descriptors* (D) which can be used for the description of the various features of the multimedia content.

b) Predefined descriptor structures and their relations, which are called *Description Schemes* (DS).

c) A language for the determination of the descriptors and the description schemes, which is called *Description Definition Language* (DDL).

d) The encoded representation of descriptors for efficient storage and fast access to multimedia data.

## 14.6.1  MPEG-7 parts

The MPEG-7 standard is organized in parts, as shown in Table 14.6.1. The basic functional parts which comprise the MPEG-7 standard are described in the following sections.

Table 14.6.1: MPEG-7 standard parts.

| Part number | Title |
|:---:|:---:|
| 1 | Systems |
| 2 | Description Definition Language |
| 3 | Visual Description Tools |
| 4 | Audio Description Tools |
| 5 | Multimedia Description Schemes |
| 6 | Reference Software |
| 7 | Conformance |
| 8 | Extraction/use of descriptors |
| 9 | Profiles and levels |
| 10 | Schema definitions |

The MPEG-7 *Systems* part includes the tools required for the preparation of the MPEG-7 descriptions for the more efficient transfer and storage of digital media, the terminal architecture and the regulative interfaces.

The MPEG-7 Description Definition Language part allows for the creation of new description schemes and new descriptors, if needed, and the extension/modification of existing description schemes. It is based on the XML language. As XML has not been specifically designed for multimedia content description, it was extended specifically for the MPEG-7 standard. As a result, this language can be separated in the following logical components:

- structural components of the XML scheme language,

- data type components of the XML scheme language,

- specific MPEG-7 extensions.

The MPEG-7 *visual description tools* offer basic structures and descriptors for the following basic visual characteristics: color, texture, shape, motion, locality and faces. Each category consists of elementary and advanced descriptors. In the next section, the visual content description technologies of MPEG-7 will be summarized.

The MPEG-7 *audio description tools* provide structures for audio content description. A set of low-level audio descriptors uses these structures for audio features that are encountered in many applications (e.g., spectral, parametric and temporal characteristics of audio signals). MPEG-7 also provides a suit of high-level audio description tools, which are more application-dependent. These high-level tools include general audio recognition tools and description indexing tools, tools for the description of the *instrument timbre*, speech content description tools, audio signal description schemes. Melody description tools enable queries by humming (a song).

The MPEG-7 *Multimedia Description Schemes* (MDS) constitute the set of description tools (descriptors and description schemes) for both basic and multimedia entities. The basic entities are general characteristics used in all digital media, e.g., vector, time and spatial coordinates. Except for this set of general description tools, more complex description tools have been standardized for multimodal media description (e.g., video, 3D graphics and audio). These description tools can be grouped in different classes, depending on their functionality:

1) *content description*: it represents structural aspects of the multimedia content, e.g., decomposition into spatial/temporal segments;

2) *content management*: it contains information on the creation, coding, and use of the multimedia content;

3) *content organization*: it analyzes and clusters multimedia content, e.g., into collections;

4) *navigation and access*: it specifies summaries and other ways to access, browse and navigate in the multimedia content;

5) *user interaction*: it describes user interface issues, user preferences and usage record, related to the audiovisual material consumption.

The MPEG-7 *reference software*, also called *eXperimentation Model* (XM) simulation platform, provides simulation for MPEG-7 Ds, DSs and DDLs. Beyond normative components, several non-normative components may be needed during simulation. The applications consisting of the corresponding data structures and programs are divided in two types: server applications (retrieval) and client applications (search, filtering).

The part of MPEG-7 *conformance* contains instructions and compatibility check procedures of each MPEG-7 implementation.

MPEG-7 *extraction and use of descriptions* presents, in an informative way, how some descriptions can be extracted and used. Since MPEG-7 is a vast collection or more than 1500 multimedia descriptors, *Profiles* and *MPEG-7 Levels* have been proposed, so that limited sets of MPEG-7 descriptors and tools are tuned to particular application needs. Such standard profiles and levels are collected in the respective MPEG-7 part. Finally, all MPEG-7 schemes are collected in the MPEG-7 *Schema Definition* part.

## 14.6.2    The MPEG-7 visual standard

A very important aim of MPEG-7 is to provide standardized descriptions of stored image or video streams and standardized headers (low-level visual descriptors), which help the user, or the applications, to identify, classify or filter images or video. These low-level descriptors can be used to compare, filter or display images or video, based only on visual content descriptions, or, if necessary, in combination with plain text-based searches.

MPEG-7 descriptors can be grouped in two categories: generic visual descriptors and specialized visual descriptors. The former ones include color, shape and motion characteristics, while the latter ones include, e.g., detection, localization and identification of human faces. This section focuses on generic descriptors, which can be used in most applications.

A particular effort has been made in the design of efficient color descriptors to be used in the detection of chromatically similar images. There is no generic color descriptor that can be used for all applications. Therefore many generic descriptors were standardized, each one being appropriate for a special visual similarity function. For example, several color spaces are included in the standard, notably RGB, $YC_bC_r$, HMMD and HSV. Descriptors for dominant color and color layout (spatial color distribution) are also supported.

MPEG-7 has defined appropriate texture descriptors, which can be used in various applications. The *homogeneous texture descriptors* describe texture directionality, roughness and regularity and are mostly suitable for the quantitative characterization of homogeneous texture. They use frequency characteristics to describe the image texture, its energy and energy variability. They are based on filter banks, which are sensitive to scaling and orientation (e.g., Gabor filters). Other suitable descriptors are acquired in the frequency domain, by calculating the mean value and standard deviation of transform (e.g., DFT) coefficients. *Non-homogeneous texture descriptors* (e.g., edge histograms) capture the spatial edge distribution, towards describing directional textures existing, e.g., in images of wood, sea waves and cloth.

Finally, MPEG-7 has defined a number of shape descriptors, which can be used to describe 2D and 3D shapes. Objects, whose shape features are best expressed by contour information, as the one shown in Figure 14.6.1a, can be described using the MPEG-7 *contour shape descriptors*. Objects, whose shape is best described by the region they occupy, like the one shown in Figure 14.6.1b, can be described by the MPEG-7 *region shape descriptor*. *2D/3D shape descriptors* can be used when the shape of a

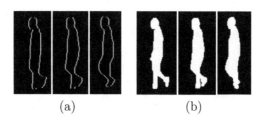

(a)          (b)

Figure 14.6.1: a) Contour-based shape description, b) region-based shape description.

three-dimensional object can be approximately described by a limited number of 2-dimensional projections, which are taken as its two-dimensional snapshots from different view angles. Thus, the two-dimensional MPEG-7 shape descriptors can be used to describe each one of the two-dimensional shapes, which are projections of the three-dimensional object. Therefore, the detection of similarities between three-dimensional objects can be performed by matching multiple pairs of two-dimensional shots, one for each object. 3D object shapes can be described by polygonal (e.g., triangular) meshes, as done in VRML files.

Motion description in a video sequence, by using motion fields, can be particularly heavy in terms of bits per video frame, even if the motion fields are sparse. MPEG-7 has developed descriptors which capture basic motion characteristics from the motion field in concise and effective descriptions.

*Motion activity descriptors.* In a video segment (e.g., a scene, a shot or a given set of consecutive frames), the overall motion activity level or speed is captured by the motion activity descriptor. It describes if a scene is slow, fast or very fast. Examples of high activity are sport or action scenes. Furthermore, scenes from news broadcasts can be considered as low-activity ones, especially the anchorperson shots. The motion activity intensity descriptor measures the motion intensity. Optionally, the motion direction, the spatial distribution of the motion activity and the temporal distribution of the motion activity can also be extracted as motion activity descriptors and be used for motion similarity detection.

*Camera motion descriptor*. The motion of the physical or virtual camera can be described by the camera motion descriptor. This descriptor yields information on total camera motion parameters, which exist at a given time instance in a shot. These parameters can, in certain applications, be supplied directly by the camera. It is also possible that these camera parameters are estimated from the video sequence itself, using an appropriate camera model and camera motion estimation. The descriptor can be used for searching video sequences based on certain total motion parameters, such as shots with a high zooming activity or shots with mainly camera pan motion.

*Motion trajectory descriptor*. The object motion can also be described separately for each independently moving object, using the motion trajectory descriptor. The object trajectory is typically found by object tracking, as described in Chapter 5. It describes object displacement as a function of time and allows object trajectory matching for object motion-based video search. One possible application is visual surveillance, e.g., searching for objects which move close to a specific region, or objects (e.g., cars) which move faster than a speed limit. Another application is human activity or gesture recognition, where hand/limb/foot trajectories can be employed to this end.

# 14.7    MPEG-7 based audiovisual content description

A considerable amount of research effort has been invested over the last years to improve MPEG-7 ability to deal with semantic video content description. For example, an anthropocentric description scheme for video content analysis, called ANTHROPOS-7 has been proposed. Its main assumption is that humans (actors) are the most important entity in most movies. The basic idea is to observe humans and their environment in video shots and organize the video content description according to our perception about humans (and their context/background). Therefore, this description introduces an MPEG-7 structure for semantic video content description regarding humans, their status/activities and the relevant context (scene background, props, objects). The so-called *Detailed Audio Visual Profile* (DAVP) MPEG-7 profile has also been proposed, which is based mainly on the MPEG-7 part 5 (MDS) and provides a way to describe single multimedia content entities, based on a comprehensive structural description of the content. Finally, an industrial application of the *Core Description Profile* (CDP), namely the *Metadata Production Framework* (MPF) has been proposed.

The MPEG-7 Audio Visual Description Profile (AVDP) provides a standard way to store high- and low-level video descriptions that are extracted either by (semi)automatic video content analysis or by manual annotation. AVDP is based on the previous DAVP and MPF description schemes and was designed to benefit both broadcasters and media industry, by creating a normative layer for video content description. Such descriptions are useful in video archival, search and retrieval, either in production archives or in broadcasting archives or even in user-fed social media video content search, e.g., in YouTube. For example, humans and their activities can be detected and tracked in a video, using automatic face detection, tracking and recognition and the appropriate descriptions can be stored in XML files. Then, we can search these files instead of searching the raw video content, e.g., for finding videos depicting person X, while walking or smiling. Needless to say that text or keyword search is impossible in many cases, since manual annotations are either completely missing or inadequate. Even if such manual annotations do exist, e.g., in production or broadcasting archives, their granularity is very gross. For example, we can retrieve videos where person X walks, but we cannot spot the exact video segment where this event happens indeed.

AVDP was introduced so as to solve two main problems arising form the MPEG-7 architecture, namely complexity and interoperability. It is well known that MPEG-7 is a vast collection of (more than 1500) multimedia descriptors and description schemes. Therefore, its use (as is) in video content description is questionable. Moreover, interoperability issues arise, since full interoperability between two different MPEG-7 documents is only assured by having knowledge on how the standard has been used. Profiles are a rather old mechanism, which restricts standards to a specific set of applications. This is done (e.g., in the case of MPEG-7) by selecting appropriate subsets of Ds and DSs from MPEG-7 and by defining new constraints on their use. For instance, interoperability can be considered in a profile by restricting the use of several DSs to follow a single and unambiguous operational way. AVDP provides all Ds and DSs, as well as corresponding constraints, needed for audiovisual content description. The most important AVDP aspects are the following ones. *TemporalDecomposition DS* (TD) decomposes a video stream in scenes, shots, or video segments. *SpatialDecomposition DS* (SD) describes regions of interest (ROIs) corresponding to objects within frames. *SpatioTemporalDecomposition DS* (STD) describes moving regions of interest over time, corresponding to object trajectories. In this case, objects can be

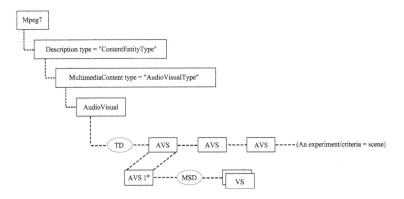

Figure 14.7.1: Schematic representation of scene/shot and key frame/key segment description in AVDP.

human bodies, faces, or scene props, or any other physical object. *MediaSourceDecomposition DS* (MSD) decomposes an audiovisual segment in its constituent audio and video channels. Video events and concepts can be described by using the MPEG-7 *StructuredAnnotation* (SA). It contains several fields that can be used for VideoSegment description, e.g., Who, WhatObject, How, WhatAction.

In Table 14.7.1, some of the most important MPEG-7 descriptors are illustrated that are used in AVDP for the above-mentioned decompositions. In the following, we shall concentrate on video content description, because audio content description is beyond the scope of this book. An illustrative example of the schematic representation of an AVDP descriptor for shot description is shown in Figure 14.7.1. In scene/shot boundary detection, we try to detect boundaries of scenes/shots, aiming at a temporal decomposition of the audiovisual content into different scenes/shots. Its results can be stored in an AudioVisual Temporal Decomposition (TD). Each resulting AVS will include only some temporal information, e.g., time codes for shot start/end.

# 14.8    Manual and semiautomatic video annotation

Video content description can typically have a header providing general information, such as:

Table 14.7.1: MPEG-7 Description Schemes used in the AVDP MPEG-7 profile.

| Description scheme | Summary |
|---|---|
| TemporalDecomposition (TD) | This description scheme (DS) acts as a tool that performs temporal decomposition of the video in multiple temporal segments, such as Video Segments (VS) or Audio-Visual Segments (AVS). |
| MediaSourceDecomposition (MSD) | It is used in the AVDP context to decompose an audiovisual segment (or an entire audiovisual content) into its audio and video channels. |
| VideoSegment (VS) | It provides a way to describe a video segment in the visual content. Each segment is defined by the starting time point of the VS and its time span. |
| SpatioTemporalDecomposition (STD) | It enables a video segment to be decomposed into spatiotemporal parts, namely MovingRegions, in order to store information related to moving objects. |
| MovingRegion (MR) | It is used to describe, for example, a moving object by storing the spatiotemporal object behavior, e.g., the spatial coordinates of the bounding box of the object and their change over time. |
| SpatialDecomposition (SD) | It is used for the spatial decomposition of a frame. The result is one or more regions of interest (StillRegion) within a video frame that may depict an object, face etc. |
| StillRegion (SR) | It is used to describe a still object, by defining its spatial region within a video frame. A StillRegion can also denote an entire video frame. |
| StructuredAnnotation | It is used to annotate concepts, events, human actions etc. |
| FreeTextAnnotation | It can be used to annotate a video segment with free text. |

- Movie information

  - Title
  - Genre (comedy, drama, action, documentary, sport, etc.)
  - Date of release
  - Director
  - Cast (actors/actresses, athletes, etc.);

- Date of ingestion

- Movie rating (e.g., appropriate for adults only)

- Target audience (men/women, adults, elderly etc.)

- Technical data (bit-rate, video resolution, type of compression, etc.)

The above information is typically manually fed or updated during content ingestion and is contained in the header of the XML file describing the video.

Most videos are annotated manually. Different people may have different semantic interpretations for the same video scene. Thus, to eliminate this confusion, adaptive and flexible approaches can be used in a semi-automatic way for video annotation. One approach is to use automatic tools for video analysis and description, as presented in previous sections. Then the human annotator can edit and amend the automatically extracted video descriptions. Another approach is to let an annotator annotate one video or some of it scenes/shots/frames/objects and then use *label propagation* tools to propagate annotations from one video to another one or from one shot to another one and so on, at varying granularity levels.

Another approach is to continue annotating the video during video search. Each time a user searches for a video with text-based query, text annotation tables are searched. When the query is satisfied, the query terms are added to the annotation text. Using such relevance feedback mechanisms that combine retrieval and annotation, the system can include different descriptions for the same video clip, preserving at the same time semantic soundness.

Information concerning the use of the audiovisual content can be archived as well, such as:

- Number of views

- Views frequency

- Views per user group

- Relevance feedback information, if available

- Quality of experience, e.g., likes/dislikes

- Engagement information

- Geographic provenance of audience.

The last three entries are very frequently used in social media data bases, such as YouTube. In this case, users provide also other forms of free-text annotations, such as tags and comments that can be valuable in content description, despite the inaccuracies existing in user-fed data.

## 14.9   Audiovisual content archives

Currently, the audiovisual archives in broadcasters all over the world are migrated from analogue to digital storage technologies. In parallel, the audio and video channels are enriched with different kinds of meta-data, ranging from basic technical information up to sophisticated levels of automatic feature extraction and content description. There are various workflows for archive data storage, search and retrieval. The most common workflows are based on a two-step approach, where a first search is based on a highly compressed mirror image (proxy or low-res) of the original file, providing faster search results and less load for the storage devices and networks. In a second step, the original file (high-res) is retrieved from the archive. Such workflows utilize the different quality levels of hierarchical compression schemes, like JPEG2000 used in digital cinema. For content search, lower quality levels of the JPEG2000 file can be used.

In many broadcasters, audiovisual content archiving is still tape-based. However, most of them are in the process of migrating to file-based audio-visual content handling. In tape-based systems, content search is realized with the help of proprietary, sometimes "home-grown", systems, which link assets to the tape archive. As part of the above-mentioned migration to file-based content handling, they are partially replaced/amended by digital *Media Asset Management* (MAM) systems. Such systems facilitate the work of editors, schedulers, material administrators, etc., within all processes of digital movie scheduling. They are modular, flexible and extensible software systems. They handle movie documentation, license management, material management, trailer production, retrieval, slot scheduling, programme scheduling, trailer scheduling and, possibly, content editing. The scheduling carried out within programme and trailer scheduling is based on the movie documentation data saved in the MAM system. For movies, data such as reference numbers, broadcasting and scheduling information, cast lists, texts, awards, etc., are maintained. Material management involves the recording of and dealing with data connected with movie material (material sets, time code locations etc.). Material managers request material for scheduled movies via an interface and assign it to the scheduled film version. Material information comprises, among others, the exact film length, time code locations, video and audio formats (4:3 or 16:9, Dolby Digital or stereo, etc.). There are different possibilities for audiovisual data retrieval, e.g., by starting queries for a detailed search, full-text search or combined search. For example, scheduling data, broadcasting data, license information, etc., can be retrieved. For a combined search, a filter can be used to narrow down the search area. MAMs can support either SDTV or HDTV content. Sometimes, content archiving can be performed via two MAM systems, one for the production/post-production domain and one specific for the program domain (ingestion, check, transmission). The metadata archived for describing the audiovisual content in the production/post-production domain can be: a) technical metadata (e.g., time code, audio/video quality, duration) documented by technicians before ingestion and during post-production and b) content-related metadata (mainly used when searching for news programs) documented by specialized personnel, after ingestion and post-production. The metadata archived for the audiovisual content in the program domain are mainly technical ones, whereas content-related data are very basic ones (name of the director, etc.). In general, so far, metadata creation/annotation is mostly manual, error-prone and very time consuming. To make things more complicated, various broadcasters use rather proprietary or very customized MAM solutions. Even language thesauri are not standardized. Therefore, metadata interoperability and transfer from one MAM system to another one is generally difficult. Furthermore, the current metadata granularity is a far cry from the one that can provided, e.g., by AVDP in conjunction with automated video analysis tools.

In terms of systems that can allow TV viewers to browse and search for broadcasted conventional TV content, there has certainly been some progress in the interaction between users and content, starting from the inclusion of *Electronic Program Guides* (EPG) services, as part of DVB or other DTV systems. EPG allows the users to browse through all the different services being broadcasted along a timeline, which extends from now to a time in the (near) future. Certainly, more advanced features can be added to the EPG, like programming of future recordings or alerts, or more information regarding the movie scenario, cast and awards.

Finally, 3DTV content archiving provides additional requirements and open questions, which are not yet addressed by the workflows and procedures that are currently in place for SDTV and HDTV. While archival of 3DTV material is pretty much manageable now, since only limited 3DTV content is available and produced, it is foreseen that proper procedures for archiving, indexing and retrieval of 3DTV content that takes into account the particularities of this medium, the rich information that it caries (depth being the most obvious one) and the needs of end users (broadcasters, production and post-production houses) and of the general public (in terms of 3D quality) should be set in place. 3D video content analysis and description is also very useful in the production of classical (single video channel) movie and SDTV/HDTV content, since in many cases, multiview camera setups are used in production and 3D video metadata are essential during post-production. The EU funded 3DTVS project aimed at providing solutions for 3DTV content description, archival and search. To this end, it extended the AVDP profile to cover 3DTV content.

## 14.9.1 Visual content indexing techniques

In the previous sections, various techniques were presented for analyzing video streams and extracting semantic information. The next step is to present techniques for creating the appropriate indexing structure of the acquired information to facilitate video retrieval. *Hashing* is a widely known technique for data indexing. Indexing techniques are different if we use low-level video descriptors (e.g., color, motion, or shape histograms) than high-level (semantic) video descriptors (e.g., based on face/person detection and tracking). In the following, we shall present the principles for low-level video indexing. Indexing can be done either at video segment or video frame level.

Low-level video indexing uses color, motion, or shape/texture video descriptors, e.g., in the form of histograms. Grayscale or color histograms can be used to this end, having a number of bins. Local edge directions in predefined image regions can be used for texture description. For each region, the histograms of four edge directions (horizontal, vertical and two diagonal) can be calculated using an edge detector, e.g., a Sobel or Canny one. Motion vector histograms can be used as well. By performing histogram quantization, we expect that visually similar video frames correspond to the same hash table entries. Each entry may have multiple indices to the video frames, which are stored in the database. When the database is queried using an image as the query example, the query image is subjected to analysis, using the same procedure and video frames, which have the same index in the hash table, are retrieved.

## 14.9.2 Relevance feedback and user profiling

Using a *relevance feedback* mechanism in an audiovisual database, a user can assign the relevance factor to a video returned to him after a query. This mechanism is useful for the efficiency of the audiovisual content search system, since it facilitates the refinement of the search and retrieval routines. The information that could be stored in the database, in order to be used by this relevance feedback mechanism should generally contain the following information:

- information about all queries submitted by the users (e.g., type of query, textual data or fields included in the query);

- relations between a user and his queries (a user may be related to multiple queries);

- relations between a query and the resulting content (multiple videos may be the result of a query);

- the relevance factor that a user assigns to a resulting video of one of his/her queries.

Given this structure in the database, the relevance feedback mechanism is described as follows. Firstly, a user submits a query to the search system and a list of videos is returned to him/her. Then, the user rates each video with a factor that indicates the relevance of his/her expected output with the results provided by the system. Then, the query and its relevance to a resulting video (provided by the user) can be stored. This information can be used to assess the efficiency of the retrieval mechanism and to refine it accordingly.

*User profiling* and *personalization* can be another feature of an audiovisual content search system. It describes the ability of the search and retrieval system to act in a user-specific manner, i.e., according to user preferences. This means that the results of a query of a specific user depend on the information about his/her preferences and his role. To this end, for every user, two types of information, namely user personal details (e.g., identity, role) and user preferences must be stored in the database. This is accomplished through user profiling. Personal details rarely change. However, in contrast, user preferences change over time and should be always updated, according to the user's activity. An example of the first type of information is the role of the user in terms of system usage; for instance, he/she can be an archivist, journalist, etc. Thus, depending on his/her role, the provided system functionalities and access rights can vary with the user. As for the second type of information, it can indicate how much a user is interested in specific video genres (e.g., documentaries or sports video). Also, a history of the queries he/she has submitted must be stored as well. To facilitate the initial profiling procedure, example user profiles can be provisioned, so that a profile can be assigned to each new user, automatically or manually. Later on, user profiles can be automatically or manually altered, depending on the overall users' activity. Preference information can be extracted by analyzing the user queries, search and retrieval results and viewing history. The query history provides raw information about the user preferences. The search and retrieval results, on the other hand, provide a direct way to infer user preferences by examining, for example, his/her relevance feedback on videos returned to a user during his search. Lastly, the viewing history of a user is also a direct way to infer preference information.

## 14.10   Conclusions

Today, thanks to the abundance of audiovisual content in the Internet, the actual use and value of digital video depends on the development of efficient description, storage, indexing and retrieval techniques. Content-based retrieval is an active research and development field. Many research prototypes and innovative techniques have been developed during the last decade, notably MPEG-7 and AVDP. Some of these have been incorporated in commercial products. Some of the audiovisual content description tools have affected the MPEG-7 standardization activities and were incorporated in its current version.

MAM systems used in production and in broadcasting offer audiovisual metadata storage. Users are provided such metadata, e.g., in the form of EPGs during broadcasting. However, the capabilities of existing systems are only a far cry of the potential in this area. The *semantic gap* between the users' needs (mainly semantic video search/description) and the currently available technology (mainly low- to middle-level video characteristics) continues to exist. Strong research and development effort is needed, in order to develop fully operational tools for video description and retrieval.

# BIBLIOGRAPHY

[1] E. Albuz, E. Kocalar, and A. A. Khokhar, "Scalable color image indexing and retrieval using vector wavelets," *IEEE Trans. on Knowledge and Data Engineering*, vol. 13, no. 5, pp. 851–861, 2001.

[2] M. S. Alencar, *Digital Television Systems.* Cambridge University Press, 2009.

[3] J. F. Arnold, M. R. Frater, and M. R. Pickering, *Digital Television: Technology and Standards.* J. Wiley, 2007.

[4] Y. A. Aslandogan and C. T. Yu, "Techniques and systems for image and video retrieval," *IEEE Trans. on Knowledge and Data Engineering*, vol. 11, no. 1, pp. 56–63, 1999.

[5] K. Bardosh, *The Complete Idiot's Guide to Digital Video.* Alpha Books, 2007.

[6] H. Benoît, *Digital Television: MPEG-1, MPEG-2 and Principles of the DVB System.* Focal Press, 2002.

303

[7]  H. Benoît, *Digital Television: Satellite, Cable, Terrestrial, IPTV, Mobile TV in the DVB Framework.* Focal Press, 2008.

[8]  C. L. Book, *Digital Television: DTV and the Consumer.* J. Wiley, 2004.

[9]  J. S. Boreczky and L. A. Rowe, "Comparison of video shot boundary detection techniques," *Storage and Retrieval for Still Image and Video Databases IV*, pp. 170–179, 1996.

[10]  D. Borth, A. Ulges, C. Schulze, and T. M. Breuel, "Keyframe extraction for video tagging and summarization," in *Proc. Informatiktage*, 2008, pp. 45–48.

[11]  J. Boston, *DTV survival guide.* McGraw-Hill, 2000.

[12]  A. C. Bovik, *The Essential Guide to Video Processing.* Academic Press/Elsevier, 2009.

[13]  R. Brice, *Newnes Guide to Digital TV.* Elsevier Science, 2002.

[14]  Z. Cernekova, C. Kotropoulos, and I. Pitas, "Video shot-boundary detection using singular-value decomposition and statistical tests," *J. Electronic Imaging*, vol. 16, no. 4, 2007.

[15]  Z. Cernekova, I. Pitas, and C. Nikou, "Information theory-based shot cut/fade detection and video summarization," *IEEE Trans. on Circuits and Systems for Video Technology*, vol. 16, no. 1, pp. 82–91, 2006.

[16]  S. F. Chang, T. Sikora, and A. Puri, "Overview of the MPEG-7 standard," *IEEE Trans. on Circuits and Systems for Video Technology*, vol. 11, no. 6, pp. 688–695, 2001.

[17]  B. W. Chen, J. C. Wang, and J. F. Wang, "A novel video summarization based on mining the story-structure and semantic relations among concept entities," *IEEE Trans. on Multimedia*, vol. 11, no. 2, pp. 295–312, 2009.

[18]  P. J. J. Cianci, *HDTV and the Transition to Digital Broadcasting: Understanding New Television Technologies.* Taylor & Francis, 2012.

[19]  G. W. Collins, *Fundamentals of Digital Television Transmission.* J. Wiley, 2000.

[20]  T. N. Cornsweet, *Visual perception.* Academic Press, 1970.

[21] C. Cotsaces, N. Nikolaidis, and I. Pitas, "Video shot detection and condensed representation: a review," *Signal Processing Magazine, IEEE*, vol. 23, no. 2, pp. 28–37, 2006.

[22] N. Culkin and K. Randle, *Digital Cinema: Opportunities and Challenges*. University of Hertfordshire Business School, 2004.

[23] N. Dalal and B. Triggs, "Histograms of oriented gradients for human detection," in *Proc. CVPR*, 2005, pp. 886–893.

[24] R. de Bruin and J. Smits, *Digital video broadcasting: technology, standards, and regulations*. Artech House, 1999.

[25] G. M. Drury, G. Markarian, and K. Pickavance, *Coding and Modulation for Digital Television*. Springer, 2000.

[26] G. Dudek, *Digital Television at Home: Satellite, Cable and Over-The-Air*. Yld Books, 2008.

[27] P. S. Eatherson, *Digital Television and Its Status*. Novinka Books, 2006.

[28] B. Evans, *Understanding digital TV: the route to HDTV*. IEEE Press, 1995.

[29] B. Fasel and J. Luettin, "Automatic facial expression analysis: a survey," *Pattern Recognition*, vol. 36, no. 1, pp. 259–275, 2003.

[30] O. Faugeras, *Three-Dimensional Computer Vision: A Geometric Viewpoint*. MIT Press, 1993.

[31] C. Fehn, P. Kauff, M. O. D. Beeck, F. Ernst, W. IJsselsteijn, M. Pollefeys, L. V. Gool, E. Ofek, and I. Sexton, "An evolutionary and optimised approach on 3DTV," in *Proc. of International Broadcast Conference*, 2002, pp. 357–365.

[32] W. Fischer, *Digital Video and Audio Broadcasting Technology: A Practical Engineering Guide*. Springer, 2008.

[33] D. M. Gavrila, "A Bayesian, exemplar-based approach to hierarchical shape matching," *IEEE Trans. on Pattern Analysis and Machine Intelligence*, vol. 29, pp. 1408–1421, 2007.

[34] N. Gkalelis, A. Tefas, and I. Pitas, "Combining fuzzy vector quantization with linear discriminant analysis for continuous human movement recognition." *IEEE Trans. on Circuits and Systems for Video Technology*, vol. 18, no. 11, pp. 1511–1521, 2008.

[35] K. Grimme, *Digital Television Standardization and Strategies.* Artech House, 2002.

[36] A. Hanjalic, *Content-based analysis of digital video.* Kluwer, 2004.

[37] A. Hanjalic, R. L. Lagendijk, and J. Biemond, "Automated high-level movie segmentation for advanced video-retrieval systems," *IEEE Trans. on Circuits and Systems for Video Technology*, pp. 580–588, 1999.

[38] J. A. Hart, *Technology, Television, and Competition: The Politics of Digital TV.* Cambridge University Press, 2004.

[39] R. L. Hartwig, *Basic TV Technology: Digital and Analog.* Elsevier Science, 2005.

[40] J. Hjelm, *Why IPTV: Interactivity, Technologies, Services.* J. Wiley, 2009.

[41] E. Hjelmås and B. K. Low, "Face detection: A survey," *Computer vision and image understanding*, vol. 83, no. 3, pp. 236–274, 2001.

[42] J. Hunter, "MPEG-7 Behind the Scenes," *D-Lib Magazine*, vol. 5, no. 9, 1999.

[43] K. F. Ibrahim, *Digital Television.* Longman, 2001.

[44] K. F. Ibrahim, *DVD Players and Drives.* Elsevier Science, 2003.

[45] K. F. Ibrahim, *Newnes Guide to Television and Video Technology: The Guide for the Digital Age - from HDTV, DVD and flat-screen technologies to Multimedia Broadcasting, Mobile TV and Blu Ray.* Elsevier Science, 2007.

[46] A. Iosifidis, N. Nikolaidis, and I. Pitas, "Movement recognition exploiting multi-view information." in *Proc. IEEE MMSP*, 2010, pp. 427–431.

[47] I.S.O, "Information technology – multimedia content description interface - part 1 - part 6," no. ISO/IEC JTC 1/SC 29 N 4153 - 4163, 2001.

[48] K. Jack, *Digital Video and DSP: Instant Access.* Newnes/Elsevier, 2008.

[49] J. Keith, *Video Demystified: A Handbook for the Digital Engineer, 2nd Edition.* LLH Technology Publishing, 1995.

[50] D. H. Kelly, "Visual responses to time-dependent stimuli. i. amplitude sensitivity measurements," *Journal of the Optical Society of America*, vol. 51, no. 4, pp. 422–429, 1961.

[51] A. C. Kokaram, *Motion picture restoration: digital algorithms for artefact suppression in degraded motion picture film and video*. Springer, 1998.

[52] G. Lekakos, K. Chorianopoulos, and G. I. Doukidis, *Interactive Digital Television: Technologies and Applications*. IGI Global, 2007.

[53] Z. Lin and L. S. Davis, "Shape-based human detection and segmentation via hierarchical part-template matching," *IEEE Trans. on Pattern Analysis Machine Intelligence*, vol. 32, no. 4, pp. 604–618, 2010.

[54] L. I. Lundström, *Understanding Digital Television: An Introduction to DVB Systems with Satellite, Cable, Broadband and Terrestrial TV Distribution*. Elsevier Science, 2006.

[55] L. I. Lundström, *Digital Signage Broadcasting: Content Management and Distribution Techniques*. Focal Press, 2008.

[56] A. C. Luther and A. F. Inglis, *Video Engineering*. McGraw-Hill, 1999.

[57] S. Mack, *Streaming Media Bible*. J. Wiley, 2002.

[58] B. S. Manjunath, J. R. Ohm, V. V. Vasudevan, and A. Yamada, "Color and texture descriptors," *IEEE Trans. on Circuits and Systems for Video Technology*, vol. 11, pp. 703–715, 1998.

[59] P. E. Mattison, *Practical digital video with programming examples in C*. J. Wiley, 1994.

[60] B. Mendiburu, *3D movie making: Stereoscopic digital cinema from script to screen*. Focal Press, 2009.

[61] B. Mendiburu, Y. Pupulin, and S. Schklair, *3D TV and 3D cinema. Tools and processes for Creative Stereoscopy*. Focal Press, 2012.

[62] M. Miller and M. Troller, *How Home Theater And HDTV Work*. Que, 2006.

[63] N. Nikolaidis and I. Pitas, *3-D Image Processing Algorithms*. J. Wiley, 2000.

[64] M. Orzessek and P. Sommer, *ATM & MPEG-2: Integrating Digital Video Into Broadband Networks*. Prentice Hall, 1998.

[65] M. Pagani, *Multimedia and Interactive Digital TV: Managing the Opportunities Created by Digital Convergence.* IGI Publishing, 2003.

[66] S. Papathanassopoulos, *European Television in the Digital Age: Issues, Dynamics and Realities.* J. Wiley, 2002.

[67] J. Penttinen, P. Jolma, E. Aaltonen, and J. Väre, *The DVB-H Handbook: The Functioning and Planning of Mobile TV.* J. Wiley, 2009.

[68] I. Pitas, *Digital Image Processing Algorithms and Applications.* J. Wiley, 2000.

[69] I. Pitas and A. N. Venetsanopoulos, *Nonlinear Digital Filters: Principles and Applications.* Springer, 1990.

[70] C. Poole and C. P. Janette Bradley, *Developer's Digital Media Reference: New Tools, New Methods.* Focal Press, 2003.

[71] C. A. Poynton, *Digital Video and HDTV: Algorithms and Interfaces.* Morgan Kaufmann, 2003.

[72] W. K. Pratt, *Digital Image Processing: PIKS Inside.* J. Wiley, 2012.

[73] I. E. G. Richardson, *H.264 and MPEG-4 Video Compression: Video Coding for Next-generation Multimedia.* J. Wiley, 2003.

[74] M. Robin and M. Poulin, *Digital Television Fundamentals.* McGraw-Hill, 2000.

[75] J. G. Robson, "Spatial and temporal contrast-sensitivity functions of the visual system," *J. Opt. Soc. Am.*, vol. 56, no. 8, pp. 1141–1142, 1966.

[76] M. Rubin, *The Little Digital Video Book.* Pearson Education, 2008.

[77] C. P. Sandbank, *Digital television.* J. Wiley, 1990.

[78] M. Sano, Y. Kawai, H. Sumiyoshi, and N. Yagi, "Metadata production framework and metadata editor," in *Proc. of the 14th annual ACM International Conference on Multimedia*, 2006, pp. 789–790.

[79] S. Schaefermeyer, *Digital Video Basics.* Course Technology PTR, 2007.

[80] J. Schaeffler, *Digital Video Recorders: DVRs Changing TV and Advertising Forever.* Focal Press, 2009.

[81] P. Schallauer, W. Bailer, R. Troncy, and F. Kaiser, "Multimedia metadata standards," *Multimedia Semantics*, pp. 129–144, 2011.

[82] O. Schreer, P. Kauff, and T. Sikora, *3D Videocommunication: Algorithms, concepts and real-time systems in human centred communication.* J. Wiley, 2005.

[83] G. Sfiris, N. Nikolaidis, and I. Pitas, "Multi-view object and human body part detection utilizing 3D scene information." in *Proc. IEEE ICIP*, 2010, pp. 29–32.

[84] M. Silbergleid and M. J. Pescatore, *The Guide to Digital Television: Understanding Digital, Pre-production, Production, Audio, Graphics & Compositing, Post Production, Duplication & Delivery, Engineering & Transmission.* Miller Freeman, 2000.

[85] W. Simpson, *Video Over IP: IPTV, Internet Video, H.264, P2P, Web TV, and Streaming.* Focal Press, 2008.

[86] A. Smolic, K. Mueller, P. Merkle, C. Fehn, P. Kauff, P. Eisert, and T. Wiegand, "3D video and free viewpoint video-technologies, applications and MPEG standards," in *Proc. IEEE International Conference on Multimedia (ICME)*, 2006, pp. 2161–2164.

[87] M. Sonka, V. Hlavac, and R. Boyle, *Image Processing, Analysis, and Machine Vision.* Thomson-Engineering, 2007.

[88] G. Stamou, M. Krinidis, E. Loutas, N. Nikolaidis, and I. Pitas, "2d and 3d motion tracking in digital video," in *Handbook of Image and Video Processing*, 2005.

[89] G. Stamou, M. Krinidis, N. Nikolaidis, and I. Pitas, "A monocular system for automatic face detection and tracking," in *Proc. of Visual Communications and Image Processing (VCIP)*, 2005.

[90] P. D. Symes, *Digital Video Compression.* McGraw-Hill, 2003.

[91] J. Taylor and C. Armbrust, *DVD Demystified, Third Edition.* McGraw-Hill, 2005.

[92] A. M. Tekalp, *Digital video processing.* Prentice Hall, 1995.

[93] R. Troncy, W. Bailer, M. Höffernig, and M. Hausenblas, "Vamp: a service for validating MPEG-7 descriptions wrt to formal profile definitions," *Multimedia Tools and Applications*, vol. 46, no. 2, pp. 307–329, 2010.

[94] E. Trucco and A. Verri, *Introductory Techniques for 3-D Computer Vision.* Prentice Hall, 1998.

[95] N. Tsapanos, A. Tefas, N. Nikolaidis, and I. Pitas, "Shape matching using a binary search tree structure of weak classifiers," *Pattern Recognition*, vol. 45, no. 6, pp. 2363–2376, 2012.

[96] N. Tsapanos, A. Tefas, and I. Pitas, "Online shape learning using binary search trees," *Image Vision Computing*, vol. 28, no. 7, pp. 1146–1154, 2010.

[97] S. Tsekeridou and I. Pitas, "Audio-visual content analysis for content-based video indexing," in *Proc. IEEE International Conference on Multimedia Computing and Systems*, 1999, pp. 667–672.

[98] S. Tsekeridou and I. Pitas, "Content-based video parsing and indexing based on audio-visual interaction," *IEEE Trans. on Circuits and Systems for Video Technology*, vol. 11, no. 4, pp. 522–535, 2001.

[99] I. Tsingalis, N. Vretos, N. Nikolaidis, and I. Pitas, "Anthropocentric descriptors and description schemes for multi-view video content," in *16th IEEE Mediterranean Electrotechnical Conference (MELECON)*, 2012, pp. 133–136.

[100] P. Turaga, R. Chellappa, V. S. Subrahmanian, and O. Udrea, "Machine recognition of human activities: A survey," *IEEE Trans. on Circuits and Systems for Video Technology*, vol. 18, no. 11, pp. 1473–1488, 2008.

[101] K. Underdahl, *Digital Video For Dummies*. J. Wiley, 2006.

[102] J. M. Van Tassel, *Digital TV Over Broadband: Harvesting Bandwidth*. Focal Press, 2001.

[103] P. Viola and M. Jones, "Robust real-time face detection," *International Journal of Computer Vision*, vol. 57, pp. 137–154, 2004.

[104] N. Vretos, V. Solachidis, and I. Pitas, "An anthropocentric description scheme for movies content classification and indexing," in *Proc. EUSIPCO*, 2005.

[105] N. Vretos, V. Solachidis, and I. Pitas, "Anthropocentric semantic information extraction from movies," *Computational Intelligence in Multimedia Processing: Recent Advances*, pp. 437–492, 2008.

[106] N. Vretos, V. Solachidis, and I. Pitas, "A mutual information based face clustering algorithm for movie content analysis," *Image and Vision Computing*, pp. 693–705, 2011.

[107] Y. Wang, Y. Q. Zhang, and J. Ostermann, *Video Processing and Communications*. Prentice Hall, 2001.

[108] J. Watkinson, *The Art of Digital Video, Fourth Edition.* Focal Press, 2007.

[109] J. W. Weber and T. Newberry, *IPTV Crash Course.* McGraw-Hill, 2006.

[110] P. Wheeler, *Digital Cinematography.* Focal Press, 2001.

[111] J. C. Whitaker, *DTV: the revolution in electronic imaging.* McGraw-Hill, 1998.

[112] J. C. Whitaker, *DTV: The Revolution in Digital Video.* McGraw-Hill, 2001.

[113] J. W. Woods, *Multidimensional Signal, Image, and Video Processing and Coding.* Elsevier/Academic Press, 2006.

[114] C. Wootton, *A Practical Guide to Video and Audio Compression: From Sprockets and Rasters to Macro Blocks.* Taylor & Francis, 2012.

[115] G. Wyszecki and W. S. Stiles, *Color Science: Concepts and Methods, Quantitative Data and Formulae, 2nd Edition.* Wiley-Interscience, 2000.

[116] M. Xu, J. Orwell, and G. Jones, "Tracking football players with multiple cameras," in *IEEE International Conference on Image Processing*, 2004, pp. 2909–2912.

[117] A. Yilmaz, O. Javed, and M. Shah, "Object tracking: A survey," *ACM Computing Surveys*, vol. 38, no. 4, 2006.

[118] A. Yoshitaka and T. Ichikawa, "A survey on content-based retrieval for multimedia databases," *IEEE Trans. on Knowledge and Data Engineering*, vol. 11, pp. 81–93, 1999.

[119] S. Zafeiriou, A. Tefas, I. Buciu, and I. Pitas, "Exploiting discriminant information in nonnegative matrix factorization with application to frontal face verification," *IEEE Trans. on Neural Networks*, vol. 17, no. 3, pp. 683–695, 2006.

[120] W. Zhao, R. Chellappa, P. J. Phillips, and A. Rosenfeld, "Face recognition: A literature survey," *ACM Computing Surveys*, vol. 35, no. 4, pp. 399–458, 2003.

# GLOSSARY

**3DAV:** 3-dimensional Audio Visual.

**3DTV:** 3-dimensional Television.

**3DVC:** 3-dimensional Video Coding.

**AAC:** Advanced Audio Coding.

**ABR:** Average Bit Rate.

**AES:** Advanced Encryption Standard.

**AFX:** Animation Framework eXtension.

**ANSI:** American National Standards Institute.

**ASF:** Advanced Systems Format.

**ATC:** Authorized Testing Center.

**ATSC:** Advanced Television System Committee.

**AU:** Action Units.

**AVC:** Advanced Video Coding.

**AVDP:** Audio Visual Description Profile.

**AVI:** Audio Video Interleave.

**BAB:** Binary Alpha Block.

**BAP:** Body Animation Parameters.

**BD:** Blu-ray Disc.

**BDA:** Blu-ray Disc Association.

**BER:** Bit Error Rate.

**BWF:** Broadcast Wave Format.

**CABAC:** Context-Adaptive Binary Arithmetic Coding.

**CAVLC:** Context-Adaptive Variable-Length Coding.

**CBR:** Constant Bit Rate.

**CCD:** Charge Coupled Device.

**CCIR:** Comite Consultatif International pour la Radio.

**CCITT:** Consultative Committee for International Telephone and Telegraph.

**CD:** Compact Disc.

**CDFS:** Compact Disc File System.

**CDP:** Core Description Profile.

**CEC:** Consumer Electronics Control.

**CELP:** Code Excited Linear Predictive.

**CGI:** Computer Generated Imagery.

**CIE:** Commission Internationale de l'Eclairage.

**CIF:** Common Intermediate Format.

**CMOS:** Complimentary Metal Oxide Sensor.

**CNR:** Carrier-to-Noise Ratio.

**COD:** Cinema On Demand.

**cpd:** cycles per degree.

**CRT:** Cathode Ray Tube.

**CS-ACELP:** Conjugate Structure Algebraic Code-Excited Linear Prediction.

**CSV:** Conventional Stereo Video.

**CTS:** Compliant Test Specification.

**D-ILA:** Direct-drive Image Light Amplifier.

**D:** Descriptor.

**DAVP:** Detailed Audio Visual Profile.

**DCCJ:** Digital Cinema Consortium of Japan.

**DCDM:** Digital Cinema Distribution Master.

**DCI:** Digital Cinema Initiatives.

**DCL:** Digital Cinema Lab.

**DCP:** Digital Cinema Package.

**DCT:** Discrete Cosine Transform.

**DD+:** Dolby Digital Plus.

**DD:** Dolby Digital.

**DDL:** Description Definition Language.

**DDWG:** Digital Display Working Group.

**DES:** Depth Enhanced Stereo.

**DFD:** Displaced Frame Difference.

**DFT:** Discrete Fourier Transform.

**DIBR:** Depth-Image Based Rendering.

**DL:** Dual Layer.

**DLDS:** Dual Layer Double Sided.

**DLP:** Digital Light Processing.

**DMB:** Digital Multimedia Broadcasting.

**DMD:** Digital Micromirror Device.

**DPX:** Digital Picture Exchange.

**DRM:** Digital Rights Management.

**DS:** Description Scheme.

**DSD:** Direct Stream Digital.

**DSM:** Digital Source Master.

**DTV:** Digital Television.

**DVB-H:** Digital Video Broadcasting to a Handheld.

**DVB-T:** Digital Video Broadcasting Terrestrial.

**DVB:** Digital Video Broadcasting.

**DVD:** Digital Video Disc.

**DVI:** Digital Visual Interface.

**EBU:** European Broadcasting Union.

**ECC:** Error Correction Code.

**EDCF:** European Digital Cinema Forum.

**EGM:** Elastic Graph Matching.

**EPG:** Electronic Program Guides.

**ES:** Elementary Stream.

**FACS:** Facial Action Coding System.

**FAP:** Facial Animation Parameters.

**FDP:** Facial Definition Parameters.

**FEC:** Forward Error Correction.

**FFT:** Fast Fourier Transform.

**FRExt:** Fidelity Range Extensions.

**GOP:** Group Of Pictures.

**GVOP:** Group of Video Object Planes.

**HBBTV:** Hybrid Broadcast Broadband Television.

**HD:** High Definition.

**HDCP:** High-definition Digital Content Protection.

**HDMI:** High-Definition Multimedia Interface.

**HDTV:** High Definition Television.

**HEVC:** High Efficiency Video Coding.

**HiP:** High Profile.

**HOG:** Histogram of Oriented Gradients.

**HSB:** Hue-Saturation-Brightness.

**HSV:** Hue-Saturation-Value.

**HTTP:** HyperText Transfer Protocol.

**HVS:** Human Visual System.

**IETF:** Internet Engineering Task Force.

**IF:** Intermediate Frequency.

**IP:** Internet Protocol.

**ISDB:** Integrated Multimedia Broadcasting.

**ISO:** International Organization for Standardization.

**ITU-R:** International Telecommunications Union-Radio Sector.

**ITU-T:** International Telecommunication Union Telecommunication Standardization Sector.

**JMVM:** Joint Multi-view Video Model.

**JPEG:** Joint Photographic Experts Group.

**JVT:** Joint Video Team.

**KDM:** Key Delivery Message.

**LAN:** Local Area Network.

**LCD:** Liquid Crystal Display.

**LCOS:** Liquid Crystal On Silicon.

**LDA:** Linear Discriminant Analysis.

**LDV:** Layered-Depth-Video.

**LED:** Light Emitting Diodes.

**LFE:** Low Frequency Effects.

**LNB:** Low Noise Block Converter.

**LNC:** Low Noise Block Converter.

**LoG:** Laplacian-of-Gaussian.

**MAM:** Media Asset Management.

**MBR:** Multiple Bit Rate.

**MDS:** Multimedia Description Scheme.

**MIME:** Multipurpose Internet Mail Extensions.

**MMS:** Microsoft Media Server.

**MPEG:** Motion Pictures Experts Group.

**MPF:** Metadata Production Framework.

**MR:** Moving Region.

**MRF:** Mixed Resolution Format.

**MS ADPCM:** Microsoft Adaptive Differential Pulse Code Modulation.

**MSD:** Mean Square Difference.

**MSD:** Media Source Decomposition.

**MSE:** Mean Square Error.

**MTP:** Media Transfer Protocol.

**MVC:** Multi-View Coding.

**MVD:** Multi-view Video-plus-Depth.

**MVV:** Multi View Video.

**MXF:** Material eXchange Format.

**NATO:** National Association of Theater Owners.

**NMF:** Nonnegative Matrix Factorization.

**NTSC:** National Television Systems Committee.

**NURBS:** Non-Uniform Rational Basis Spline.

**OFDN:** Orthogonal Frequency Divided Multiplexing.

**OMA:** Open Mobile Alliance.

**OSTA:** Optical Storage Technology Association.

**OTP:** Opposite Track Path.

**PAL:** Phase Alternation Line.

**PCA:** Principal Component Analysis.

**PCM:** Pulse Code Modulation.

**PDP:** Plasma Display Panels.

**PES:** Packets of Elementary Streams.

**PNA:** Progressive Network Audio.

**PNG:** Portable Network Graphics.

**POV:** Point-Of-View.

**PSNR:** Peak Signal to Noise Ratio.

**PSTN:** Public Switched Telephone Network.

**PTP:** Parallel Track Path.

**PTP:** Picture Transfer Protocol.

**Qpel:** Quarter pixel.

**QPSK:** Quadrature Phase Shift Keying.

**RA:** Real Audio.

**RAM:** Real Audio Metadata.

**RBE:** Rainbow Effect.

**RDT:** Real Data Transport.

**RGB:** Red-Green-Blue.

**RIFF:** Resource Interchange File Format.

**RM:** Real Media.

**RMVB:** Real Media Variable Bitrate.

**ROI:** Region Of Interest.

**RS:** Reed-Solomon.

**RTCP:** Real-time Transport Control Protocol.

**RTMP:** Real Time Messaging Protocol.

**RTP:** Real-time Transport Protocol.

**RTSP:** Real Time Streaming Protocol.

**RV:** Real Video.

**SA-DCT:** Shape Adaptive Discrete Cosine Transform.

**SA:** Structured Annotation.

**SACD:** Super Audio Compact Disc.

**SD:** Spatial Decomposition.

**SDE:** Screen Door Effect.

**SDTV:** Standard Definition Television.

**SECAM:** System Electronique Color Avec Memoire.

**SFN:** Single Frequency Networks.

**SIFT:** Scale-Invariant Feature Transform.

**SIP:** Session Initiation Protocol.

**SL:** Single Layer.

**SLDS:** Single Layer Double Sided.

**SMIL:** Synchronized Multimedia Integration Language.

**SMPTE:** Society of Motion Pictures and Television Engineers.

**SMS:** Screen Management System.

**SMS:** Short Message Service.

**SR:** Still Region.

**STFT:** Short Term Fourier Transform.

**SVM:** Support Vector Machine.

**SVOPC:** Sinusoidal Voice Over Packet Coder.

**SWF:** ShockWave File.

**SWV:** Stereoscopic Window Violation.

**TCP:** Transmission Control Protocol.

**TD:** Temporal Decomposition.

**TFT:** Thin Film Transistor.

**TMDS:** Transition Minimized Differential Signalling.

**TMS:** Theater Management System.

**TN:** Twisted Nematic.

**TS:** Transport Streams.

**TTS:** Text To Speech.

**UDF:** Universal Disc Format.

**UDP:** User Datagram Protocol.

**UHDTV:** Ultra High Definition TeleVision.

**URL:** Uniform Resource Locator.

**USB:** Universal Serial Bus.

**V+D:** Video-plus-Depth.

**VBR:** Variable Bit Rate.

**VCEG:** Video Coding Experts Group.

**VESA:** Video Electronic Standards Association.

**VFX:** Visual Effects.

**VGA:** Video Graphics Array.

**VLC:** Variable-Length encoder.

**VO:** Video Object.

**VOD:** Video-On-Demand.

**VoIP:** Voice Over Internet Protocol.

**VOP:** Video Object Plane.

**VQA:** Video Quality Assessment.

**VRML:** Virtual Reality Modeling Language.

**VS:** Video Segment.

**VSB:** Vestigial Sideband Modulation.

**WMA:** Windows Media Audio.

**WMP:** Windows Media Player.

**WMV:** Windows Media Video.

**WWW:** World Wide Web.

**XM:** eXperimentation Model.

**XML:** eXtensible Markup Language.

# INDEX

www.ingramcontent.com/pod-product-compliance
Lightning Source LLC
LaVergne TN
LVHW022301060326
832902LV00020B/3206